# ROMAN NUMERALS
## ~ Conversion ~

$$i = 1$$
$$v = 5$$
$$x = 10$$
$$l = 50$$
$$c = 100$$

The letters composing a number are ranged in order of value and the number meant is found by addition.

If a letter or a set of letters is placed before a letter of higher value it is to be subtracted from it before the addition is done.

# LIFE OF JOHN FOXE.

JOHN FOXE was born in Lincolnshire, in the year 1517.   At the age of sixteen he went to Brazenose College, Oxford, where he took his degree of M.A.   While at the University, and for some time after, he was a zealous Papist, and was strictly moral in his life.   Being led to read church history, and also to study the Bible, he became convinced of the errors of the Romish Church.   The bigoted Romanists soon discovered the change in his opinions, and had him expelled from the University. Oppressed and forsaken, he was in great need, when Sir Thomas Lucy, of Warwickshire, befriended him, and engaged him as tutor in his family.

After remaining some time at Coventry, he removed to London; but being a stranger, and without money, he was soon reduced to great want.   From this he was relieved in the following extraordinary manner.   Sitting one day in St. Paul's church, and looking like a spectre, being almost starved, a stranger, whom he did not remember having ever seen before, sat down by him, and, putting a large sum of money into his hand, exhorted him to be of good cheer, for God would, in a few days, give him more certain means of subsistence.   The prophecy was fulfilled; for, within three days, he was appointed by the Duchess of Richmond tutor to her nephew's family.

But Mary was now on the throne, and the persecution carried on against the Protestants became at length so bitter, that Foxe was forced to leave England. He betook himself to Basle, in Switzerland; and it was in this city, famous for printing, that he began his well-known work on Martyrology. When Elizabeth ascended the throne he returned to England. The Duke of Norfolk, one of his former pupils, received him into his house, and at his death left Foxe a pension. He was afterwards settled at Salisbury, where he revised and completed his Book of Martyrs.

There can be no doubt as to its substantial accuracy throughout, as has been most satisfactorily shown by the late Canon Townsend and other writers. It has become quite a fashion in these days to decry Foxe as unworthy of credit; but what is the result of more thorough investigation? Froude, one of our ablest living historians, in his recent essay on "The Dissolution of the Monasteries," says that he was taught to believe, like other modern students of history, that the papal dispensations for immorality, of which we read in Foxe and other Protestant writers, were calumnies; but he had been forced, against his will, to believe that the supposed calumnies were but the plain truth.

After a long life of piety and usefulness, Foxe died on the 18th April, 1587, and was interred in the chancel of St. Giles's, Cripplegate, of which parish, during the reign of Elizabeth, he had for some time been vicar. A plain tablet, bearing a Latin inscription, was erected by his son to his memory.

# CONTENTS.

# ILLUSTRATIONS.

---

# FOXE'S BOOK OF MARTYRS.

## CHAPTER I.

THE dreadful martyrdoms we shall now describe arose from the persecution of the Christians by pagan fury in the primitive ages of the church, during three hundred years, until the time of Constantine the Great.

The first martyr to our holy religion was its blessed Founder Himself, who was betrayed by Judas Iscariot, condemned under Pontius Pilate, and crucified on Calvary.

Stephen, a deacon of the first Christian church, was the next martyr. He was stoned to death. Then followed James, the brother of John, who was killed by the sword.

With the exception of John, who narrowly escaped, and lived to a great age, all the other apostles seem to have been called to lay down their lives for the sake of Christ.

### The first Primitive Persecution, beginning in the year 67, under the Reign of the Emperor Nero.

The first persecution in the primitive ages of the church was under Nero Domitius, the sixth emperor of Rome, A.D. 67. This monarch reigned five years tolerably well; but then gave way to the greatest extravagance of temper, and the most atrocious barbarities. Among other diabolical outrages, he ordered the city of Rome to be set on fire, which was done by his officers, guards, and servants. While the city was in flames, he went up to the tower of Mæcenas, played upon his harp, sang the song of the Burning of Troy, and declared, " That he wished the ruin of all things before his death." This dreadful conflagration continued nine days.

Nero charged this deed upon the Christians, at once to excuse himself and have an opportunity for persecution. The barbarities inflicted were such as excited the sympathy of even the Romans themselves. Nero nicely refined upon cruelty, and contrived all manner of punishments for his victims. He had some sewed up in the skins of wild beasts, and then worried by dogs till they expired; and others dressed in shirts stiff with wax, fixed to axle-trees, and set on fire in his garden. This persecution was general throughout the Roman empire ; but it increased rather than diminished the spirit of Christianity.

## Second Primitive Persecution under Domitian.

The emperor Domitian, naturally of a cruel disposition, raised a second persecution against the Christians; among the numerous martyrs that suffered under him was Simeon, bishop of Jerusalem, who was crucified. Flavia, the daughter of a Roman senator, was banished to Pontus; and a cruel law was made, " That no Christian, once brought before the tribunal, should be exempted from punishment without renouncing his religion."

Third Primitive Persecution under the Roman Emperors.

Upon Nerva succeeding Domitian, he gave a respite to the Christians; but, reigning only thirteen months, his successor Trajan, in the year 108, began the third persecution. While this persecution raged, Plinius Secundas, a heathen philosopher, wrote to the emperor in favour of the Christians. To his epistle, Trajan returned this indecisive answer: "That Christians ought not to be sought after, but when brought before the magistracy they should be punished." Provoked by this reply, Tertullian exclaimed: " O confused sentence; he would not have them sought for, as innocent men, and yet would have them punished as guilty."

The emperor Trajan was succeeded by Adrian, who continued the persecution with the greatest rigour. Phocas, bishop of Pontus, refusing to sacrifice to Neptune, was, by his immediate order, cast first into a hot lime-kiln, and, being drawn from thence, was thrown into a scalding bath, where he expired.

Ignatius, bishop of Antioch, boldly vindicated the faith of Christ before the emperor, for which he was cast into prison and cruelly tormented ; for, after being scourged, he was compelled to hold fire in his hands, while papers dipped in oil were put to his sides and lighted ! His flesh was then torn with hot pincers, and at last he was dispatched by wild beasts.

During the martyrdom of Faustinus and Jovita, brothers and citizens of Brescia, their torments were so many, and their patience so firm, that Calocerius, a pagan, beholding them, was struck with admiration, and exclaimed in ecstacy, " Great is the God of the Christians ! " for which he was apprehended and put to death.

Adrian was succeeded by Antoninus Pius, so amiable a monarch that his people gave him the title of "The Father of Virtues." Immediately on his accession he published an edict forbidding further persecution of the Christians, and concluded it in these words : "If any hereafter shall vex or trouble the Christians, having no other cause but that they are such, let the accused be released and the accusers be punished."

### Fourth Primitive Persecution under the Roman Emperors, which commenced A.D. 162.

Antoninus Pius was succeeded by Marcus Aurelius Antoninus Verus, who began the fourth persecution, in which many Christians were martyred, particularly in Asia and France. The greatest cruelties were used in this persecution. Some of the martyrs were obliged to pass, with their already wounded feet, over thorns, nails, sharp shells, etc. ; other were scourged till their sinews and veins lay bare ; and, after suffering most excruciating tortures, were destroyed by the most terrible deaths.

Germanicus, a young Christian, being delivered to the beasts, behaved with such astonishing courage, that several pagans became converts to a faith which inspired so much fortitude.

Polycarp, hearing that persons were seeking to apprehend him, escaped, but was discovered by a child. He was carried before the pro-consul, condemned, and put to death in the market-place. Twelve other Christians, who had been intimate with him, were soon after martyred.

Justin, the celebrated philosopher, and the author of an apology for Christianity, fell a martyr in this persecution. Having been apprehended, with six of his companions, they were commanded to deny their faith, and sacrifice to the pagan idols. They refused, and were therefore condemned to be first scourged and then beheaded.

Circumstances occasioned the persecution to subside for some time, at least in those parts immediately under the inspection of the emperor; but we find that it soon after raged in France, particularly at Lyons, where the tortures to which many Christians were put almost exceeds the powers of description. The martyrs of Lyons are said to have been forty-eight in number. They all died with great fortitude, glorifying God and the Redeemer. In this reign Apollonius, a Roman senator, became a martyr. Eusebius, Vincentius, Potentianus, for refusing to worship Commodus as Hercules, were likewise put to death. Julius, a Roman senator, was ordered by the emperor to sacrifice to him as Hercules. This Julius absolutely refused, and publicly professed himself a Christian. On this account, after remaining in prison a considerable time, he was beat to death with a club.

Irenæus, bishop of Lyons, was born in Greece, and received a Christian education. He was a zealous opposer of heresies in general, and wrote a tract against heresy, which had great influence at the time. This pointed him out as an object of resentment to the emperor; he was accordingly beheaded in A.D. 202.

The persecutions about this time extended to Africa, and many were martyred in that part of the globe; the principal of whom was Perpetua, a married lady of about twenty-six years of age, with an infant child at her breast. She was seized for being a Christian.

Her father, who tenderly loved her, tried to persuade her to renounce Christianity. Perpetua, however, resisted every entreaty. On being carried before the pro-consul Minutius, she was commanded to sacrifice to the idols: refusing, she was ordered to a dark dungeon, and deprived of her child. Perpetua gave the strongest proof of fortitude and strength of mind on her trial. The judge entreated her to consider her father's tears, her infant's helplessness, and her own life; but, triumphing over all the sentiments of nature, she forgot the thought of pain in the prospect of that immortality offered by Christ. She was first torn by wild beasts, and then killed by the sword.

Callistus, bishop of Rome, was martyred in 224; and in 232 Urban, one of his successors, met the same fate. Agapetus, a boy of Præneste, in Italy, who was only fifteen years of age, refusing to sacrifice to the idols, was severely scourged and then hanged up by the feet, and boiling water poured over him. He was afterwards worried by wild beasts, and at last beheaded.

### Sixth General Persecution under the Roman Emperors.

Maximus, who became Emperor in the year 235, began to persecute the Christians; and in Cappadocia the president Semiramus made great efforts to exterminate them from that kingdom. A Roman soldier who refused to wear a laurel crown bestowed by the emperor, and confessed himself a Christian, was scourged and put to death. Pontianus, bishop of Rome, for preaching against idolatry, was banished to Sardinia, and there destroyed. Anteros, a Grecian, who succeeded this bishop in the see of Rome, gave so much offence to the government by collecting the acts of the martyrs, that he suffered martyrdom, after having held his dignity only forty days.    Pammachius, a Roman senator, with his family and other Christians, to the number of forty-two, were all beheaded in one day, and their heads fixed on the city gates.    Hippolitus, a Christian prelate, was tied to a wild horse, and dragged through fields, stony places, and brambles, till he died.

While this persecution continued, numerous Christians were slain without trial, and buried in heaps; sometimes fifty or sixty being cast into a pit together.

Maximus died in A.D. 238; and was succeeded by Gordian, during whose reign, and that of his successor, Philip, the church was free from persecution for more than ten years; but in the year 249 a violent persecution broke out in Alexandria.   The fury of the people being great against the Christians, they broke open their houses, stole the best of their property, destroyed the rest, and murdered the owners; the universal cry was, "Burn them, burn them! kill them!"   The names of the martyrs, and the particulars of this affair, however, have not been recorded.

### Seventh General Persecution under the Roman Emperors.

In the year 249, Decius being emperor of Rome, a dreadful persecution was begun against the Christians.   Fabian, bishop of Rome, was the first person of eminence who felt its severity.   The deceased emperor, Philip, had committed his treasure to the care of this good man; but Decius, not finding as much as he expected, determined to wreak his vengeance on him.   He was accordingly seized, and suffered martyrdom by decapitation.   Abdon and Semen, two

Persians, were apprehended as strangers; but being found Christians, were put to death. Moyses, a priest, was beheaded for the same reason. Julian, a native of Cilicia, was seized for being a Christian. He was frequently tortured, but remained inflexible; and, though often brought from prison for execution, was again remanded, to suffer greater cruelties. He was, at last, put into a leathern bag, with a number of serpents and scorpions, and thrown into the sea. Peter, a young man at Lampsacus, on being commanded by Optimus, the pro-consul, to sacrifice to Venus, said, "I am astonished that you should wish me to sacrifice to an infamous woman, whose debaucheries even your own historians record, and whose life consisted of such actions as your laws would punish. No! I shall offer the true God the sacrifice of praise and prayer." Optimus, on hearing this, ordered him to be broken on a wheel; but his torments only inspired him with fresh courage; he even smiled on his persecutors. He was at length beheaded.

In the island of Crete persecution raged with great fury, the governor being exceedingly active in executing the imperial decrees.

The emperor Decius, having erected a pagan temple at Ephesus, in the year 251, commanded all who were in that city to sacrifice to the idols. This order was nobly refused by seven of his own soldiers. The emperor, wishing to spare them, gave them a respite till he returned from a journey. In his absence they escaped, and hid themselves in a cavern; but he was informed of it on his return, the mouth of the cavern was closed up, and they were starved or smothered to death.

After persecution had raged in Cappadocia, Phrygia, and other districts, and when Gallus had concluded his wars, a plague broke out in the empire; and sacrifices to the pagan deities were ordered by the emperor to appease their wrath. The Christians, refusing to comply with these rites, were charged with being the authors of the calamity: thus the persecution spread from the interior to the extreme parts of the empire, and many fell martyrs to the impetuosity of the rabble, as well as the prejudice of the magistrates. At length, the emperor having been murdered by his general, Æmilian, a profound peace succeeded throughout the empire, and the persecution was suffered to subside.

### Eighth General Persecution under the Roman Emperors.

After the death of Gallus, Valerian was chosen emperor. For the space of four years he governed with moderation, and treated the Christians with peculiar lenity; but in the year 257 an Egyptian, named Macriamus, gained a great ascendancy over him, and persuaded him to persecute the Christians. Edicts were accordingly published, and the persecution, which began in the month of April, continued for three years and six months.

Among the martyrs that fell in this persecution were Rufina and Secunda, two beautiful and accomplished ladies, daughters of a gentleman of eminence in Rome. They were beheaded in the year 257. In the same year Stephen, bishop of Rome, was beheaded, and about that time Saturninus, bishop of Thoulouse, was attacked and seized by the rabble of that place, for preventing, as they alleged, their oracles from speaking. On refusing to sacrifice to the idols, he was treated with barbarous indignity, and then fastened by the feet to the tail of a bull. On a signal, the enraged animal was driven down the steps of the temple, by which the martyr's brains were dashed out. Stephen was succeeded by Sextus as bishop of Rome. Marcianus, who had the management of the Roman government in the year 258, procured an order from the emperor Valerian to put to death all the Christian clergy in Rome, and Sextus was one of the first who felt the severity of the edict. He was beheaded August 6th, 258, and six of his deacons suffered with him.

Laurentius, commonly called St. Laurence, the principal of the deacons who taught and preached under Sextus, followed him to the place of execution, when Sextus predicted that he should meet him in heaven three days after. Laurentius considering this as a certain indication of his own approaching martyrdom, at his return collected all the Christian poor, and distributed amongst them the treasures of the church. Having been commanded to give an account of them to the emperor, he collected together a great number of aged, helpless, and impotent poor, and repaired to the magistrates, saying, " These are the true treasures of the church." Provoked at the disappointment, the governor ordered him to be scourged. He was beaten with iron rods, set upon a wooden horse, and had his limbs dislocated. He endured these tortures with such fortitude and perseverance, that he was ordered to be fastened to a large gridiron, with a slow fire under it, that his death might be more tedious. But his astonishing constancy and serenity of countenance under such excruciating torments, gave the spectators so exalted an idea of the dignity and truth of the Christian religion, that many became converts.

Among these was a soldier called Romanus. He declared himself a Christian immediately after the death of Laurentius, and soon followed him by a less lingering and torturing martyrdom to the world of blessed spirits in heaven. On his avowal of the Christian faith, he was scourged and beheaded.

Fourteen years before this persecution raged in Africa with great violence, and many thousands received the crown of martyrdom, among whom was Cyprian, bishop of Carthage, an eminent prelate, and a pious ornament of the church. Before his baptism he studied the Scriptures with care, and being struck with the excellence of their truths, determined to practise the virtues they recommended. He sold his estate, distributed the money among the poor, dressed himself in plain attire, and commenced a life of austerity and solitude. In the year 257 he was brought before the pro-consul Aspasius Paternus. When commanded to conform to the religion of the empire, he boldly confessed his faith. He was therefore exiled to a little city on the Libyan sea. On the death of the pro-consul he returned to Carthage, but was soon after seized, and carried before the new governor, who condemned him to be beheaded; and on the 14th of September, 258, this sentence was executed.

Perhaps one of the most dreadful events in the history of martyrdom was that which took place at Utica, where 300 Christians were, by the orders of the pro-consul, placed around a burning lime-kiln. A pan of coals and incense being prepared, they were commanded either to sacrifice to Jupiter, or be thrown into the kiln. Unanimously refusing, they bravely jumped into the pit, and were suffocated immediately.

### Ninth General Persecution under the Roman Emperors.

In the year 274 the emperor Aurelian began to persecute the Christians; the principal sufferer was Felix, bishop of Rome, who was advanced to the Roman see in 274, and was beheaded in the same year. Diocletian, mounting the imperial throne in 284, at first showed great favour to the Christians. In the year 286 he associated Maximian with him in the empire; when Felician and Primus, two Christian brothers, were put to death before any general persecution broke out. They were seized by an order from the imperial court, and, owning themselves Christians, were scourged, tortured, and finally beheaded. Marcus and Marcellianus, twin natives of Rome, and of noble descent, were also apprehended, severely tortured, and then condemned to death. A respite of a month was obtained for them, that their parents and relations might try to bring them back to paganism, but it was vain. At last their constancy subdued their persuaders, and the whole family became converts.

Tranquillinus, the father, was sent for by the prefect, when he confessed that, so far from having been able to persuade his sons to forsake Christianity, he had become a Christian himself. In accounting for the change, he used such powerful arguments that he made a convert of the prefect, who soon after sold his estate, resigned his command, and spent the remainder of his days in pious retirement.

Tibertius, a native of Rome, was of a family of rank and distinction. Being accused as a Christian, he was commanded either to sacrifice to idols, or to walk upon burning coals. He chose the latter, and is said to have walked over them without damage, when Fabian passed sentence upon him that he should be beheaded.

A remarkable affair occurred in the year 286. A legion of soldiers, consisting of 6,666 men, contained none but Christians. This was called the Theban legion, because the men had been raised in Thebais; they at length joined the emperor in Gaul. About this time Maximian ordered a general sacrifice, at which the whole army was to assist; at the same time the soldiers were to swear to aid him in extirpating Christianity from Gaul. Every man in the legion nobly refused to engage in this cruel enterprise, and for this refusal were all put to death.

Alban—from whom St. Albans received its name—was the first British martyr. He was originally a pagan, but being of a very humane disposition, he sheltered a Christian ecclesiastic, named Amphibalus, whom some officers were in pursuit of on account of his religion. The pious example and edifying discourses of the refugee made a great impression on the mind of Alban, and he became a Christian. The enemies of Amphibalus learning where he was secreted, came to the house of Alban to apprehend him. The noble host, desirous of protecting his guest, changed clothes with him. He was carried before the governor, who determined to wreak his vengeance on him; with this view, he commanded him to advance to the altar, and sacrifice to the pagan deities. The brave Alban boldly professed himself a Christian. The governor therefore first scourged and afterwards beheaded him. The venerable Bede states, that upon

this occasion the executioner suddenly became a convert to Christianity, and entreated permission either
to die for Alban or with him.   Obtaining the latter
request, they were beheaded by a soldier on the 22nd
of June, 287, at Verulam, now St. Albans, where a
magnificent church was erected to the memory of
Alban about the time of Constantine the Great.

### Tenth General Persecution under the Roman Emperors,

Notwithstanding the efforts of the heathen to exterminate the Christians, they increased so greatly as
to render themselves formidable by their numbers.
Galerius, the adopted son of Diocletian, stimulated
by his mother, persuaded the emperor to commence
another persecution.   It began on the 23rd of February, 303, and opened in Nicomedia.   The prefect
of that city repaired one morning to the Christians'
church, which his officers were commanded to break
open, and then commit the sacred books to the flames.
Diocletian and Galerius, who were present, ordered
their attendants to level the church with the ground.
This was followed by a severe edict, commanding
the destruction of all other Christian churches and
books; and an order soon succeeded, the object of
which was to render Christians outlaws, and consequently incapable of holding any place of trust,
profit, or dignity, or of receiving any protection
from the legal institutions of the realm.   An immediate martyrdom was the result of this edict; for a
bold Christian not only tore it down, but execrated
the emperor for his injustice and cruelty; he was in
consequence seized, tortured, and then burnt alive.
The Christian prelates were likewise apprehended
and imprisoned; and Galerius privately ordered the

imperial palace to be set on fire, that the Christians might be charged as the incendiaries, and a plausible pretext given for carrying on the persecution with severity. A general sacrifice was then commanded, which occasioned various martyrdoms. Among others, a Christian named Peter was tortured, and then burnt; several deacons and presbyters were seized and executed, and the bishop of Nicomedia himself was beheaded. So great was the persecution, that there was no distinction made of age or sex. Many houses were set on fire, and whole Christian families perished in the flames; others had stones fastened about their necks, and were driven into the sea. The persecution became general in all the Roman provinces, but more particularly in the East, and lasted ten years.

About this time the Christians thought it unlawful to bear arms under a heathen emperor. Maximilian, the son of Tabius Victor, was ordered by Dion, the pro-consul, to be measured, that he might be enlisted. He, however, declared himself a Christian, and refused to do military duty. Being found of the proper height, Dion ordered that he should be marked as a soldier. He told Dion that he could not possibly engage in the service. The pro-consul instantly replied that he should either serve as a soldier, or die for disobedience. "Do as you please with me," replied Maximilian; "behead me if you think proper. I am already a soldier of Christ, and cannot serve any other power." The pro-consul then pronounced this sentence upon him: "that for refusing to bear arms, and professing the Christian faith, he should lose his head." This sentence he heard with great intrepidity, exclaiming, "God be praised!" At

the place of execution he exhorted those that were
Christians to remain so; and such as were not, to
embrace a faith which led to eternal salvation.   He
then received the fatal stroke.

At length the emperors Diocletian and Maximian
resigned the imperial diadem, and were succeeded by
Constantius and Galerius; the former a prince of
most mild and humane disposition, and the latter
remarkable for his tyranny and cruelty.  These divided
the empire into two equal governments; Galerius
ruling in the East, and Constantius in the West.
The people felt the effects of the different disposi-
tions of the emperors; for those in the West were
governed in the mildest manner, but such as resided
in the East felt all the miseries of cruelty and
oppression.

As Galerius bore an implacable hatred to Christians, we are informed that "he not only condemned
them to tortures, but to be burnt in slow fires.
They were first chained to a post, then a gentle
fire put to the soles of their feet, which contracted
the callus till it fell off from the bone; then flam-
beaux just extinguished were put to all parts of
their bodies, so that they might be tortured all
over; and care was taken to keep them alive,
by throwing cold water in their faces, and giving
them some to wash their mouths, lest their throats
should be dried up with thirst and choke them.
Thus their miseries were lengthened out, till
at last, their skins being consumed, and they
just ready to expire, they were thrown into a
great fire and had their bodies burned to ashes,
after which their ashes were thrown into some
river."

### Constantine the Great.

Constantine the Great at length determined to redress the grievances of the Christians. For this purpose he raised an army of 30,000 foot and 8,000 horse, with which he marched towards Rome against Maxentius the emperor. He considered that while his father adored only one God he continually prospered; he therefore rejected idols and implored the assistance of the Almighty, who heard his prayers, and answered them in a manner so surprising, that Eusebius said he could not have believed it had he not received it from the emperor's own mouth, who publicly and solemnly ratified its truth. The extraordinary narrative is as follows:—" The army arriving near Rome, the emperor was employed in devout ejaculations on the 27th of October, about three o'clock in the afternoon, when, the sun declining, there suddenly appeared to him a pillar of light in the heavens, in the form of a cross, with this plain inscription—*In hoc signo vinces:* ' In this sign thou shalt conquer.' Constantine was greatly surprised at the astonishing sight, which was also visible to the whole army, who equally wondered at it with himself. The officers and commanders, prompted by the augurs and soothsayers, looked upon it as an inauspicious omen, portending an unfortunate expedition. The emperor himself did not understand it, till at length CHRIST appeared to him in a vision, with the cross in his hand, commanding him to make it a royal standard, and cause it to be continually carried before his army as an ensign both of victory and safety. Early the next morning Constantine informed his friends and officers of what he had seen in the night, and sending for proper workmen, described to them the form of the standard, which he then ordered them to make with the greatest art and magnificence. They made it thus: a long spear, plated with gold, with a traverse piece at the top in the form of a cross, to which was fastened a four-square purple banner, embroidered with gold, and beset with precious stones, which reflected the brightest lustre; towards the top was depicted the emperor between his two sons; above the cross stood a crown, overlaid with gold and jewels, within which was placed the sacred symbol—namely, the two first letters of Christ in Greek, X and P, one intersecting the other. This device he afterwards bore, not only upon his shields, but also upon his coins, many of which are still extant."

In the battle that followed Constantine defeated Maxentius, and entered Rome in triumph. A law was now published in favour of the Christians, and a copy of it sent to Maximus in the East.

We cannot close our account of these persecutions under the Roman emperors, without calling attention to the evident indignation which the Almighty manifested towards the persecutors. History shows that no nation or individual can prosper where Christ Jesus, the Son of God, is contemned. During these events, the Romans were not only plagued and destroyed by their own emperors, but also by civil wars, three of which happened in two years at Rome after the death of Nero. In the days of Tiberius 5,000 Romans were maimed or slain at one time by the fall of a theatre. Of the Jews, about this time, there were destroyed by Titus and Vespasian 11,000, besides those whom Vespasian slew in subduing Galilee, and those who were sent into Egypt and other

provinces to slavery to the number of 17,000.  Two
thousand were brought with Titus in his triumph;
many of whom he gave to be devoured by wild
beasts, while the rest were cruelly slain.   By this all
nations may see what it is to reject God's truth, and
much more to persecute those who are sent by God
for their salvation.

# CHAPTER II.

JULIAN THE APOSTATE was the nephew of Constantine the Great. Constantius died in the year 361, when Julian succeeded him; but he no sooner attained the imperial dignity than he renounced Christianity for paganism. He restored idolatrous worship, re-opening temples that had been shut up, rebuilding such as were destroyed, and ordering the magistrates and people to follow his example; but he issued no public edicts against Christianity. He recalled all banished pagans, allowed the free exercise of religion to every sect, but deprived all Christians of office at court, in the magistracy, or in the army. He was chaste, temperate, vigilant, laborious, and apparently pious; so that by his pretended virtues he for a time did more mischief to Christianity than the most profligate of his predecessors.

The most famous martyr during his reign was Basil, who, by his opposition to Arianism, had made himself known. This brought upon him the vengeance of the Arian bishop of Constantinople, who issued an order to prevent him from preaching. He continued, however, to perform his duty at Ancyra, the capital of Galatia, till his enemies accused him of being an incendiary and a disturber of the public peace.

One day, meeting with a number of pagans going in procession to a sacrifice, he boldly expressed his abhorrence of their idolatrous proceedings. This provoked the people to seize him and carry him before the governor, who, finding him a strenuous Christian, ordered him first to be put on a rack and then committed to prison. Basil, however, not only continued firm, but with a prophetic spirit foretold the death of the emperor, and that he would be tormented in the other world. Julian then told Basil in great anger, that though he had an inclination to pardon him at first, he had put it out of his power by his behaviour. He then commanded that the body of Basil should be torn every day in seven different parts till the skin and flesh were entirely mangled. The inhuman sentence was executed with rigour, and the martyr expired under its severities on the 28th of June, 362.

Urbanus, Menidemus, and Theodorus, with fourscore other clergymen at Constantinople, petitioned the emperor to relieve them from the oppressions and cruelties of the Arians. But the tyrant, instead of this, ordered them to be embarked in a ship, which was to be set on fire. This order being executed, they all perished in the flames.

## The Persecutions of the Christians by the Goths, &c.

During the reign of Constantine the Great several Scythian Goths embraced Christianity, the light of the gospel having spread considerably in Scythia, though the two kings who ruled that country and the majority of the people continued pagans. Fritegern, king of the Western Goths, was an ally of the Romans; but Athanaric, king of the Eastern Goths, was at war with them. The Christians in the dominions of the former lived unmolested; but the latter, having been defeated by the Romans, wreaked his vengeance on his Christian subjects.

Eusebius, bishop of Samosatia, a distinguished writer of ecclesiastical history, was an eminent champion of Christ against the Arian heresy. The Arians therefore looked on him as a dangerous enemy, and at length persuaded the emperor to banish him into Thrace. He was afterwards restored to his see, which, however, he did not long enjoy, for an Arian woman threw a tile at him from the top of a house, fracturing his skull and terminating his life, in the year 380.

# CHAPTER III.

## THE PERSECUTIONS OF THE WALDENSES AND ALBIGENSES.

BERENGARIUS, about the year 1000, boldly preached the truth according to its primitive simplicity. Many from conviction embraced his doctrine, and were hence called Berongarians. He was succeeded by Peter Bruis, who preached at Toulouse, under the protection of the earl Hildephonsus; and the tenets of the reformers, with the reasons of their separation from the church of Rome, were published in a book written by Bruis, under the title of THE ANTI-CHRIST. In the year 1140 the number of the reformed was so great as to alarm the pope, who wrote to several princes to banish them from their dominions, and employed learned men to write against them. Peter Waldo, a native of Lyons, at this time became a strenuous opposer of popery; and from him the reformed received the appellation of Waldoys, or Waldenses. When pope Alexander III. was informed of these transactions, he excommunicated Waldo and his adherents, and commanded the bishop of Lyons to exterminate them. Thus began the papal persecutions against the Waldenses.

Waldo remained three years undiscovered in Lyons, though the utmost diligence was used to apprehend him, but at length he escaped to the mountains of Dauphiny. He soon after found means to propagate his doctrines in Dauphiny and Picardy, which so exasperated Philip, king of France, that he put the latter province under military execution: destroying above 300 gentlemen's seats, erasing some walled towns, burning many of the reformed, and driving others into Normandy and Germany.

Notwithstanding these persecutions, the reformed religion continued to flourish, and the Waldenses became more numerous than ever. At length the pope accused them of heresy, and used all manner of acts for their extirpation: such as excommunication, anathemas, canons, constitutions, decrees, etc., by which they were rendered incapable of holding places of trust, honour, or profit; their lands were seized, their goods confiscated, and they were not permitted to be buried in consecrated ground.

The reformed ministers continued to preach boldly against the Romish church; and Peter Waldo in particular, wherever he went, asserted that the pope was anti-christ, that mass was an abomination, that the host was an idol, and that purgatory was a fable. These proceedings originated the inquisition, for pope Innocent III. elected certain monks inquisitors, to find and deliver over the reformed to the secular power. These monks, upon the least surmise or information, delivered over the reformed to the magistrate, and the magistrate delivered them to the executioner. The process was short, as an accusation was deemed adequate to guilt, and a fair trial was never granted to the accused.

In the year 1380 a monk inquisitor, named Francis Boralli, had a commission granted him by pope Clement VII. to search for and punish the Waldenses in various places. He went to Ambrone, and summoned all the inhabitants to appear before him : those of the reformed religion were delivered over to the secular power and burnt ; and those who did not appear were excommunicated, and had their effects confiscated. In the distribution of these effects, the clergy had the lion's share, more than two-thirds going to them.

In the year 1400 the Waldenses residing in the valley of Pragela were suddenly attacked by a body of troops, who plundered their houses, murdered the inhabitants, or drove them to the Alps, where great numbers were frozen to death, it being in the depth of winter. In 1460 a persecution was carried on in Dauphiny by the archbishop of Ambrone, who employed a monk, named John Vayleti, who proceeded with such violence, that not only the Waldenses, but even many papists were sufferers; for if any of them expressed compassion or pity for the unoffending people, they were sure to be accused of partiality to heretics, and to share their fate. At length Vayleti's proceedings became so intolerable that a great number of papists signed a petition against him to Louis XI., king of France, who sent an order to the governor of Dauphiny to stop the persecution. Vayleti, however, by order of the archbishop, still continued it; for taking advantage of the last clause of the edict, he pretended that he did nothing contrary to the king's precept, who had ordered punishment to such as affirmed anything against the holy catholic faith. This persecution at length concluded with the death of the archbishop in 1487.

In 1488 pope Innocent VIII. determined to persecute the Waldenses. and craved the assistance of

the king of France, who sent his lieutenant into the
valley of Loyse for the purpose of exterminating
them. The Waldenses escaped into dens and caves,
and other retreats; but their cruel enemies placed
fagots at the mouths of these, and set fire to them.
It is computed that 3,000 were suffocated in this
cruel manner.

About the close of the fifteenth century, the heads
of the families of Merindol were summoned to appear
before the ecclesiastical court. When they confessed
themselves Waldenses, they were ordered to be
burnt, their families outlawed, their habitations laid
waste, and the woods that surrounded the town cut
down, so that the whole should be desolate. The
king, however, being informed of this barbarous
decree, countermanded the execution of it; but his
order was suppressed by Cardinal Tournon, and the
greatest cruelties were perpetrated with impunity.

The president of Opede sent soldiers to burn some
villages occupied by protestants: this commission
they too faithfully executed, exceeding it by a brutal
treatment of the inhabitants, in which neither infancy, age, nor sex, was spared. He also prohibited
all from giving assistance or sustenance to the
sufferers. He next marched against Cabrieres, and
began to cannonade it. At this time there were not
above sixty poor peasants with their families in the
town: and they sent him word that he need not
expend powder and shot upon the place, as they
were willing to open the gates and surrender, provided they might be permitted to retire unmolested
to Geneva or Germany. This was promised them;
but the gates were no sooner opened than the president ordered all the men to be cut to pieces, which

cruel command was immediately executed. Several women and children were driven into a large barn, which was set on fire, and every one perished in the flames.

At length the judgment of God overtook this monster of cruelty; he was afflicted with a most dreadful and painful disease. In his extremity he sent for a surgeon from Arles, who, on examining his disorders, told him they were of a singular nature, and much worse than he had ever seen in any other person. He then reprehended him for his cruelties, and told him that unless he repented, he might expect the hand of Heaven to fall still heavier upon him. On hearing this the president flew into a passion, and ordered his attendants to seize the surgeon; but he found means to escape, and soon after the president's disorder increased to a terrible degree. As he had found some little relief from the surgical operations, he again sent for the operator, having been informed of the place of his retirement: his message was accompanied with an apology for his former behaviour, and a promise of security. The surgeon, forgiving what was past, went to him, but too late to be of any service; for he found the tyrant raving like a madman, and crying out that he had a fire within him. After blaspheming for some time he expired in dreadful agonies; and his body in a few hours became so offensive that hardly any one could endure the place where it lay.

## The Persecution of the Albigenses.

The Albigenses were a people of the reformed religion who inhabited the country of Albi. They were condemned in the council of Lateran, by order

of pope Alexander III.; but they increased so
rapidly, that many cities were inhabited exclusively
by persons of their persuasion, and several eminent
noblemen embraced their doctrines.    Among the
latter were the earls of Toulouse and Foix.    The
pope pretended that he wished to draw them to the
Romish faith by argument and reasoning, and for
this end ordered a general conference; in which,
however, the popish doctors were entirely overcome by the arguments of Arnold, a reformed
clergyman.

A friar, named Peter, having been murdered in
the dominions of the earl of Toulouse, the pope
made the murder a pretence to persecute that nobleman and his subjects.    The earl, hearing of this,
wrote to the pope, assuring him that he had not the
least hand in Peter's death; for that friar was killed
by a gentleman, who, immediately after, fled out of
his territories.    But the pope being determined on
his destruction, a formidable army, with several
noblemen and prelates at the head of it, began their
march against the Albigenses.    The pope's legate
being at Valence, the earl repaired thither, and said
he was surprised that armed men should be sent
against him, before any proof of his guilt had been
produced.    He therefore voluntarily surrendered
himself, armed with the testimony of a good conscience, and hoped that the troops would thus be
prevented from plundering his innocent subjects.
The legate replied that he could not countermand
the orders to the troops, unless he would deliver up
seven of his best fortified castles as securities.    The
earl now perceived his error in submitting, but it
was too late; he therefore sent authority for the

surrender of the castles. The pope's legate had no sooner garrisoned these places, than he ordered their governors to appear before him. When they came, he said that, " the earl of Toulouse having delivered up his castles to the pope, they must consider that they were now the pope's subjects, and not the earl's; and that they must therefore act conformably to their new allegiance." The governors were astonished to see their lord in captivity, and themselves compelled into a new allegiance. But what afflicted them still more were the affronts put upon the earl; for he was stripped, led nine times round the grave of friar Peter, and severely scourged before the people. The army proceeded to besiege Bezieres; and the earl of Bezieres, thinking it impossible to defend the place, came out, and implored mercy for the inhabitants; intimating that there were as many Roman catholics as Albigenses in the city. The legate replied that all excuses were useless; that the place must be delivered up at discretion, or the most dreadful consequences would ensue.

The earl of Bezieres, returning to the city, told the inhabitants he could obtain no mercy, unless the Albigenses would abjure their religion and conform to the church of Rome. The Roman catholics pressed the Albigenses to comply; but the Albigenses nobly answered that they would not forsake their religion for the base price of a frail life; that God was able, if he pleased, to defend them: but if he would be glorified by the confession of their faith unto death, it would be an honour to them to die for his sake. Their enemies, finding importunity ineffectual, sent their bishop to the legate,

beseeching him not to include them in the chastise-
ment of the Albigenses; and urging him to try to
win the latter over by gentleness, and not by rigour.
On hearing this the legate flew into a passion, and
declared that "if all the city did not acknowledge
their fault, they should all taste of one curse, without distinction of religion, sex, or age." The inhabitants refusing to yield on such terms, the place
was taken by storm, when every cruelty was practised; nothing was to be heard but the groans of
men who lay weltering in their blood; the lamentations of mothers, who, after being cruelly ill-treated
by the soldiery, had their children taken from them,
and dashed to pieces before their faces. The city
being fired in various parts, those who hid themselves in their dwellings had either to remain and
perish in the flames, or rush out and fall by the
swords of the soldiers. The bloody legate, during
these infernal proceedings, enjoyed the carnage, and
even cried out to the troops, "Kill them, kill them
all; kill man, woman, and child; kill Roman
catholics as well as Albigenses, for when they are
dead the Lord knows how to select his own."
Thus the beautiful city of Bezieres was reduced to a
heap of ruins; and sixty thousand persons of different ages and both sexes were murdered.

The earl and a few others escaped to Carcasson,
which they put into the best posture of defence.
The legate, not willing to lose an opportunity of
shedding blood during the forty days which the
troops were to serve, led them immediately against
Carcasson. A furious assault was made, but the be-
siegers were repulsed with great slaughter; and
upon this occasion the earl gave the greatest proofs

of his courage, animating the besieged by crying out, "We had better die fighting than fall into the hands of such bigoted and bloody enemies." Two miles from Carcasson was a small town of the same name, which the Albigenses had likewise fortified. The legate, enraged at the repulse he had received, determined to wreak his vengeance on this town; the next morning he made an assault, and though the place was bravely defended, took it by storm, and put all within it to the sword. He now determined to get the earl of Bezieres into his power: and by the most solemn promises of personal security, succeeded in accomplishing his object. The earl believed the perjured legate, was seized and cast into prison, where he soon after died. The legate called the prelates and lords of his army together, telling them that it was necessary that there should be a secular general, wise and valiant, to command in their affairs. This charge was accepted by Simon, earl of Montfort. Four thousand men were left to garrison Carcasson; and the deceased earl of Bezieres was succeeded by earl Simon, a bigoted Roman catholic, who threatened vengeance on the Albigenses unless they conformed. But the king of Arragon, who was in his heart of the reformed persuasion, secretly encouraged the Albigenses, and gave them hopes that, if they acted with prudence, they might cast off the yoke of Simon. They took his advice, and while Simon was gone to Montpellier, surprised some of his fortresses, and were successful in several expeditions against his officers.

These proceedings so enraged the earl, that, returning from Montpellier, he collected together some

forces, marched against the Albigenses, and ordered
every prisoner he took to be immediately burnt.
Receiving further assistance, he attacked the castle
of Beron, and making himself master of it, ordered
the garrison to be cruelly mutilated and deprived of
sight—one person alone excepted, and he was but
partially blinded, in order that he might conduct
the rest to Cabaret.  Simon then undertook the
siege of Menerbe, which, on account of the want of
water, was obliged to yield to his forces.  The lord
of Termes, the governor, was put in prison, where
he died; his wife, sister, and daughter were burnt,
and 180 persons were committed to the flames.
Many other castles surrendered to him: the inhabitants of which were butchered in the most barbarous
manner.

Soon after the pope's legate called a council at
Montpellier for renewing military operations against
the Albigenses, and for doing proper honour to earl
Simon.  On meeting the council, the legate paid
many compliments to the earl, and declared that he
should be prince of all countries that might in future
be taken from the Albigenses; at the same time, by
order of the pontiff, he styled him the active and
dexterous soldier of Jesus Christ, and the invincible
defender of the catholic faith.  Just as the earl was
going to return thanks, a messenger brought word
that the people had heard earl Simon was in council, and that they had taken up arms and were
coming to destroy him.  This intelligence threw
the council into confusion; and Simon, though a
minute before styled an invincible defender of the
faith, was glad to jump out of the window and steal
away from the city.  The affair becoming serious,

the pope called a council at Lateran, in which great powers were granted to Roman catholic inquisitors, and many Albigenses were put to death. This council likewise confirmed to Simon the honours intended him, and empowered him to raise another army. He immediately repaired to court, received his investiture from the French king, and began to levy forces. Having now a number of troops, he determined, if possible, to exterminate the Albigenses, when he received advice that his countess was besieged in Narbonne by the earl of Toulouse. He proceeded to her relief, when the Albigenses met him, gave him battle, and defeated him; but he found means to escape into the castle of Narbonne. After this Toulouse was recovered by the Albigenses; but the pope, espousing earl Simon's cause, enabled him once more to undertake the siege of that city. The earl assaulted the place furiously, but was repulsed with great loss. By the legate's advice, however, he made another assault, and was again repulsed. To complete his misfortune, before the troops could recover from their confusion, the earl of Foix made his appearance at the head of a formidable army, attacked his already dispirited forces, and put them to rout. The earl narrowly escaped drowning in the Garonne, into which he had hastily plunged to avoid being captured. This discomforture almost broke his heart; but the pope's legate continued to encourage him, and offered to raise another army, which promise, after three years' delay, he at length performed, and that bigoted nobleman was once more enabled to take the field. On this occasion he turned his whole forces against Toulouse, which he besieged

for nine months, when, in one of the sallies made
by the besieged, his horse was wounded. The animal being in great anguish, ran away with him,
and bore him directly under the ramparts of the
city, when an archer shot him in the thigh with an
arrow; and a woman immediately after throwing a
large stone from the wall, it struck him upon the
head and killed him. The siege was raised; but
the legate, incensed at his disappointment, engaged
the king of France in the cause, who sent his son
to besiege the city. The French prince, with some
chosen troops, furiously assaulted it: but meeting
with a severe repulse, he abandoned Toulouse to besiege Miromand. This place he took by storm, and
put to the sword all the inhabitants, consisting of
5,000 men, women, and children.

The persecution against the Albigenses was renewed in 1620. At a town called Tell, while the
minister was preaching to a congregation of the
reformed, the papists attacked and murdered a
number of the people. A lady of eminence being
exhorted to change her religion—if not for her own
sake, at least for that of her infant—said, "I did
not quit Italy, my native country, nor forsake the
estate I had there, for the sake of Jesus Christ, to
renounce him here. With regard to my infant,
why should I not deliver him up to death, since
God gave his Son to die for me?" They then took
the child from her, delivered it to a popish nurse to
bring up, and slew the mother. Dominico Berto, a
youth of sixteen, refusing to turn papist, was set
upon an ass with his face to the tail, which he was
obliged to hold in his hand. In this condition he
was led to the market place, amidst the acclamations

of the populace; after which he was mutilated and burnt, till at last he died with pain. An Albigense young lady, of a noble family, was seized and carried through the streets with a paper mitre upon her head. After mocking and beating her, the brutal multitude told her to call upon the saints, when she replied, " My trust and salvation is in Christ only; for even the Virgin Mary, without the merits of her Son, could not be saved." On this the multitude fell upon and destroyed her.

# CHAPTER IV.

## The Origin, Progress, and Cruelties of the Inquisition.

IN the time of pope Innocent III., the reformed
religion had occasioned such a noise throughout
Europe that the catholics began to fear their church
was in danger, and the pope accordingly instituted
a number of inquisitors—persons who were to make
inquiry after, apprehend, and punish heretics. At
the head of these was Dominic, who had been
canonized. He and the other inquisitors spread
themselves into various Roman catholic countries,
and treated the protestants with the utmost severity.
At length the pope, not finding them so useful as he
hoped, resolved to establish fixed and regular courts
of inquisition; the first of them, of which Dominic
became the inquisitor-general, was in Toulouse.

These courts were soon erected in other countries;
but the Spanish inquisition became the most powerful and dreadful of all. Dominicans and Francis-
cans being the most zealous of the monks, the pope
invested them with an exclusive right of presiding
over and managing these courts. The friars of those
two orders were always selected from the very dregs
of the people, and were therefore not much troubled
with scruples of conscience; they were obliged,
however, by the rules of their orders, to lead very

austere lives, which rendered their manners unso-
cial, and better qualified them for their work.

The pope gave the inquisitors unlimited powers,
as judges delegated by him and immediately repre-
senting his person; they were permitted to excommunicate or sentence to death whom they thought
proper, upon the slightest information of heresy; they
were allowed to publish crusades against all whom
they deemed heretics, and enter into league with
sovereign princes to join these crusades with their
forces. About the year 1244 their power was further increased by the emperor Frederic II., who
declared himself the protector and friend of all inquisitors, and published two cruel edicts: that heretics who continued obstinate should be burnt, and
that those who repented should be imprisoned for life.

The officers of the inquisition are—three inquisitors, or judges, a procurator-fiscal, two secretaries, a
magistrate, a messenger, a receiver, a jailer, an
agent of confiscated possessions, and several asses-
sors, counsellors, executioners, physicians, surgeons,
door-keepers, familiars, and visitors, who are all
sworn to profound secrecy. Their chief accusation
against those who are subject to this tribunal is
heresy, which comprises all that is spoken or written
against the creed or the traditions of the Romish
church. The other articles of accusation are— renouncing the Roman catholic persuasion, and believing
that persons of any other religion may be saved, or
even admitting that the tenets of any but papists are
either scriptural or rational. Two other things
also incurred most severe punishment; to disapprove
of any action done by the inquisition, or doubt the
truth of anything asserted by inquisitors.

When the inquisitors have taken umbrage against a person, all expedients are used to facilitate condemnation; false oaths and testimonies are employed to find the accused guilty, and all laws and institutions are sacrificed to satiate the most bigoted vengeance. If a person accused be arrested and imprisoned, his treatment is deplorable. The jailers may begin by searching him for books and papers which tend to his conviction, or for instruments which might be employed in self-murder or escape; and on this pretext they often rob him of valuables and even wearing apparel. He is then committed to prison. Innocence, on such an occasion, is a weak reed; nothing being easier than to ruin an innocent person. The mildest sentence is imprisonment for life; yet the inquisitors proceed by degrees at once subtle, slow, and cruel. The jailer first insinuates himself into the prisoner's favour by pretending to advise him well; and among other hints of false kindness, tells him to petition for an audit. When he is brought before the consistory, the first demand is, "What is your request?" To this the prisoner very naturally answers, that he would have a hearing. On this, one of the inquisitors replies, "Your hearing is—confess the truth, conceal nothing, and rely on our mercy." If the prisoner makes some trifling confession, they immediately found an indictment on it; if he is mute, they shut him up without light, or any food but a scanty allowance of bread and water till he overcomes his obstinacy, as they call it; if he declares his innocence, they torment him till he either dies with the pain, or confesses himself guilty.

On the re-examination of such as confess, they

continually say, "You have not been sincere: you tell not all; you keep many things concealed, and therefore must be remanded to your dungeon." When those who have been silent are called for re-examination, if they continue mute, such tortures are ordered as either make them speak or kill them; and when those who proclaim their innocence are re-examined, a crucifix is held before them, and they are solemnly exhorted to take an oath of their confession of faith. This brings them to the test; they must either swear they are Roman catholics, or acknowledge they are not. If they acknowledge they are not, they are proceeded against as heretics: if they acknowledge they are, a string of accusations is brought against them, to which they are obliged to answer extempore, no time being given them to arrange their thoughts. On having verbally answered, pen, ink, and paper are brought them in order to produce a written answer, which must in every degree coincide with the verbal one. If the answers differ, the prisoners are charged with prevarication; if one contains more than the other, they are accused of wishing concealment; if they both agree, they are charged with premeditated artifice.

After a person impeached is condemned, he is either severely whipped, violently tortured, sent to the galleys, or sentenced to death; in either case the effects are confiscated. After judgment a procession is arranged to the place of execution, and the ceremony is called an *Auto da Fé*, or Act of Faith. The following is an exact account of one of these solemn farces, performed at Madrid in the year 1682:—

The officers of the inquisition, preceded by

trumpets, kettle-drums, and their banner, marched
on the 20th of May, in cavalcade, to the palace of the
great square, where they declared by proclamation,
that on the 30th June the sentence of the prisoners
would be executed. There had not been a spectacle of this kind at Madrid for several years, for
which reason it was expected by the inhabitants
with much impatience. When the day arrived, a
prodigious number of people appeared, dressed as
gaily as their circumstances would admit. In the
square was raised a high scaffold; and thither, from
seven in the morning till the evening, were brought
criminals of both sexes: all the inquisitions in the
kingdom sending their prisoners to Madrid. Twenty
men and women, with one renegado Mahometan,
were ordered to be burned; fifty Jews and Jewesses
were sentenced to a long confinement, and to wear
a yellow cap; and ten others, indicted for bigamy,
witchcraft, and other crimes, were sentenced to be
whipped, and then sent to the galleys; these last
wore large pasteboard caps, with inscriptions on
them, having a halter about their necks, and torches
in their hands. On this occasion the whole court of
Spain was present. The grand inquisitor's chair
was placed in a sort of tribunal, higher than that of
the king. Nobles acted the part of sheriff's officers
in England, leading such criminals as were to be
burned, and holding them when fast bound with
thick cords; the rest of the victims were conducted
by familiars of the inquisition. There was among
them a young Jewess of exquisite beauty, only
seventeen years of age. Being on the same side
of the scaffold on which the queen was seated,
she addressed her, in hope of obtaining pardon, in

TRIAL BY TORTURE BEFORE THE INQUISITION.—*See page 59.*

D

the following pathetic speech:—" Great queen! will not your royal presence be of some service to me in my miserable condition? Have regard to my youth; and, oh! consider that I am about to die for professing a religion imbibed from my earliest infancy!" Her majesty seemed to pity her, but turned away, as she did not dare to speak a word for one who had been declared heretic by the inquisition. Mass now began, in the midst of which the priest came from an altar placed near the scaffold, and seated himself in a chair prepared for that purpose. Then the chief inquisitor descended from the amphitheatre, dressed in his cope, and having a mitre on his head. After bowing to the altar, he advanced towards the king's balcony, attended by some of his officers, carrying a cross and the gospels, with a book containing the oaths by which the kings of Spain oblige themselves to protect the catholic faith, to extirpate heretics, and support with all their power the decrees of the inquisitions. On the approach of the inquisitor, presenting his book to the king, his majesty rose up bare-headed and swore to maintain the oath; after which the king continued standing till the inquisitor had returned to his place, when the secretary of the holy office mounted a pulpit and administered a like oath to the whole assembly. Mass commenced about twelve at noon, and did not end till nine in the evening, being protracted by a proclamation of the sentences of the several criminals. Next followed the burning of the twenty-one men and women, whose intrepidity was truly astonishing: some thrust their hands and feet into the flames with the most dauntless fortitude; while all acted with such resolution, that many of the amazed spectators lamented that such heroic souls *had not been more enlightened.* The king was so near the criminals, that their dying groans were audible to him; his coronation oath obliges him to sanction by his presence all the acts of the tribunal.

The inquisition belonging to Portugal is on a similar plan to that of Spain, having been instituted about the same time, and put under the same regulations. The house, or rather palace, is a noble edifice. It contains four courts, each about forty feet square, round which are about 300 dungeons or cells. The dungeons on the ground floor are for the lowest class of prisoners, and those on the second storey for superior rank. The galleries are built of freestone, and hid from view both within and without by a double wall about fifty feet high. So extensive is the whole prison, which contains so many turnings that none but those acquainted with it can find their way through. The apartments of the chief inquisitor are spacious and elegant; the entrance is through a large gate, which leads into a court-yard, round which are several chambers, and some large saloons for the king, royal family, and the rest of the court to stand and observe the executions.

A testoon, which is sevenpence-halfpenny, is allowed every prisoner daily; and the principal jailer, accompanied by two other officers, visits every prisoner monthly to know how he would have his allowance laid out. Sentinels walk about continually to listen, and if the least noise is heard, to address and threaten the prisoner; if the noise is repeated, a severe beating ensues. The following is said to be a fact:—A prisoner having a violent cough, one of the guards came and ordered him not to make a noise; to which he replied it was not in his power to forbear. The cough increasing, the guard went into the cell, stripped the poor creature naked, and beat him so unmercifully that he soon died.

Sometimes a prisoner passes months without knowing of what he is accused, or having the least idea when he is to be tried. The jailer at length informs him that he must petition for a trial. This having been done, he is taken bare-headed for examination. At the door of the tribunal the jailer knocks three times, to give the judges notice of their approach. A bell is then rung by one of the judges, when an attendant opens the door, admits the prisoner, and accommodates him with a stool. The prisoner is then ordered by the president to kneel, and lay his right hand upon a book, which is presented to him close shut. This being complied with, the following question is put to him: "Will you promise to conceal the secrets of the holy office, and to speak the truth?" Should he answer in the negative, he is remanded to his cell and cruelly treated. If he answers in the affirmative, he is ordered to be again seated, and the examination proceeds; the president asks a variety of questions, and the clerk minutes both them and the answers. When the examination is closed, the bell is again rung, the jailer appears, and the prisoner is ordered to withdraw, with this exhortation: "Tax your memory, recollect all the sins you have committed, and when you are again brought here, communicate them to the holy office." The jailer and attendants, when apprised that the prisoner has made an ingenuous confession, and readily answered every question, make him a low bow, and treat him with affected kindness. He is brought in a few days to a second examination, with the same formalities as before. The inquisitors often deceive prisoners by promising the greatest lenity, and even to restore their liberty, if they will accuse themselves : the unhappy persons who are in their power frequently fall into this snare, and are sacrificed to their own simplicity.

Another artifice is used by the inquisitors when a prisoner has too much resolution to accuse himself, and too much foresight to be ensnared by their sophistry. A copy of an indictment is given him, in which, among many trivial accusations, he is charged with many enormous crimes. This rouses his temper, and he exclaims against such falsities. He is then asked which of the crimes he can deny. He naturally mentions the most atrocious, and expresses his abhorrence of them ; when, the indict-ment being snatched out of his hand, the president says, " By your denying only those crimes which you mention, you implicitly confess the rest ; we shall therefore proceed accordingly."

Though the inquisitors allow the torture to be used only three times, it is so severe that the prisoner either dies under it or ever after continues a cripple. The following is a description of the severe torments occasioned by the torture, from the account of one who suffered it the three usual times, but happily survived its cruelties.

### The First Time of Torture.

A prisoner, on refusing to comply with the iniqui-tous demands of the inquisitors, by confessing the

crimes they charged him with, was immediately conveyed to the torture-room, where no light appeared
but that of two candles. That the cries of the
sufferers might not be heard, the room is lined with
a kind of quilting, covering all the crevices and
deadening the sound. The prisoner's horror was
extreme on entering this infernal place, when suddenly he was surrounded by six wretches, who, after
preparing the tortures, stripped him naked to his
drawers. He was then laid on his back on a kind
of stand, elevated a few feet from the floor. They
began by putting an iron collar round his neck, and
a ring to each foot, which fastened him to the stand.
His limbs being thus stretched out, they wound two
ropes round each arm and each thigh; these, being
passed under the scaffold, were drawn tight at the
same instant by four of the men. The pains which
immediately succeeded were intolerable; the ropes
being of a small size, cut through the prisoner's
flesh to the bone, making the blood gush out. As
he persisted in not confessing what the inquisitors
required, the ropes were drawn in this manner
four times successively. A physician and surgeon
attended, and often felt his temples, to judge of his
danger. By these means his tortures were for a
short time suspended, but only that he might recover to sustain further torture. During this extremity of anguish, while the tender frame is tear-
ing, as it were, in pieces, while at every pore it feels
the sharpest pangs, and the agonized soul is ready to
burst from its wretched mansion, the ministers of the
inquisition look on without emotion, and calmly
advise the poor distracted creature to confess his guilt,
that he may obtain pardon and receive absolution.

All this, however, was ineffectual with the prisoner, whose mind was strengthened by a sweet conscious- ness of innocence, and' the divine consolation of religion. Amidst his bodily suffering, the physician and the surgeon were so barbarous as to declare that if he died under the torture he would be guilty, by his own obstinacy, of self-murder. The last time the ropes were drawn tight he grew so exceedingly weak, by the stoppage of the circulation of his blood, and the pains he endured, that he fainted away, upon which he was unloosed and carried back to his dungeon.

## The Second Time of Torturing.

The inhuman wretches, finding that all the tor- tures they inflicted, instead of extorting a confession from the prisoner, only served to excite his suppli- cations to Heaven for patience and power to perse- vere in truth and integrity, were so inhuman, six weeks after, as to expose him to another kind of torture, more severe, if possible, than the former, the manner of inflicting which was as follows: they forced his arms backwards, so that the palms of his hands were turned outward behind him; when, by means of a rope that fastened them together at the wrists, and which was turned by an engine, they drew them by degrees nearer each other, in such a manner that the back of each hand touched, and stood parallel to each other. Both his shoulders were thus dislocated, and a considerable quantity of blood issued from his mouth. This torture was repeated thrice, after which he was taken to the dungeon, and delivered to the physician and

MARTYRDOM OF JOHN HUSS.—*See page* 89.

surgeon, who, in setting the dislocated bones, put him to the most exquisite torment.

## The Third Time of Torturing.

About two months after the second torture the prisoner, being recovered, was again ordered to the torture-room ; and there, for the last time, made to undergo another kind of punishment, which was inflicted twice without intermission. The executioners fastened a thick iron chain twice round his body, which, crossing upon his stomach, terminated at the wrists. They then placed him with his back against a thick board, at each extremity whereof was a pulley, through which there run a rope that caught the ends of the chain at his wrists. Then the executioner, stretching the end of this rope by means of a roller placed at a distance behind him, pressed or bruised his stomach in proportion as the ends of the chain were drawn tighter. They tortured him in this manner to such a degree, that his wrists, as well as his shoulders, were dislocated. They were, however, soon set by the surgeons ; but the barbarians, not yet satisfied, made him immediately undergo the torture a second time, which he sustained with equal constancy and resolution. He was then remanded to his dungeon, attended by the surgeon to dress his bruises and adjust the parts dislocated ; and here he continued till their gaol delivery restored him to a miserable freedom in this world, or their *Auto da Fé* removed him to a better state.

It may be judged from these accounts what dreadful agony the sufferer must have laboured

under, by being so frequently put to the torture.
Most of his limbs were disjointed; so much was he
bruised and exhausted as to be unable for weeks to
lift his hand to his mouth, and his body became
greatly swelled by frequent dislocations.   After his
discharge he felt the effect of the cruelty for the remainder of his life, being frequently seized with
thrilling and excruciating pains, to which he had
never before been subject.   The unhappy females
who fall into the hands of the inquisitors, have no
favour shown them on account of sex, but are tortured with as much severity as the male prisoners.

Should the prisoner still refuse to confess, he is
remanded to his dungeon; but a stratagem is used
to draw from him what the torture fails to do.   A
companion is allowed to attend him; this person
insinuates himself into the good graces of the prisoner, sympathises with him, and, taking advantage
of the hasty expressions forced from him by pain,
does all he can to dive into his secrets.   This companion sometimes pretends to be a prisoner like
himself, to draw the unhappy person to betray his
private sentiments.

Francis Romanus, a native of Spain, was employed by the merchants of Antwerp to transact
some business for them at Bremen.   He had been
educated in the Romish persuasion, but going one
day to a protestant church, he was struck with the
truths which he heard, and on perusing the scriptures, and the writings of some protestant divines,
he perceived the falsehood of the principles he
had formerly held.   Resolved to think only of his
eternal salvation, he resigned his agency to the
merchants of Antwerp, giving them an account of

his conversion; and then, resolved on the conversion of his parents, he returned without delay to Spain. But the Antwerp merchants writing to the inquisitors, he was seized, imprisoned for a time, and then condemned to the flames as a heretic. He was led to the place of execution in a garment painted with demon figures, and had a paper mitre put on his head by way of derision. As he passed by a wooden cross, one of the priests bade him kneel to it; but he absolutely refused to do so, saying, "It is not for Christians to worship wood." Having been placed on a pile of fagots, the fire quickly reached him, when he suddenly lifted up his head. The priests, thinking he meant to recant, ordered him to be taken down. Finding, however, that they were mistaken, and that he still retained his constancy, he was placed again upon the pile, where, as long as he had life and voice remaining, he kept repeating these verses of the seventh Psalm —" O Lord my God, in thee do I put my trust. O let the wickedness of the people come to an end, but establish thou the just. My defence is of God, who saveth the upright in heart. I will praise the Lord according to his righteousness; and will sing praise to the name of the Lord most high!"

At St. Lucar, in Spain, resided a carver named Rochus, whose principal business was to make images of saints and other popish idols. Becoming, however, convinced of the errors of Rome, he embraced the protestant faith, left off carving images, and, for subsistence, followed the business of a seal engraver only. But having retained one image of the Virgin Mary for a sign, an inquisitor, passing by, asked if he would sell it. Rochus mentioned a

price; the inquisitor objected to it, and offered half
the money. Rochus replied, "I would rather break
it to pieces than take such a trifle." "Break it to
pieces!" said the inquisitor: "break it to pieces if
you dare!" Rochus, being provoked at this ex-
pression, snatched up a chisel, and cut off the nose
of the image. This was sufficient; the inquisitor
went away in a rage, and soon after sent to have
him apprehended. In vain did he plead that what
he defaced was his own property; and that if it was
not proper to do as he would with his own, it was
not proper for the inquisitor to bargain for the image in the way of trade. Nothing, however, availed
him; his fate was decided; he was condemned to be
burnt, and the sentence was executed without delay.

A Spanish Roman catholic, named Juliano, travelling into Germany, became a convert to the
protestant religion, and undertook to convey to his
own country a great number of Bibles, concealed in
casks, and packed up like Rhenish wine. He succeeded so far as to distribute the books. A pretended
protestant, however, who had purchased one of the
Bibles, betrayed him. Juliano was seized, and,
means being used to find out the purchasers of the
Bibles, 800 persons were apprehended. Juliano was
burnt, 20 were roasted on spits, several imprisoned
for life, some were publicly whipped, many sent to
the galleys, and a very small number were acquitted.

A young lady, named Maria de Coccicao, was
taken up by the inquisitors, and ordered to be put to
the rack. The torments she felt made her confess
the charges against her. The cords were then
slackened, and she was reconducted to her cell,
where she remained till she recovered the use of her

MURDER OF THE ADMIRAL, PRINCE OF NAVARRE AND CONDÉ.—*See page 69.*

limbs; she was then brought again before the tribunal, and ordered to ratify her confession. This she absolutely refused to do, telling them that what she had said was forced from her by the excessive pain she underwent. The inquisitors, incensed at this reply, ordered her again to be put to the rack, when the weakness of nature once more prevailed, and she repeated her former confession. She was immediately remanded to her cell; and being a third time brought before the inquisitors, they ordered her to sign her first and second confessions. She answered as before, but added, " I have twice given way to the frailty of the flesh, and perhaps may, while on the rack, be weak enough to do so again; but depend upon it, if you torture me a hundred times, as soon as I am released from the rack I shall deny what was extorted from me by pain." The inquisitors then ordered her to be racked a third time; and during this last trial she bore the torments with the utmost fortitude, and could not be persuaded to answer any of the questions put to her. As her courage and constancy increased, the inquisitors, instead of putting her to death, condemned her to a severe whipping through the public streets, and banished her for ten years.

A lady of a noble family of Seville, named Jane Bohorquia, was apprehended on the information of her sister, who had been tortured and burnt for professing the protestant religion. While on the rack, she confessed she had frequently conversed with her sister on protestantism; and upon this extorted confession, Jane was seized, and ordered to be racked, which was done with such severity, that she expired a week after of the wounds and bruises.

E

Isaac Orobio, a learned physician, having beaten a Moorish servant for stealing, was accused by him of professing Judaism, and the inquisitor seized the master upon the charge. He was kept three years in prison before he had the least intimation of what he had to undergo, and then suffered the following modes of torture:—A coarse coat was put upon him and drawn so tight that the circulation of the blood was nearly stopped, and the breath almost pressed out of his body. After this the strings were suddenly loosened, when the air, forcing its way hastily into his stomach, and the blood rushing into its channels, he suffered incredible pain. He was seated on a bench, his back against a wall, to which iron pulleys were fixed. Ropes being fastened to several parts of his body and limbs, were passed through the pulleys, and being suddenly drawn with great violence, his whole frame was forced into a distorted mass. After having suffered for a considerable time the pains of this position, the seat was suddenly removed, and he was left suspended against the wall. The executioners fastened ropes round his wrists, and then drew them about his body. Placing him on his back, with his feet against the wall, they pulled with their utmost violence, till the cord had penetrated to the bone. He suffered the last torture three times, and then lay seventy days before his wounds were healed. He was afterwards banished, and in his exile wrote the account of his sufferings.

It is wonderful that superstition has—with respect to the inquisition especially—always overcome common sense, and custom operated against reason. One prince, indeed, Don Carlos, the amiable son of Philip II., king of Spain, and grandson of the

celebrated emperor, Charles V.—intended to abolish
this cruel court, but he lost his life before he became
able to accomplish the merciful purpose. He possessed all the good qualities of his grandfather, without any of the bad ones of his father. He had sense
enough to see the errors of popery, and abhorred
the very name of the inquisition. He inveighed
publicly against the court, ridiculed the affected
piety of the inquisitors, and declared that if he ever
came to the crown, he would abolish the inquisition
and exterminate all its agents. This irritated the
inquisitors against him, and they accordingly determined on his destruction. They employed their
emissaries to spread the most artful insinuations
against the prince, and at length raised such a spirit
of discontent among the people that the king was
under the necessity of removing Don Carlos from
the court.

Shortly after the prince having shown great favour
to the protestants in the Netherlands, the inquisition
loudly declared, that as the persons in question were
heretics, the prince himself must be one, since he
gave them countenance. Thus they gained such an
ascendancy over the mind of the king, that he sacrificed the feelings of nature to the force of bigotry,
and passed sentence of death on his only son. The
prince had what they called an indulgence—that
is, he was permitted to choose the manner of his
death. He chose bleeding and the hot bath. On
an early day everything was prepared as he wished,
when veins in his arms and legs were opened, and
he gradually sank to death without apparent pain,
falling a martyr to inquisitorial malice, strangely
sanctioned by parental bigotry.

# CHAPTER V.

## Horrible Massacres in France, anno 1572.

AFTER a long series of troubles in France, the papists, seeing they could not overcome the protestants by open force, began to devise how they might entrap them by subtlety, and that by two ways: first by a pretended commission sent into the Low Countries, which the prince of Navarre and Conde was to command. This was merely to learn what power and force the admiral had under him, who they were, and what were their names. The second was by a marriage between the prince of Navarre and the king's sister; to which were to be invited all the chief protestants of France. Accordingly they first began with the queen of Navarre, mother to the prince who was to espouse the king's sister. Allured by fair words, she consented to come to Paris. Shortly after she fell sick, and died within five days, not without suspicion of poison.

Notwithstanding, the marriage still proceeded. The admiral, prince of Navarre and Conde, and many other protestant chiefs, were induced by the king's letters and promises to proceed to Paris, and were received with great solemnity. The marriage took place on the 19th of August, 1572, and was solemnized by the cardinal of Bourbonne.

Afterwards they resorted to the bishop's palace to dinner. In the evening they were conducted to a palace in the centre of the city, to supper. Four days after this the admiral, coming from the council table, was shot at with a pistol charged with three bullets, and wounded in both his arms. He still remained in Paris, although his friends advised him to flee. Soldiers were appointed in different places of the city to be ready at the command of the king; and upon the watchword being given, they burst out to the slaughter of the protestants, beginning with the admiral himself, who, being wounded, was cast out of the window into the street, where his head being struck off, was embalmed and sent to the pope. The savage people then cut off his arms, and drew his mangled body three days through the streets of Paris, after which they took it to the place of execution, and there hanged it by the heels, to the scorn of the populace.

The martyrdom of this virtuous man had no sooner taken place, than the troops, with rage and violence, ran about slaying all the protestants they knew or could find within the city gates. This continued many days; but the greatest slaughter was in the first three days, in which were said to be murdered above 10,000 men and women, old and young, of all sorts and conditions. The bodies of the dead were carried in carts and thrown into the river, which, with other whole streams in certain places of the city, was reddened with the blood of the slain. In the number of eminent men who fell in this dreadful slaughter were Petrus Ramus, Lambinus, Plateanus, Lomenius, Chapesius, and others.

The brutal deeds of this period were not confined

within the walls of Paris, but extended to other
cities and quarters of the realm, especially at Lyons,
Orleans, Toulouse, and Rouen, where the cruelties
were, if possible, even greater than in the capital.
Within the space of one month 30,000 religious protestants are said to have been slain.    When intelligence of the massacre was received at Rome, the
greatest rejoicings took place.  The pope and his cardinals went in procession to the church of St. Mark,
to give thanks to God; and a medal was struck to
commemorate the event.   A jubilee was also published, and the ordnance fired from the castle of St.
Angelo.   To the person who brought the news the
cardinal of Lorraine gave 1,000 crowns.   Similar
rejoicings were also made all over France for this
imagined overthrow of the faithful.

MEDAL STRUCK BY POPE GREGORY XIII., TO COMMEMORATE THE
MASSACRE OF ST. BARTHOLOMEW.

The enemies of the truth began now to think that
they were the sole lords of men's consciences; and
truly, it did seem as if God had abandoned the
earth to the ravages of his enemy.   But he had
otherwise decreed, and thousands who had not
*bowed the knee to Baal* were called forth *to glory and
virtue.*

The year following died Charles IX. of France, the tyrant who had been instrumental in these calamities. He was only in the 28th year of his age, and his death was remarkable and dreadful. When lying on his bed, the blood gushed from various parts of his body. At length, after violent convulsions, and the utterance of the most horrid blasphemies, it issued in such quantities from his mouth that he expired.

### Robert Oguier, his Wife, and their Sons, who were burned at Lisle.

On Saturday, March 6th, 1556, about ten o'clock at night, the provost of the city, with his sergeants, went to seek protestants met in houses; but there was no assembly. They therefore came to the house of Robert Oguier, which was a little church, where both rich and poor were familiarly instructed in the scriptures. Having entered, they found books, which they carried away. But he whom they principally sought was not there, namely, Baudicon, the son of Oguier, who had gone out to talk of the word of God with some of the brethren. On his return, he knocked, when Martin, the younger brother, bade him be gone; but Baudicon, thinking he mistook him for some other, said, "It is I, open the door;" with that the sergeants opened, saying, "Ah, sir, you are well met!" to whom he answered, "I thank you, my friends; you are also welcome hither." Then said the provost, "I arrest you all, in the emperor's name;" and with that commanded the husband, his wife, and their two sons to be bound and imprisoned, leaving their two daughters to look to the house. A few days after the prisoners were

brought before the magistrates, who examined them.
They directed their speech to Robert Oguier, in
these words: "It is told us that you never come to
mass, yea, and also dissuade others. We are further
informed that you maintain conventicles in your
house, causing erroneous doctrines to be preached
there, contrary to the ordinance of our holy mother
the church."

He confessed the first charge, and justified his
conduct, by proving from the scriptures, that the
saying of mass was contrary to the ordinances of
Jesus Christ; and he defended the religious meetings in his house by showing that they were commanded by our blessed Saviour himself.

One of the magistrates asked what they did when
they met. To which Baudicon answered, "If it
please you, I will open the business at large." The
sheriffs said, "Well, let us hear it." Baudicon,
lifting up his eyes to heaven, began thus:—" When
we meet together in the name of our Lord Jesus
Christ, we first of all prostrate upon our knees before God, and in the humility of our spirits do make
a confession of our sins before his Divine Majesty.
Then we pray that the word of God may be rightly
divined and purely preached: we also pray for our
sovereign lord the emperor, and for his honourable
counsellors, that the commonwealth may be peaceably governed to the glory of God; yea, we forget
not you whom we acknowledge our superiors, en-
treating our God for you and for this city, that you
may maintain it in all tranquillity. Thus I have
exactly related unto you what we do: think you
now, whether we have offended so highly in the
matter of our assembling."

Each of them made an open confession of their
faith; and, being returned to prison, they were put
to the torture to make them confess who frequented
their house; but they would discover none, unless
such as were well known to the judges, or were at
that time absent. Four or five days after they were
convened again before their judges, and asked
whether they would submit to the will of the magistrates. Robert Oguier, and Baudicon his son, said,
"Yea, we will." Then, demanding the same of
Martin, the younger brother, he answered that he
would accompany his mother; so he was sent back
to prison, whilst the father and the son were sentenced to be burnt alive to ashes. One of the judges,
after sentence was pronounced, said, "To-day you
shall go to dwell with all the devils in hell-fire."
Having received sentence of death, they returned to
prison, joyful that the Lord did them the honour to
enrol them among his martyrs.

As they were about to separate Baudicon from his
father, he said, "Let my father alone, and trouble
him not: he is an old man, and hath an infirm
body; hinder him not, I pray you, from receiving
the crown of martyrdom." Baudicon was then conveyed to a chamber apart, and there, being stripped
of his clothes, was prepared to be sacrificed. While
one brought him gunpowder to put to his breast, a
fellow standing by, said, "Wert thou my brother, I
would sell all I am worth to buy fagots to burn thee
—thou findest too much favour." The young man
answered, "Well, sir, the Lord show you more
mercy." Whilst they spake thus to Baudicon, some
of the friars pressed about the old man, persuading
him at least to take a crucifix into his hands, lest

the people should murmur against him; adding further, that he might for all that lift up his heart to
God.   Then they fastened it between his hands;
but as soon as Baudicon was come down and espied
what they had done, he said, "Alas! father, what
do you now? will you play the idolater at our last
hour?"   And then, pulling the idol out of his
hands, which they had fastened therein, he threw it
away, saying, "What cause hath the people to be
offended at us for not receiving a Christ of wood?
We bear upon our hearts the cross of Christ, the Son
of the ever-living God."

A band of soldiers attended them to execution.
Being come to the place, they ascended the scaffold;
Baudicon then asked leave of the sheriffs to confess
his faith before the people; answer was made that
he was to look unto his spiritual father, and confess
to him.   He was then dragged to the stake, where
he began to sing the 16th Psalm.   The friar cried
out, "Do you not hear, my master, what wicked
errors these heretics sing, to beguile the people
with?"   Baudicon hearing him, replied, "Callest
thou the Psalms of David errors?   But no wonder,
for thus you are wont to blaspheme against the
Spirit of God."   Then turning his eyes toward his
father, who was about to be chained to the stake,
he said, "Be of good courage, father; the worst
will soon be past."   He often reiterated these short
breathings: "O God, Father everlasting, accept
the sacrifice of our bodies, for thy well-beloved Son
Jesus Christ's sake."   One of the friars cried out,
"Heretic, thou liest; he is none of thy father: the
devil is thy father."   During these conflicts he
lifted his eyes upwards, and speaking to his father,

said, "Behold I see the heavens open, and millions of angels ready to receive us, rejoicing to see us thus witnessing the truth before the world. Father, let us be glad and rejoice, for the joys of heaven are set upon us." Fire was forthwith put to the straw and wood, which burnt beneath, whilst they, not shrinking from the pains, spake to one another; Baudicon often repeating this in his father's ears, "Faint not, father, nor be afraid; yet a very little while, and we shall enter the heavenly mansions." In the end, the fire growing hot upon them, the last words they were heard to say were, "Jesus Christ, thou Son of God, into thy hand do we commend our spirits." And thus these two slept sweetly in the Lord.

Eight days after Jane the mother, and Martin her son, were executed in the same city. Many attempts were made to cause them to waver in their faith; and the mother for a short time manifested weakness, but, through the efforts of Martin, she regained her former steadfastness. Not long after the emissaries of Satan came in, supposing to find her in the mind wherein they left her, when she said, "Away, Satan, get thee behind me; for henceforth thou hast neither part nor portion in me. I will, by the help of God, stand to my first confession; and if I may not sign it with ink, I will seal it with my blood." And from that time this frail vessel grew stronger and stronger.

Soon after Martin and his mother were bound and brought to the place of their martyrdom. His mother ascending the scaffold, cried to Martin, "Come up, come up, my son." As he was speaking to the people, she said, "Speak out, Martin, that it

may appear to all that we die for the truth."
Martin would have made a confession of his faith,
but he was not permitted to speak. His mother,
being bound to the stake, said, in the hearing of
the spectators, "We are Christians, and that which
we now suffer is not for murder or theft, but
because we believe that which the word of God
teacheth us; we both rejoice that we are counted
worthy to suffer for the same." The fire being
kindled, the vehemency thereof did not abate the
fervency of their zeal; they continued constant in
the faith, and with uplifted hands said, "Lord
Jesus, into thy hands we commend our spirits."
And thus they blessedly slept in the Lord.

### Massacre of the Huguenots at Vassy, in Champaigne.

The duke of Guise, on his arrival at Joinville,
asked whether those of Vassy had sermons preached
constantly by their minister. He was told they
had, and that they increased daily. On hearing
this he fell into a grievous passion; and on Saturday, the last day of February, 1562, he departed
from Joinville, and lodged in the village of Damar-
tin, distant about two miles and a half. The next
day, having heard mass in the morning, he went on
to Vassy, attended by 200 armed men. Command
was given to such as were papists to retire into the
monastery, unless they would venture the loss of
their lives. The duke then marched on towards
the place where the sermon was, being a barn about
100 paces from the monastery. By this time Mr.
Leonard Morel, the minister, after the first prayer,
had begun his sermon before auditors, who might

amount to 1,200 men, women, and children. The horsemen first approaching the barn, shot off two arquebuses upon those who were in the galleries joining the windows. The people perceiving their danger, endeavoured to shut the door, but were prevented by the ruffians rushing in upon them, drawing their swords, and crying out, "Death of God! kill, kill these Huguenots." The duke of Guise, with his company, violently entered, striking down the poor people with their swords, daggers, and cutlasses, not sparing age or sex; the whole assembly were so astonished, that they knew not which way to turn, but ran hither and thither, flying as sheep before ravening wolves. Some of the murderers shot off their carbines against them that were in the galleries; others cut in pieces such as were below; some had their heads cleft in twain, their arms and hands cut off; so that many of them died instantly on the spot. The walls and galleries of the place were dyed with the blood of those who were murdered; and so great was the fury of the murderers, that part of the people within were forced to break open the roofs of the houses, in hope of saving themselves upon the top. Being got thither, and then fearing to fall again into the hands of these cruel tigers, some of them leapt over the walls of the city, which were very high, flying wounded into the woods and amongst the vines. The duke charged his soldiers to kill especially the young men. Pursuing those who went on the housetops, they cried, "Come down, ye dogs, come down;" using many cruel speeches to them. The cause why some women escaped was, as the report went, for the duchess's sake, his wife, who, passing

by the walls of the city, and hearing hideous out-
cries, with the noise of the carbines and pistols
continually discharging, sent in haste to the duke,
her husband, with much entreaty to cease his persecution.

The minister at first. ceased not to preach, till
one discharged his piece against the pulpit where
he stood: after which, falling upon his knees, he
entreated the Lord to have mercy on himself, and
also on his flock. Having prayed, he left his gown
behind him, thinking thereby to keep himself unknown; but as he approached the door he stumbled
upon a dead body, where he received a blow with a
sword upon his right shoulder. Getting up again,
and then thinking to go forth, he was immediately
laid hold of, and grievously hurt on the head with a
sword; whereupon, being felled to the ground, and
thinking himself mortally wounded, he cried,
"Lord, into thy hands I commend my spirit, for
thou hast redeemed me, God of truth." While he
thus prayed one of the bloody crew ran upon him,
intending to hamstring him; but it pleased God
that his sword broke in the hilt. Two gentlemen
taking knowledge of him, said, "He is a minister,
let him be conveyed to my lord duke." Leading
him away by the arms, they brought him before the
gate of the monastery, whence the duke and the
cardinal his brother coming forth, asked him, "Art
thou the minister of this place? Who made thee so
bold as to seduce this people thus?" "Sir," said
the minister, "I am no seducer; I have preached to
them the gospel of Jesus Christ." The duke, perceiving that this answer condemned his cruel
outrages, began to curse and swear, saying, "Death

of God! doth the gospel preach sedition ? Provost, go and let a gibbet be set up, and hang this fellow." At which words the minister was delivered into the hands of two pages, who cruelly misused him. The women of the city, being ignorant papists, caught up dirt to throw in his face, and with extended out-cries, said, " Kill him, kill this varlet, who hath been the cause of the death of so many."

This massacre continued a full hour, the duke's trumpeters sounding the while several times. When any of the victims desired to have mercy shown them for the love of Jesus Christ, the murderers in scorn would say unto them, " You use the name of Christ, but where is your Christ now ? " There died in this massacre, within a few days, fifty or threescore persons; besides these, there were about 250 men and women that were injured, whereof some died, one losing a leg, another an arm, another his fingers. The poor's-box, which was fastened to the door of the church with two iron hooks, contain-ing £12, was wrested thence, and never restored. The minister was closely confined, and frequently threatened to be inclosed in a sack and drowned. He was, however, on the 8th of May, 1563, liberated at the earnest suit of the prince of Portien.

# CHAPTER VI.

## Persecutions in Bohemia and Germany.

THE severity exercised over the churches of the Bohemians induced them to send two ministers and four laymen to Rome, in the year 977, to seek relief from the pope. After some delay their request was granted, and the grievances redressed. Two things in particular were permitted them—viz., to have divine service in their own language, and to give the cup in the sacrament to the laity. Succeeding popes, however, exerted all their power to fetter their prejudices on the minds of the Bohemians; while the latter with great spirit aimed to preserve their religious liberties. Some friends, zealous for the gospel, applied to Charles, king of Bohemia, in 1375, to call a council for inquiry into the abuses which had crept into the church, and to make a thorough reformation. Charles sent to the pope for advice; the latter only replied, " Punish severely those presumptuous heretics." The king accordingly banished those who had made the application, and imposed additional restraints on the religious liberties of the country.

The martyrdom of John Huss and Jerome of Prague—two great men brought to the truth by the writings of our countryman, John Wickliffe, the

morning star of the reformation—gave great anima-
tion to the cause. These two distinguished reformers
were condemned by the council of Constance, when
fifty-eight Bohemian noblemen interposed in their
favour. Nevertheless, they were burnt; and the
pope, with the council of Constance, ordered the
Romish clergy to excommunicate all who adopted
their opinions or pitied their fate. Hence arose
great contentions between the papists and reformed
Bohemians, which produced a violent persecution
against the latter. At Prague it was extremely
severe. At length the reformed, driven to despera-
tion, armed themselves, attacked the senate-house,
and cast twelve of its members, with the speaker,
out of the windows. The pope, hearing of this,
came to Florence, and publicly excommunicated the
reformed Bohemians, exciting the emperor of Germany, and other kings, princes, dukes, &c., to take
up arms to extirpate them, promising full remission
of sins to every one who should kill a Bohemian
protestant. The result of this was a bloody war;
for several popish princes undertook the extirpation,
or at least expulsion, of the proscribed people;
while the Bohemians, arming themselves, prepared
vigorously to repel the assault. The popish army
overcame the protestant forces at the battle of Cut-
tenburg; they conveyed their prisoners to three
deep mines near the town, and threw several hundred into each, where they perished miserably.

A bigoted popish magistrate, name Pichel, seized
twenty-four protestants, among whom was his
daughter's husband. On their professing themselves
of the reformed religion, he sentenced them to be
drowned in the river Abbis. On the day of the

F

execution a great concourse of people attended, among whom was Pichel's daughter. Seeing her husband prepared for death, she threw herself at her father's feet, bedewed them with tears, and implored him to pardon her husband. The obdurate magistrate sternly replied, " Intercede not for him, child : he is a heretic—a vile heretic ! " To which she nobly answered, " Whatever his faults may be, or however his opinions may differ from yours, he is still my husband." Pichel flew into a passion, and said, " You are mad ! Cannot you, after his death, have a much worthier husband ? " " No, sir," she replied, " my affections are fixed upon him, and death shall not dissolve my marriage vow." Pichel continued inflexible, and ordered the prisoners to be tied with their hands and feet behind them, and thrown into the river. This being done, the young lady leaped into the waves, and embracing the body of her husband, both sank together.

The emperor Ferdinand, who bitterly hated the protestants, instituted a high court of judges, on the plan of the inquisition, with this difference, that the new court was to move from place to place, attended by a body of troops. The greater part of this court consisted of Jesuits, from whose decision there was no appeal. This bloody tribunal, attended by its ferocious guard, made the tour of Bohemia.

The first who fell a victim was an aged minister, whom they killed as he lay sick in bed. Next day they robbed and murdered another, and soon after shot a third while preaching. They tied a minister and his wife back to back and burnt them. Another minister they hung upon a cross-beam, and making a fire under him, broiled him to death. One gentleman they hacked into small pieces; they filled a young man's mouth with gunpowder, and blew his head to atoms. Their principal rage was directed against the clergy. They seized a pious protestant minister, whom they tormented daily for a month. They derided and mocked him; hunted him like a wild beast, till ready to expire with fatigue; they made him run the gauntlet, each striking him with their fists, or with ropes; they scourged him with wires; they tied him up by the heels till the blood started out of his nose and mouth; they hung him up by the arms till they were dislocated, and then had them set again. Burning papers, dipped in oil, were placed to his feet; his flesh was torn with red-hot pincers; he was put to the rack, and most cruelly mangled. Boiling lead was poured upon his feet; and, lastly, a knotted cord was twisted about his forehead in such a manner as to force out his eyes. In the midst of these enormities particular care was taken lest the wounds should mortify, and his sufferings be shortened, till the last day, when forcing out his eyes proved fatal. At length, winter being far advanced, the high court of judges, with their military ruffians, returned to Prague; but on their way, meeting with a protestant pastor, they stripped him naked, and covered him alternately with ice and burning coals. The unhappy victim expired beneath the torments, seemingly to the delight of his inhuman persecutors.

### Life, Sufferings, and Martyrdom of John Huss.

John Huss was a Bohemian, and was born about the year 1380. His parents had him educated at a private school; he was then sent to the university

of Prague, where he soon became conspicuous. The
English reformer, Wickliffe, had so kindled the
light of reformation, that it began to illumine even
Bohemia. His doctrines were received with avidity
by great numbers of people; especially by John
Huss, and his friend and fellow-martyr Jerome of
Prague. The reformists daily increasing, the archbishop of Prague issued a decree to suppress Wickliffe's writings. This, however, had the effect of
stimulating the converts to greater zeal, and at
length almost the whole university united in promoting them. In that institution the influence of
Huss was very great, not only from his learning,
eloquence, and exemplary life, but also on account
of valuable privileges he had obtained from the king
in behalf of the Bohemians.

Strongly attached to the doctrines of Wickliffe,
Huss strenuously opposed the decree of the archbishop, who, notwithstanding, obtained a bull from
the pope, to prevent the publishing of Wickliffe's
writings in his province. Against these proceedings
Dr. Huss, with other members of the university,
protested, appealing from the sentence of the archbishop. The pope no sooner heard of this, than he
granted a commission to cardinal Colonno, to cite
Huss to appear at the court of Rome. From this
Dr. Huss desired to be excused, and so greatly was
he favoured in Bohemia, that king Winceslaus, the
queen, the nobility, and the university, desired the
pope to dispense with his appearance; as also that
he would not suffer the kingdom of Bohemia to lie
under the accusation of heresy, but permit all to
preach the gospel with freedom, according to their
honest convictions.

Three proctors appeared for Dr. Huss before cardinal Colonno. They pleaded an excuse for his absence, and said they were ready to answer in his behalf. But the cardinal declared him contumacious, and excommunicated him. On this the proctors appealed to the pope, who appointed four cardinals to examine the process: the commissioners confirmed the sentence, and extended the excommunication to the friends and followers of Huss. From this unjust sentence Huss appealed to a future council, but without success; and being expelled from his church in Prague, he retired to Hussenitz, his native place, where he continued to promulgate the truth, in his writings as well as in his public ministry.

He was now summoned to appear at the council at Constance; and to dispel any apprehension of danger, the emperor sent him a passport, promising him safety. He told the person who delivered it, that he desired nothing more than to purge himself publicly of the imputation of heresy, and that he felt happy to have an opportunity for doing so at the council.

At the end of November he set out for Constance, accompanied by two Bohemian noblemen, eminent among his disciples, who followed him through respect and affection. He caused placards to be fixed on the gates of the churches at Prague, and also declared, in the cities through which he passed, that he was going to vindicate himself at Constance, and invited his adversaries to be present. On his way he met with every mark of affection and reverence from people of all descriptions.

Arriving in Constance, he took lodgings in a remote part of the city. Soon after there came to

him one Stephen Paletz, who was engaged by the
city of Prague to manage the prosecution.  Paletz
was afterwards joined by Michael de Cassis, on the
part of the court of Rome.  These two drew up
articles against him, which they presented to the
pope and prelates of the council.  Notwithstanding
the promise of the emperor, to give him safe conduct
to and from Constance, according to the maxim of the
council, that "Faith is not to be kept with heretics,"
when it was known he was in the city, he was immediately arrested, and committed prisoner to a
chamber in the palace.  Upon this, one of Huss's
friends urged the imperial passport; but the pope
replied he had not granted one, and was not bound
by that of the emperor.

The nobility of Bohemia and Poland used all their
interest for Huss; and so far prevailed as to prevent
his being condemned unheard, which appeared to
have been resolved on by the commissioners.  Before his trial a Franciscan friar was employed to
entangle him in his words, and then appear against
him.  This man came to him in the character of an
idiot, and, with seeming sincerity and zeal, requested
to be taught his doctrines.  But Huss soon detected
him, and told him that while his manners wore a
semblance of simplicity, his questions discovered a
depth and design beyond the reach of an idiot.  He
afterwards found this pretended fool to be Didace,
one of the deepest logicians in Lombardy.

At length Huss was brought before the council,
when the articles against him were read : they were
upwards of forty in number, and chiefly extracted
from his writings.  The following extract, forming
the eighth article of impeachment, will give a sample

of the ground on which this infamous trial was conducted. "An evil and a wicked pope is not the
successor of Peter, but of Judas." Answer—"I wrote
this in my treatise: If the pope be humble and
meek, despising the honour and lucre of the world;
if he be a shepherd, feeding the flock of God with
the word, and with virtuous example, and diligently
and carefully labour and travail for the church,
then he is without doubt the true vicar of Christ.
But if he walk contrary to these virtues, so much as
there is no society between Christ and Belial, and
Christ himself saith, 'He that is not with me is
against me,' how is he then the true vicar of Christ
or Peter, and not rather the vicar of antichrist?
Christ called Peter himself, Satan, when he opposed
Him only in one word. Why, then, should not any
other, being more opposed to Christ, be called Satan,
and consequently antichrist, or at least the principal
minister or vicar of antichrist? Infinite testimonies
to this effect are found in St. Augustine, St. Jerome,
Cyprian, Chrysostom, Bernard, Gregory, Remigius,
Ambrose, and all the holy fathers of the Christian
church."

After his examination a resolution was come to
by the council, to burn him as a heretic unless he re-
tracted. He was then committed to a filthy prison,
where, in the daytime, he was so laden with fetters
that he could hardly move; and every night he was
fastened by his hands to a ring against the wall.
He continued some days in this situation, while
many noblemen of Bohemia interceded in his behalf.
They drew up a petition for his relief, which was
presented to the council by several of the most illus-
trious men of the country; but no attention was

paid to it. Shortly after four bishops and two lords were sent by the emperor to the prison, to prevail on Huss to make a recantation. But he called God to witness, with tears in his eyes, that he was not conscious of having preached or written anything against the truth of God, or the faith of the true church. The deputies then represented the great wisdom and authority of the council; to which Huss replied, "Let them send the meanest person of that council, who can convince me by argument from the word of God, and I will submit my judgment to him." This faithful answer had no effect, and the deputies, finding they could make no impression on him, departed, astonished at his resolution.

On the 4th of July he was, for the last time, brought before the council. After a long examination he was desired to abjure, which he refused without the least hesitation. The bishop of Lodi then preached a bloody persecuting sermon, from the text, "Let the body of sin be destroyed." The sermon was the usual prologue to a cruel martyrdom; his fate was now fixed, his vindication rejected, and judgment pronounced. The council censured him for being obstinate and incorrigible, and ordained that he should be degraded from the priesthood, his books publicly burnt, and himself delivered to the secular power. He received the sentence without the least emotion; and at the close of it kneeled down, and, with all the magnanimity of a primitive martyr, exclaimed: " May thine infinite mercy, O my God, pardon this injustice of my enemies. Thou knowest the iniquity of my accusations: how deformed with crimes I have been represented: how I have been oppressed by worthless

witnesses, and a false condemnation: yet, O my
God, let that mercy of thine, which no tongue
can express, prevail with thee not to avenge my
wrongs."

These excellent sentences were received as so
many expressions of treason, and only tended to
inflame his adversaries. Accordingly, the bishops
appointed by the council stripped him of his priestly
garments, degraded him, and put a paper mitre on
his head, on which were painted devils, with this
inscription : " A ringleader of heretics." This
mockery was received by the heroic martyr with
an air of unconcern, and it seemed to give him
dignity rather than disgrace. A serenity appeared
in his looks, which indicated that his soul had cut
off many stages of a tedious journey in her way to
the realms of everlasting happiness.

The ceremony of degradation being over, the
bishops delivered him to the emperor, who put him
into the care of the duke of Bavaria. His books
were consumed at the gates of the church; and on
the 6th of July he was led to the suburbs of
Constance to be burnt alive. When he reached the
place he fell on his knees, sung several portions of
the Psalms, looked steadfastly towards heaven, and
said, " Into thy hands, O Lord, do I commit my
spirit : thou hast redeemed me, O most good and
faithful God ! " As soon as the chain was put about
him at the stake, he said, with a smiling countenance, " My Lord Jesus Christ was bound with a
harder chain than this for my sake; why, then,
should I be ashamed of this old rusty one ? "
When the fagots were piled around him, the duke
of Bavaria was so officious as to desire him to

abjure. His noble reply was, "No, I never preached any doctrine of an evil tendency; and what I taught with my lips I now seal with my blood." He then said to the executioner, "You are now going to burn a goose (the name of Huss signifying goose, in the Bohemian language), but in a century you will have a swan which you can neither roast nor boil." If this were spoken in prophecy, he must have meant Martin Luther, who shone about a hundred years after, and who had a swan for his arms—whether suggested by this circumstance, or on account of family descent and heraldry, is not known. As soon as the fagots were lighted, the heroic martyr sung a hymn, with so loud and cheerful a voice, that he was heard through all the crackling of the combustibles and noise of the multitude. At length his voice was interrupted by the flames, which soon put an end to his mortal life, and wafted his undying spirit, which no fire on earth could subdue or touch, to the regions of ever-lasting glory.

MARTYRDOM AT VENICE.

## CHAPTER VII.

THIS hero in the cause of truth was born at Prague, and educated in its university, where he soon became distinguished for his learning and eloquence. Having completed his studies, he travelled over a great part of Europe, and visited many seats of learning, particularly the universities of Paris, Heidelberg, Cologne, and Oxford. At the latter he became acquainted with the works of Wickliffe, and being a person of uncommon application, translated many of them into his own language.

On the 4th of April, 1415, Jerome went to Constance. This was about three months before the death of Huss. He entered the town privately, and consulting some of the leaders of his party, was convinced that he could render his friend no service. Finding that his arrival at Constance was known, and that the council intended to seize him, he went to Iberling, an imperial town at a short distance. While here he wrote to the emperor, and avowed his readiness to appear before the council, if he would give a safe conduct; this however was refused. He then applied to the council, but met with an answer equally unfavourable. After this he caused papers to be put up in all the public places of Constance, particularly on the door of the cardinal's house. In these he professed his willingness to appear at Constance in defence of his character and doctrine. He further declared that if any error should be proved against him he would retract it, desiring only that the faith of the council might be given for his security.

Receiving no answer he set out on his return to Bohemia, taking with him a certificate signed by several of the Bohemian nobility then at Constance, testifying that he had used every prudent means to procure an audience. Notwithstanding this he was seized on his way by an officer, who hoped thus to receive commendation from the council. The council desired him immediately to be sent to Constance. He was accordingly conveyed in irons, and on his way was met by the elector palatine, who caused a long chain to be fastened to Jerome, by which he was dragged like a wild beast to the cloister, whence, after some insults and examinations, he was conveyed to a tower, and fastened to a block with his legs in the stocks. In this manner he remained eleven days and nights, till, becoming dangerously ill, they, in order to satiate their malice still further, relieved him from that painful state. He remained confined till the martyrdom of his friend Huss; after which he was brought forth and threatened with torments and death if he remained obstinate. In a moment of weakness he forgot his manliness and resolution, abjured his doctrines, and confessed that Huss merited his fate, and that both he and Wickliffe were heretics. In consequence of this his chains were taken off, and this harsh treatment done away. He was, however, still confined, with daily hopes of liberation. But his enemies suspecting his sincerity, another form of recantation was drawn up and proposed to him. He, however, refused to answer this, except in public, and was brought before the council, when, to the astonishment of his auditors and to the glory of truth, he renounced his recantation, and requested permission to plead his own cause, which was refused.

They proceeded with the charges, which were reduced to five articles:—That he was a derider of the papal dignity, an opposer of the pope himself, an enemy to the cardinals, a persecutor of the bishops, and a despiser of Christianity! To these charges Jerome answered with an amazing force of eloquence and strength of argument: "Now, whither shall I turn me? To my accusers? My accusers are as deaf as adders. To you, my judges? You are all prepossessed by the arts of my accusers." After this speech he was remanded to prison. The third day after his trial was brought on, and witnesses were examined in support of the charge. The prisoner was prepared for his defence, which appears almost incredible, when we consider he had been nearly a year shut up in loathsome dungeons, deprived of daylight, and almost starved for want of common necessaries. But his spirit soared above these disadvantages.

The most bigoted of the assembly were unwilling he should be heard, dreading the effects of his eloquence in the cause of truth. This was such as to excite the envy of the greatest persons of his time. "Jerome," said Gerson, the chancellor of Paris, at his accusation, "when thou wast in Paris thou wast, by means of thine eloquence, an angel, and didst trouble the whole university." At length it was carried by the majority that he should have liberty to proceed in his defence, which he began in such an exalted strain, and continued with such a torrent of elocution, that the obdurate heart was seen to melt, and the mind of superstition seemed to admit a ray of conviction. He began to deduce from history the number of great and virtuous men who had, in their time, been condemned and punished as evil persons, but whom after-generations had proved to have deserved honour and reward. He laid before the assembly the whole tenour of his life and conduct. He observed that the greatest and most holy men had been known to differ in points of speculation, with a view to distinguish truth, not to keep it concealed. He proceeded to defend the doctrines of Wickliffe, and concluded with observing that it was far from his intention to advance anything against the church of God; that it was only of the abuses of the clergy he complained; and that it was certainly impious that the patrimony of the church, which was originally intended for charity and benevolence, should be prostituted to "the lust of the flesh, the lust of the eye, and the pride of life," which the apostle declares "are not of the Father, but of the world."

The trial being ended, Jerome received the same sentence as had been passed on his martyred countryman, and was, in the usual style of popish duplicity, delivered over to the civil power; but being a layman, he had not to undergo the ceremony of degradation. His persecutors, however, prepared for him a cap of paper, painted with red devils, which being put upon his head, he said,

" Our Lord Jesus Christ, when he suffered death
for me, a most miserable sinner, did wear a crown
of thorns upon his head; and I, for his sake, will
wear this adorning of derision and blasphemy."
Two days they delayed the execution in hope that
he would recant; meanwhile the cardinal of
Florence used his utmost endeavours to bring him
over, but they all proved ineffectual; Jerome was
resolved to seal his doctrine with his blood.

On his way to the place of execution he sang
several hymns; and on arriving at the spot, the
same where Huss had suffered, he kneeled down
and prayed fervently. He embraced the stake with
great cheerfulness and resolution; and when the
executioner went behind him to set fire to the
fagots, he said, " Come here, and kindle it before
my eyes; for had I been afraid of it, I had not
come here, having had so many opportunities to
escape." When the flames began to envelope him,
he sung another hymn; and the last words he was
heard to say were—

"This soul in flames I offer, Christ, to thee!"

He was of a fine and manly form, and possessed
a strong and healthy constitution, which served to
render his death extremely painful, for he was observed to live an unusual time among the flames.
He, however, sang till his aspiring soul took its
flight, as in a fiery chariot, from earth to heaven.

### Persecutions in the Netherlands.

The light of the gospel spreading over the con-
tinent, and chasing thence the dark night of
ignorance, increased the alarm of the pope, who

G

urged the emperor to persecute the protestants; many thousands fell martyrs, among whom were the following :—

A pious protestant widow, named Wendelinuta, being apprehended, several monks tried to persuade her to recant. Their attempts, however, proving ineffectual, a Roman catholic lady of her acquaintance desired to be admitted to her dungeon, promising to exert herself to induce the prisoner to abjure her religion. On being admitted she did her utmost to perform the task; but finding her endeavours fruitless, she said, " Dear Wendelinuta, if you will not embrace our faith, at least keep these things secret, and strive to prolong your life." To which the widow replied, " Madam, you know not what you say; for with the heart we believe to righteousness, but with the tongue confession is made unto salvation." Still holding her faith, her goods were confiscated, and she was condemned to be burnt. At the place of execution a monk presented a cross to her; she answered, " I worship no wooden god, but the eternal God, who is in heaven." She was then executed, by being strangled before the fagots were kindled.

At Colen two protestant clergymen were burnt; a tradesman of Antwerp, named Nicholas, was tied up in a sack, thrown into the river, and drowned; and Pistorius, an accomplished scholar and student, was burnt in the market of a Dutch village.

A minister of the reformed church was ordered to attend the execution of sixteen protestants by beheading. This gentleman performed the melancholy office with great propriety, exhorted them to repentance, and gave them comfort in the mercies of their

Redeemer. As soon as they were beheaded, the magistrate cried out to the executioner, "You must behead the minister; he can never die better than with such excellent precepts in his mouth, and such laudable examples before him." He was accordingly beheaded, though many of the Roman catholics themselves reprobated this piece of barbarity.

George Scherter, a minister of Saltzburg, was committed to prison for instructing his flock in the truth of the gospel. While in confinement he wrote a confession of his faith; soon after which he was first beheaded, and afterwards burnt to ashes. Percival, a learned man of Louviana, was murdered in prison; and Justus Insparg was beheaded for having Luther's sermons in his possession. Giles Tolleman, a cutler of Brussels, was apprehended as a protestant, and many attempts were made by the monks to persuade him to recant. Once a fair opportunity of escaping offered itself, but of which he did not avail himself. Being asked the reason, he replied, "I would not do the keepers so much injury; as they must have answered for my absence." When he was sentenced to be burnt he fervently thanked God for allowing him, by martyrdom, to glorify his name. Observing at the place of execution a great quantity of fagots, he desired the principal part of them to be given to the poor, saying, "A small quantity will suffice to consume me." The executioner offered to strangle him before the fire was lighted, but he would not consent, telling him that he defied the flames; and, indeed, he died with such composure amidst them, that he hardly seemed sensible of pain.

In Flanders, about 1543 and 1544, persecution

raged with great violence. Many were doomed to
perpetual imprisonment, others to perpetual banish-
ment; but the greater number were put to death
either by hanging, or drowning, burning, the rack,
or burying alive. John de Boscane was apprehended in the city of Antwerp. On his trial he
undauntedly professed himself of the reformed religion, on which he was immediately condemned.
The magistrate, however, was afraid to execute the
sentence publicly, as he was universally revered for
his inoffensive life and exemplary piety. An order
was, therefore, given to drown him in prison. The
executioner accordingly forced him into a large
tub; but Boscane struggling, and getting his head
above the water, the executioner stabbed him in
several places with a dagger till he expired. John
de Buisons was, about the same time, secretly apprehended. In this city the number of protestants
being great, and the prisoner much respected, the
magistrates, fearful of an insurrection, ordered him
to be beheaded in prison.

In 1568 were apprehended at Antwerp, Scoblant,
Hues, and Coomans. Scoblant, who was first
brought to trial, persisting in his faith, received
sentence of death. On his return to prison he requested the gaoler not to permit any friar to come
near him; saying, " They can do me no good, but
may greatly disturb me. I hope my salvation is
already sealed in heaven, and that the blood of
Christ, in which I firmly trust, hath washed me
from my iniquities. I am now going to throw off
this mantle of clay to be clad in robes of eternal
glory. I hope I may be the last martyr of papal
tyranny, and that the blood already spilt will be

sufficient to quench its thirst of cruelty; that the
church of Christ may have rest here, as his servants
will hereafter." On the day of execution he took a
pathetic leave of his fellow-prisoners. At the stake
he uttered with great fervency the Lord's Prayer,
and sung the 40th Psalm; then commending his
soul to God, the flames soon terminated his mortal
existence.

A short time after Hues died in prison, on which
occasion Coomans thus vents his mind to his friends:
" I am now deprived of my friends and companions;
Scoblant is martyred, and Hues dead by the visitation of the Lord; yet I am not alone: I have with
me the God of Abraham, of Isaac, and of Jacob; he
is my comfort, and shall be my reward." When
brought to trial Hues freely confessed himself of the
reformed religion, and answered with manly firmness every charge brought against him. "But,"
said the judge, " will you die for the faith you profess?" " I am not only willing to die," replied
Coomans, " but also to suffer the utmost stretch of
invented cruelty for it; after which my soul shall
receive its confirmation from God himself in eternal
glory." Being condemned, he went cheerfully to
the place of execution, and died with Christian fortitude and resignation.

## Assassination of the Prince of Orange.

Baltazar Gerad, a bigoted Roman catholic, thinking to advance his own fortune and the popish
cause, resolved on the assassination of the prince of
Orange. Having provided himself with firearms,
he watched the prince as he passed through the

great hall of his palace to dinner, and demanded a passport. The princess of Orange, observing in his voice and manner something confused and singular, asked who he was. The prince said he wished a passport, which he should have presently. After dinner, on the return of the prince and princess through the hall, the assassin, from behind one of the pillars, fired at the prince, the balls entered the left side, and passing through the right, wounded the stomach and vital parts. The prince could only say, " Lord have mercy upon my soul, and upon this poor people ! " and immediately expired.

The death of this virtuous prince spread universal sorrow throughout the United Provinces. The assassin was immediately taken and sentenced to death : yet such was his enthusiasm and blindness, that he coolly said, " Were I at liberty I would repeat the same."

In different parts of Flanders numbers fell victims to popish jealousy and cruelty. In the city of Valence, in particular, fifty-seven of the principal inhabitants were butchered in one day for refusing to embrace the Romish superstition ; besides whom great numbers suffered in confinement till they perished.

# CHAPTER VIII.

PERSECUTION OF PROTESTANTS IN DIFFERENT FOREIGN COUNTRIES.

## Account of Persecutions in Calabria.

ABOUT the 14th century many Waldenses of Pragela and Dauphiny emigrated to Calabria, where, having received permission to settle, they soon, by industrious cultivation, converted several wild and barren spots into beauty and fertility. The nobles of Calabria were highly pleased, finding them honest, quiet, and industrious. Things went on peaceably for a few years, during which the Waldenses formed themselves into two corporate towns, annexing several villages to their jurisdiction. At length, they sent to Geneva for two clergymen, one to minister in each town. Intelligence of this was conveyed to pope Pius the Fourth, who determined to exterminate them from Calabria. Cardinal Alexandrino, a man of violent temper and a furious bigot, was therefore sent with two monks to Calabria, who were to act as inquisitors. These persons came to St. Xist, one of the towns built by the Waldenses, where having assembled the people, they told them that they should receive no injury if they would accept preachers appointed by the pope; but if they refused they should be deprived of their property and lives; and that, to prove them, mass should be publicly said this afternoon, at which they must attend.

The inhabitants of St. Xist, instead of obeying, fled into the woods, and thus disappointed the cardinal. He then proceeded to La Garde, the other town belonging to the Waldenses, where, to avoid a similar dilemma, he ordered the gates to be locked, and all avenues guarded. The same proposals were then made, but with this artifice: the cardinal said that the inhabitants of St. Xist had immediately acceded to his proposal, that the pope should appoint them preachers. This falsehood succeeded; for the people of La Garde thinking what the cardinal said was true, agreed to follow the example of their brethren at St. Xist.

Having gained his point by falsehood, he sent troops to massacre the people of St. Xist. He commanded the soldiers to hunt them down in the woods like wild beasts, and to spare neither age nor sex. The troops entered the woods, and many poor Xistians fell a prey to their ferocity, before the Waldenses were apprised of their design. At length, however, they determined to sell their lives as dear as possible, when several conflicts happened, in which the half-armed Waldenses performed prodigies of valour, and many were slain on both sides. At length, the greater part of the troops being killed in the different rencounters, the remainder were compelled to retreat, which so enraged the cardinal that he wrote to the viceroy of Naples for reinforcements.

The viceroy proclaimed throughout the Neapolitan territories, that all outlaws, deserters, and other proscribed persons, should be freely pardoned, on condition of making a campaign against the inhabitants of St. Xist, and continuing under arms till they were destroyed. On this, several persons of desperate fortune came in, and being formed into light companies, were sent to scour the woods, and put to death all they could meet of the reformed religion. The viceroy himself joined the cardinal, at the head of a body of regular forces, and in conjunction they strove to accomplish their bloody purpose. Some they caught, and suspending them upon trees, cut down boughs and burnt them, or left their bodies to be devoured by beasts or birds of prey. Many they shot at a distance; but the greatest number they hunted down by way of sport. A few escaped into caves; where famine destroyed them in their retreat. The inhuman chase was continued till all these people perished.

The inhabitants of St. Xist being exterminated, those of La Garde engaged attention. The fullest protection was offered them, if they would embrace the Roman catholic religion. If they refused this mercy, the utmost extremeties would be the result. The Waldenses, however, unanimously refused to renounce their religion, or embrace the errors of popery. The cardinal and viceroy were so filled with rage at this, that they ordered thirty of them to be put immediately to the rack, as a terror to the rest. Several of these died under the torture; one Charlin, in particular, was so cruelly used that his body burst, and he expired in the greatest agonies. These barbarities did not answer the end for which they were intended; those who survived the rack, and those who had not felt it, remained constant to their faith, declaring that nothing should induce them to renounce God, or bow down to idols. On this, the obdurate cardinal ordered several of them to be stripped naked, and whipped to death with iron rods: some were hewn to pieces with swords; others were thrown from a high tower; and others covered with pitch and burnt alive.

The viceroy having returned to Naples, and the cardinal to Rome, the marquis of Butiane was commissioned to complete what they had begun, which he at length affected, so that there was not a single person of the reformed religion left in Calabria.

### Account of Persecutions in the Valleys of Piedmont.

The Waldenses, in consequence of the persecutions they met with in France, fled, among other places, to the valleys of Piedmont, where they increased and flourished for a time. Notwithstanding their harmless behaviour, however, and regular payment of tithes to the Romish clergy, the latter complained to the archbishop of Turin that they were heretics.

At Turin one of the reformed had his bowels torn out and placed before his face till he expired. At Revel, Catelin Girard, being at the stake, desired the executioner to give him a stone; when Girard, looking earnestly at it, said, "When it is in the power of a man to digest this stone, the religion for which I suffer shall have an end, and not before." He then threw down the stone, and submitted cheerfully to the flames. A great many more were oppressed or put to death till, wearied with their sufferings, the Waldenses at length flew to arms.

Philip VII. was at this time duke of Savoy and supreme lord of Piedmont. He determined at length to stop these bloody wars. Unwilling to

offend the pope or the archbishop, he nevertheless
sent to them saying that he could no longer see his
dominions overrun with troops commanded by prelates instead of generals; nor would he suffer his
country to be depopulated.

During his reign the Waldenses enjoyed repose;
but on his death the scene changed, for his successor
was a bigoted papist. About this time some of the
Waldenses proposed that their clergy should preach
in public, that every one might know the purity of
their doctrines; for hitherto they had preached only
in private, and to persons of the reformed religion.
As yet they possessed only the New Testament, and
a few books of the Old, in their own language.
Anxious to have the whole, they employed a Swiss
printer, for 1,500 crowns of gold, to furnish them
with a complete edition.

When tidings of this reached the new duke, he was
greatly exasperated, and sent a large body of troops
into the valleys, swearing that if the people would
not conform, he would have them flayed alive.
The commander soon found he could not conquer
with the number of men then under him; he therefore sent word to the duke that the idea of sub-
jugating the Waldenses with so small a force was
ridiculous; that they were well acquainted with the
country, had secured all the passes, were well
armed, and determined to defend themselves; and
as to flaying them alive, that every skin he tore off
would cost him a dozen lives. Alarmed at this, the
duke recalled the troops, determining to act by
stratagem. He therefore offered rewards for any
Waldenses who might be taken, and these were
either flayed alive or burnt.

Paul III., a furious bigot, ascending the pontifical chair, solicited the parliament of Turin to persecute the Waldenses as the most pernicious of heretics. The parliament assented, and several were seized and burnt by their order. Among these was Bartholomew Hector, a bookseller and stationer of Turin. He was brought up by a Roman catholic, but treatises by some of the reformed clergy having fallen into his hands, he was convinced of the errors of the church of Rome; his mind for some time wavered between fear and duty. At length he fully embraced the reformed religion, and was apprehended and burnt.

A consultation being again held by the parliament of Turin, it was agreed that deputies should be sent to the valleys of Piedmont with the following propositions: That if the Waldenses would return to the church of Rome, they should enjoy their houses and lands, and live without molestation. That to prove their obedience they should send twelve principal persons, with all their ministers and schoolmasters, to Turin, to be dealt with at discretion. That the pope, the king of France, and the duke of Savoy approved of and authorized these proposals. That if the Waldenses rejected them, persecution and death should be their reward.

The Waldenses made the following noble reply: That no consideration should make them renounce their religion. That they would never consent to entrust their best and most valued friends to the discretion of their worst enemies. That they valued the approbation of the King of kings more than that of any temporal authority. That their souls were more precious than their bodies, and would receive their supreme regard and care.

These spirited answers greatly exasperated the parliament of Turin, which continued more eagerly than ever to secure such Waldenses as fell into their hands, and put them to the most cruel deaths. Among these was Jeffrey Varnagle, minister of Angrogne, whom they committed to the flames. They soon after begged from the king of France a body of troops, in order to exterminate them from the valleys of Piedmont; but just as the troops were about to march, the protestant princes of Germany interposed, and threatened to assist the Waldenses. On this the king of France sent word to the parliament of Turin that he could not then spare troops to act in Piedmont. Those sanguinary senators were thus disappointed, and the persecution gradually ceased, as now they could put to death only the very few they caught by chance.

After a few years' tranquillity they were again disturbed. The pope's nuncio coming to Turin, told the duke of Savoy that he was astonished the Waldenses were not yet rooted out from the valleys of Piedmont, or compelled to return to the church; that his remissness awakened suspicion; and that he should report the affair to the pope. Fearful of being misrepresented to the pope, the duke, to prove his zeal, resolved to let loose all his cruelty on the unoffending Waldenses. He issued orders for them to attend mass regularly on pain of death. This they absolutely refused, on which he entered their valleys with a great body of troops, and began a most furious persecution, in which numbers were hanged, drowned, tied to trees and pierced with prongs, thrown from precipices, burnt, stabbed, racked to death, worried by dogs, and crucified with their heads downwards. Those who fled had their goods plundered and their houses burnt. When ministers or schoolmasters were caught, they were put to the most exquisite tortures. If any wavered in their faith they sent them to the galleys, to be converted by dint of hardships.

The duke of Savoy, not being so successful as he wished, increased his forces by joining to them ruffians released from the prisons on condition of their assisting to exterminate the Waldenses. No sooner were the latter informed of this, than they secured as much of their property as they could, and quitting the valleys, retired to the rocks and caves among the Alps. The troops on reaching their country, began to plunder and burn the towns and villages; but they could not force the passes to the Alps, gallantly defended by the Waldenses, who in those attempts always repulsed their enemies; but if the troops caught any they were treated most barbarously. A soldier having caught one of them, bit his right ear off, saying, " I will carry this member of that wicked heretic with me into my own country, and preserve it as a rarity." He then stabbed the man, and threw him into a ditch.

At one time a party of the troops found a venerable man upwards of 100 years of age, with his grand-daughter, a maiden about eighteen, in a cave. They murdered the poor old man in a most inhuman manner, and would have cruelly ill-used the girl had she not escaped. Finding that she was pursued, she threw herself from a precipice and was killed. Determined, if possible, to expel their invaders, the

Waldenses entered into a league with the protestant powers in Germany, and with the reformed in Dauphiny and Pragela. These were to furnish troops; and the Waldenses resolved, when thus reinforced, to quit the Alps, where, as winter was coming on, they must soon have perished, and drive the duke's army from their native valleys.

The duke himself, however, was now tired of the war. It had been much more tedious and bloody than he expected, as well as more expensive; he had hoped the plunder would discharge the cost, but the pope's nuncio, the bishops, monks, and other ecclesiastics who attended the army under various pretences, took the greater part of the spoil for themselves. For these and other reasons, and fearing that the Waldenses, by the treaties they had entered into, would become too powerful for him, he determined to make peace with them. This he did, greatly against the will of the ecclesiastics, who by the war, both satiated their avarice and their revenge. Before the articles could be ratified, the duke died; but on his deathbed he enjoined his son to do what he had promised, and to be as favourable as possible to the Waldenses. Charles Emanuel, the duke's son, fully ratified the peace, the priests in vain trying to dissuade him.

## Persecutions at Venice and Rome.

Before the terrors of the inquisition were known at Venice, many protestants had fixed their residence there, and many converts were made by the purity of their doctrines, and the inoffensiveness of their lives. When the pope learned this, in the

year 1542, he sent inquisitors to Venice to make inquiry and to apprehend such as they might deem
obnoxious. Thus a severe persecution began, and
many were martyred for serving God with sincerity.
As soon as sentence was passed, the prisoner had an
iron chain, to which a great stone was suspended,
fastened to his body; he was then laid on a plank,
with his face upwards, and rowed between two boats
out to sea; the boats then separated, and, by the
weight of the stone, he was sunk.

If any denied the jurisdiction of the inquisitors at
Venice, they were conveyed to Rome, where, being
committed to damp and nauseous prisons, a most
miserable death ensued. A citizen of Venice, named
Anthony Ricetti, being apprehended, was sentenced
to be drowned in the manner above described. A
few days before his execution his son entreated him
to recant. His father replied, "A good Christian is
bound to relinquish not only goods and children,
but life itself for the glory of his Redeemer." The
nobles of Venice likewise sent word, that if he would
embrace the Roman catholic religion, they would
not only spare his life, but redeem for him a considerable estate which he had mortgaged. With this
proposal, however, he refused to comply. They
therefore ordered the execution of his sentence, and
he died commending his soul fervently to his Redeemer. Francis Sega, another Venetian, steadfastly
persisting in his faith, was executed a few days after
Ricetti, in the same manner.

Francis Spinola, a protestant gentleman of great
learning, was apprehended and carried before their
tribunal. A treatise on the Lord's Supper was put
into his hand, and he was asked if he knew the

author. To which he replied, "I confess myself its author; and solemnly affirm that there is not a line in it but what is authorized by and consonant to the Holy Scriptures." On this confession he was committed to a dungeon. After some days he was brought to a second examination, when he charged them with being merciless barbarians, and so represented the superstition and idolatry of the church of Rome, that, unable to refute his arguments, they recommitted him to his dungeon. Being brought up a third time, they asked him if he would recant his errors; to which he answered, that his doctrines were the same as those which Christ and his apostles had taught, and which were handed down in the sacred volume. He was then drowned in the manner already described.

The following remarkable incident took place at Rome. A young Englishman was one day passing a church when the procession of the host was coming out. A bishop carried the host, which the young man perceiving, snatched it from him, threw it on the ground, and trampling it under his feet, exclaimed, "Ye wretched idolaters, who neglect the true God to adore a morsel of bread!" The people would have torn him to pieces on the spot; but the priests persuaded them to let him abide the sentence of the pope.

The pope ordered him to be burnt immediately; but a cardinal, more refined in cruelty, dissuaded him, saying it was better to torture him, and thus find out if he had been instigated by any one to commit so atrocious an act. He was accordingly tortured with unusual severity: but they could only get these words from him, "It was the will of God

H

that I should do what I did." The pope therefore
sentenced him to be led, naked to the middle,
through the streets of Rome, by the executioner—
to wear the image of the devil upon his head—to
have his breeches painted with flames—to have his
right hand cut off, and after being carried about
thus in procession, to be burnt.

On hearing this sentence he implored God to
give him strength. As he passed through the
streets he was greatly derided by the people, to
whom he said some severe things respecting the
Romish superstition. But a cardinal overhearing,
ordered him to be gagged. When he came to the
church door where he trampled on the host, the
hangman cut off his right hand and fixed it on a
pole. Then two tormentors, with flaming torches,
scorched his flesh the rest of the way. At the place
of execution he kissed the chains that were to bind
him. A monk presenting the figure of a saint to
him, he struck it aside, and then being fastened to
the stake, the fagots were lighted, and he was burnt
to ashes.

### Further Account of Persecutions in the Valleys of Piedmont in the Seventeenth Century.

Pope Clement the Eighth sent missionaries into
the valleys of Piedmont, to induce the protestants
to renounce their religion. These missionaries,
erecting monasteries, soon became so troublesome
to the reformed, that they petitioned the duke of
Savoy for protection. But instead of this the duke
published a decree, that one witness should be
sufficient in a court of law against a protestant, and

that any witness who convicted a protestant of crime should receive a hundred crowns as a reward. In consequence of this many protestants fell martyrs to perjury and avarice; for there were papists who would swear anything against them for the sake of the reward, and then fly to their priests for absolution.

Among the victims to these persecutions were the following:—

Peter Simonds, a protestant, about eighty years of age, was bound and then thrown down a precipice. In the fall the branch of a tree caught hold of the ropes that fastened him, and suspended him midway, so that he languished for several days till he perished of hunger. A woman, named Armand, had her limbs separated from each other; the parts were then hung on a hedge. Several men, women, and children, were flung from the rocks, and dashed to pieces. Among others was Magdalen Bertino, a protestant woman of La Torre, who was bound and thrown down one of the precipices. Mary Ramondet, of the same town, had her flesh mangled till she expired. Magdalen Pilot, of Villaro, was cut to pieces in the cave of Castolus. Ann Charboniere had one end of a stake thrust into her body, and the other end being fixed in the ground, she was left to perish. Jacob Perin, the elder of the church of Villaro, with David his brother, were flayed alive.

Giovanni Andrea Michialin, an inhabitant of La Torre, with four of his children, was apprehended; three of them were killed before his eyes, the soldiers asking him on the death of each if he would recant, which he refused. One of the soldiers then took up the youngest by the legs, and putting the same question to the father, who replied as before, the inhuman brute dashed out the child's brains. The father, however, at the same moment, started from them and fled; the soldiers fired, but missed him; he escaped to the Alps. Giovanni Pelanchion, refusing to abjure his oath, was fastened to the tail of a mule, and dragged through the streets of Lucerne, amidst the acclamations of a mob, who kept stoning him, and crying out, "He is possessed of the devil." They then took him to the river side, struck off his head, and left it with his body unburied on the bank.

Peter Fontaine had a beautiful child, ten years of age, named Magdalene, who was ill-used and murdered by the soldiers. Another girl, about the same age, they roasted alive at Villa Nova: and a poor woman, hearing the soldiers were coming towards her house, snatched up the cradle in which her infant son was asleep, and fled towards the woods. The soldiers pursuing her, she put down the cradle and child; the soldiers murdered the infant, and continuing the pursuit, slaughtered the mother in a cave. Jacobo Michelino, chief elder of the church of Bobbio, and several other protestants, were hung up by hooks fixed to their bodies, and left to expire. Giovanni Rostagnal, a venerable protestant, upwards of four-score years of age, had his features mangled, and was otherwise injured by sharp weapons, till he bled to death. Daniel Saleagio and his wife, Giovanni Durant, Lodwich Durant, Bartholomew Durant, Daniel Revel, and Paul Reynaud, had their mouths stuffed with gunpowder, and their heads blown to atoms.

Jacob Birone, a schoolmaster of Rorata, refusing to change his religion, had the nails of his toes and fingers torn off with hot pincers, and holes bored through his hands with the point of a dagger. He next had a cord tied round his middle, and was led through the streets with a soldier on each side of him. At every turning the soldier on his right hand side cut a gash in his flesh, and the soldier on his left hand side struck him with a bludgeon, both saying, "Will you go to mass? Will you go to mass?" He still replied in the negative, and being at length taken to the bridge, they cut off his head on the balustrade, and threw both that and his body into the river. Paul Garnier, beloved for his piety, had his eyes put out, was then flayed alive, and divided into four parts, which were placed on the four principal houses of Lucerne. He bore his sufferings with most exemplary patience, praising God as long as he could speak. Daniel Cardon, of Rocappiata, being apprehended by some soldiers, they cut off his head. Two poor old blind women, of St. Giovanni, were burnt alive. A widow of La Torre, with her daughter, was driven into the river, and there stoned to death. Paul Giles, attempting to run away, was shot in the neck; they then mutilated and stabbed him, and gave his carcase to the dogs.

A young woman, named Susanna Ciacquin, being assaulted by a soldier, she made a stout resistance, and in the struggle pushed him over a precipice, when he was dashed to pieces by the fall. His comrades immediately fell upon her with their swords, and cut her to atoms. Giovanni Pullius was ordered by the marquis of Pianessa to be executed near the convent. When brought to the gallows, several monks attended, to persuade him to renounce his religion. But he told them he was happy in being thought worthy to suffer for the name of Christ. They then represented to him what his wife and children, who depended upon his labour, would suffer after his decease; to which he replied, "I would have my wife and children, as well as myself, to consider their souls more than their bodies, and the next world before this; and with respect to the distress I may leave them in, God is merciful, and will provide for them." Finding him inflexible, the monks commanded the executioner to perform his office, when he launched the martyr into the world of glory.

Daniel Rambaut, of Villaro, was seized, and, with several others, committed to the gaol of Paysana. Here he was visited by several priests, who strove to persuade him to turn papist; but this he refused; the priests then pretended to pity his numerous family, told him he might have his life if he would subscribe the following articles:—the real presence in the host—Transubstantiation—Purgatory—the pope's infallibility—that masses said for the dead will release souls from purgatory—that praying to the saints will procure the remission of sins. Rambaut replied that neither his religion, his understanding, nor his conscience, would suffer him to subscribe any of these articles. Filled with rage at his answer, the priests tried to shake his resolution by daily tortures; they deprived him of one limb after another so gradually as to cause him the utmost agony; finding that he bore his sufferings with unconquerable fortitude, they stabbed him to the heart, and gave his body to be devoured by dogs.

# CHAPTER IX.

CONTAINING A HISTORY OF THE REFORMATION, AND THE CIRCUMSTANCES
WHICH PRECEDED IT.

History of the English Martyrology and the Reformation,
with an Account of Wickliffe and his Doctrines.

THE first serious attempts made in England
towards the reformation of the church took
place in the reign of Edward III., about the year
1350, when the morning star of that glorious era
arose in JOHN WICKLIFFE. He was public reader of
divinity in the university of Oxford, and was
deeply versed in theology and all kinds of philosophy. This even his adversaries allowed. At
his appearing, the greatest darkness pervaded the
church. Little but the name of Christ remained
among the Christians, while his true and lively
doctrine was as unknown to the most part as his
name was common to all men.

Wickliffe boldly published his belief with regard
to the several articles of religion in which he
differed from the doctrine commonly received.
Pope Gregory XI., hearing this, condemned some
of his tenets, and commanded the archbishop of
Canterbury and the bishop of London to oblige him
to subscribe the condemnation of them; and in case
of refusal to summon him to Rome. This commission could not easily be executed, Wickliffe

having great friends, the chief of whom was John of Gaunt, duke of Lancaster, who had great power, and was resolved to protect him. The archbishop holding a synod at St. Paul's, Wickliffe appeared, accompanied by the duke of Lancaster and Lord Percy, marshal of England; when a dispute arising whether Wickliffe should answer sitting or standing, the duke of Lancaster proceeded to threats, and gave the bishop very hard words. The people present, thinking the bishop in danger, sided with him, so that the duke and the earl-marshal thought it prudent to retire, and to take Wickliffe with them.

A circumstance occurred soon after which greatly tended to help the cause of truth. After the death of pope Gregory XI., who wished to crush Wickliffe and his doctrines, the great schism took place. Urban VI., who succeeded to the papal chair, was so proud and insolent, that a large number of cardinals and courtiers set up another pope against him, named Clement, who reigned eleven years. After him, Benedictus XIII. was elected, who reigned twenty-six years. On the contrary side, Urban VI. succeeded Boniface IX., Innocentius VIII., Gregory XII., Alexander V., and John XIII. Concerning this miserable schism, it would require another Iliad to relate in order its various circumstances and tragical parts.

Wickliffe, who paid less regard to the injunctions of the bishops than to his duty to God, continued to promulgate his doctrines, and gradually to unveil the truth to the eyes of men. He wrote several works which gave great alarm and offence to the clergy; but the protection of the duke of Lancaster secured him from their malice. He translated the Bible into

English, which, amidst the ignorance of the time, had the effect of the sun breaking forth in a dark night. To this Bible he prefixed a bold preface, wherein he reflected on the bad lives of the clergy, and condemned the worship of saints, images, and the corporeal presence of Christ in the sacrament; but what offended his enemies most was, his exhorting all people to read the Scriptures for themselves.

About the same time there arose a dissension in England between the people and the nobility, which did not a little disturb the commonwealth. In this tumult Simon of Sudbury, archbishop of Canterbury, was taken by the people and beheaded. To him succeeded William Courtnay, who was no less diligent in doing his utmost to root out heretics. Notwithstanding this, the followers of Wickliffe increased, and daily grew to greater force, until Barton, vice-chancellor of Oxford, calling together eight monastical doctors and four others, with the consent of the rest, put the common seal of the university to an edict, threatening a grievous penalty to any who should hereafter associate with any of Wickliffe's favourers. To Wickliffe himself he threatened the greater excommunication and imprisonment, unless after three days he did repent and amend; which when Wickliffe understood, forsaking the pope and all the clergy, he thought to appeal unto the king; but the duke of Lancaster interposing, forbade him; whereby, being beset by troubles and vexations, he was forced again to make confesssion of his doctrine.

In consequence of Wickliffe's translation of the Bible, and his preface, his followers greatly multiplied. Many of them, indeed, were not men of learning; but being wrought upon by the conviction of plain reason, this determined them in their persuasion. In a short time his doctrines made great progress, being not only espoused by vast numbers of the students at Oxford, but also by the great men at court, particularly by the duke of Lancaster and lord Percy, together with several young and well-educated gentlemen. Hence Wickliffe may be considered as the great founder of the reformation in this kingdom. He was of Merton College, in Oxford, where he took his doctor's degree, and became so eminent for his fine genius and great learning, that Simon Islip, archbishop of Canterbury—having founded Canterbury college, now Christ Church, in Oxford—appointed him rector, which employment he filled with universal approbation till the death of the archbishop. Langham, successor to Islip, being desirous of favouring the monks, and introducing them into the college, attempted to remove Wickliffe, and put one Woodhall, a monk, in his room. But the fellows of the college refusing to consent to this, the affair was carried to Rome, and Wickliffe deprived in favour of Woodhall. However, this in no way lessened his reputation. Shortly after he was presented to the living of Lutterworth, in the county of Leicester, and he there published, in sermons and writings, his opinions, which spread widely through the land. His most bitter enemies never charged him with immorality. This great man was left in quiet at Lutterworth till his death, which happened 31st December, 1385. But after his body had lain in the grave forty-one years, his bones were taken up by decree of the synod of Constance, publicly burnt, and thrown into the river near the town. This condemnation of his doctrine did not prevent its spreading all over the kingdom, and with such success that, according to Spelman, two men could hardly be found together without one of them being a Lollard or Wickliffite.

Wickliffe wrote divers works, copies of which, in the year 1410, were burnt at Oxford. And not only in England, but in Bohemia likewise, his books were burnt, the archbishop of Prague having made diligent inquisition for them.

In the council of the Lateran a decree was made, which required all magistrates to extirpate heretics on pain of deposition. The canons of this council being received in England, the prosecution of heretics became a part of the common law; and a writ, styled *de heretico comburendo*, was issued under Henry IV., for burning them upon conviction, after which special statutes were made for the same purpose. The first was assented to only by the lords and the king. The commons did not concur in it. Yet the utmost extent of its severity was, that the laws of the church should be supported by writs. It appears that heretics were then very numerous; that they wore a peculiar habit, preached in churches and other places against the existing faith, and refused to regard ecclesiastical censures.

When Henry IV. came to the crown, in 1399, he passed an act against all who should presume to preach without the bishop's licence. All transgressors of this kind were to be imprisoned, and brought to trial within three months. If on conviction they offered to abjure, and did not relapse, they were to be imprisoned and fined at pleasure: but if they refused to abjure, or relapsed, they were to be delivered over to the secular arm to be burned in some public

place.    About this time William Sautre, a parish
priest of St. Osith, in London, being condemned as
a relapse, and degraded by Arundel, archbishop of
Canterbury, a writ was issued, wherein burning is
called the common punishment, and referred to the
customs of other nations. This was the first example
of that cruel punishment in this kingdom.

The clergy, fearful lest the doctrines of Wickliffe
should gain power, used every exertion to check
them.   In the reign of Richard II., the bishops obtained a general licence to imprison heretics without
a special order from court ; this, however, the house
of commons revoked.   But as the fear of imprisonment could not check the evil, Henry IV., who
wished the favour of the clergy, earnestly recommended to parliament the concerns of the church.
Reluctant as the house of commons was to prosecute
the Lollards, the clergy at last obtained a most detestable act for burning heretics, which was not repealed till 1677.   It was immediately after the passing of this act that the ecclesiastical court condemned
William Sautre to the flames.

Notwithstanding the opposition of the clergy,
Wickliffe's doctrine spread in Henry IV.'s reign to
such a degree, that the majority of the house of
commons were inclined to it ; whence they presented
two petitions to the king, one against the clergy, the
other in favour of the Lollards.   The first set forth,
that the clergy made use of their wealth, and consumed it in a way quite different from the intent of
the donors ; that their revenues were excessive, and
ought to be lessened.   In the second petition they
prayed that the statute passed against the Lollards
might be repealed or restricted.  As it was the king's

interest to please the clergy, he answered the commons very sharply, refusing to consent to their petitions. With regard to the Lollards, he declared that he wished they were extirpated from the land. To prove the truth of this, he signed a warrant for burning a man in humble life, but of strong mind and sound piety, named Thomas Badly, by trade a tailor. He was convicted of heresy, in the year 1409, before the bishop of Worcester. On his examination he said, that it was impossible any priest could make the body of Christ sacramentally, nor would he believe it unless he saw it manifestly on the altar; that it was ridiculous to imagine that, at the supper, Christ held in his own hand his own body, and divided it among his disciples, yet remaining whole. "I believe," said he, "the Omnipotent God in Trinity: but if every consecrated host at the altar be Christ's body, there must then be in England no less than 20,000 gods." After this he was examined before the archbishop of Canterbury, and again in the presence of a great number of bishops, the duke of York, and several of the nobility. Great pains were used to make him recant, but he remained faithful. On this the archbishop of Canterbury ratified the sentence of the bishop of Worcester. When the king signed the warrant for his death, he was brought to Smithfield, and there, being put into a tub, was bound with iron chains to a stake, and had dry wood piled around him. Before the wood was lighted, the king's eldest son came near the spot, and acting the part of the good Samaritan, endeavoured to save the life of him whom the hypocritical Levites sought to put to death. He counselled him to withdraw out of these dangerous labyrinths of opinions, adding threatenings which might have daunted any man. Courtnay also, then chancellor of Oxford, urged on him the faith of the church.

Meanwhile the prior of St. 'Bartholomew's, in Smithfield, brought the sacrament of Christ's body, with twelve torches borne before, to the poor man at the stake. He demanded of him how he believed it; he answered that it was hallowed bread, but not God's body. The fire being then applied, he cried, " Mercy!" calling likewise upon the Lord; when the prince commanded them to take away the tun, and quench the fire. He then asked him if he would forsake heresy; if he would he should have goods enough, also a yearly pension from the king's treasury. But this valiant champion of Christ refused the offer, more inflamed with the spirit of God than with any earthly desire. The prince, therefore, commanded him to be put again into the tun. As he could be allured by no reward, so he was not abashed by torments; but, as a valiant soldier of Christ, persevered till his body was reduced to ashes, and his soul rose triumphant unto God who gave it.

In the reign of Henry V., about 1413, a pretended conspiracy, evidently of priestly contrivance, was said to be discovered, in which Sir John Oldcastle and other followers of Wickliffe were implicated. Many of these were condemned, both for high treason and heresy: they were first hanged, and then burnt. A law was then made that all Lollards should forfeit their whole possessions in the fee simple, with their goods and chattels; and all sheriffs and magistrates were required to take an oath to destroy them and their heresies. The clergy made an ill use of this law, and imprisoned any who offended them; but the judges interposed for them, taking it upon them to declare what opinions were heresies by law and what were not. Thus the people found more mercy from the common lawyers than from those who ought to have been the pastors of their souls.

The persecutions of the Lollards in the reign of Henry V. were owing to the clergy, as that monarch was naturally averse to cruelty. It is supposed, that the chief cause of the hatred of the clergy to them was that they had endeavoured to strip them of part of their revenues. However this might be, they thought the most effectual way to check their progress would be to attack the chief protector of it, Sir John Oldcastle, baron of Cobham; and to persuade the king that the Lollards were conspiring to overturn the throne. It was even reported that they intended to murder the king with the princes, and most of the lords, spiritual and temporal, in hopes that the confusion thence arising would prove favourable to their religion. A false rumour was spread, that Sir John Oldcastle had got together twenty thousand men in St. Giles'-in-the-Fields, a place then overgrown with bushes. The king himself went thither at midnight, and finding no more than fourscore or a hundred persons, who were privately met for worship, he fell on them, and killed many before he knew the purpose of their meeting. Some of them being afterwards examined, were prevailed on, by promises or threats, to confess whatever their enemies desired, and these accused Sir John Oldcastle.

The king hereupon thought him guilty, and set

a thousand marks upon his head, with a promise of perpetual exemption from taxes to any which should secure him. Sir John was apprehended and imprisoned in the Tower; but escaping, he fled into Wales, where he long concealed himself. But being afterwards seized in Powisland, in North Wales, by lord Powis, he was brought to London, to the great joy of the clergy, who were resolved to sacrifice him to strike terror into the rest of the Lollards. Sir John was of a good family, had been sheriff of Hertfordshire under Henry IV., and summoned to parliament among the barons of the realm in that reign. He had been sent beyond sea with the earl of Arundel, to assist against the French. He was a man of extraordinary merit, notwithstanding which he was hanged up by the waist with a chain, and burnt alive. This most barbarous sentence was executed amidst the curses of the priests and monks, who used their utmost endeavours to prevent the people from praying for him. Such was the tragical end of Sir John Oldcastle, baron of Cobham, who left the world with a resolution which answered perfectly to the brave spirit he had ever maintained in the cause of truth and of God. This was the first noble blood shed by popish cruelty in England.

## Historical Account of the Progress of the Reformation in the Reign of King Henry VIII.

The reader will doubtless attend to the transactions recorded in this reign with peculiar interest. It was now that God, through the instrumentality of the king, liberated our country from the papal yoke.

The wars between the houses of York and Lancaster had produced such trouble, that the nation hailed with joy the accession of Henry VII. to the throne, who, being descended from the house of Lancaster, by his marriage with the heiress of the house of York, freed them from the fear of more wars by new pretenders. But the covetousness of his temper, the severity of his ministers, his ill conduct in the matter of Bretagne, and his jealousy of the house of York, made him so generally odious to his people, that his life was little respected, and his death as little lamented. Henry VIII. succeeded with every advantage. His restitution of the money that had been unjustly exacted of the people under covert of the king's prerogative made the nation conclude they should live secure under such a prince, and that violent remedies against wrong should be no more necessary. Either from the magnificence of his own temper, or from seeing the ill effects of his father's parsimony, the new king distributed his rewards with an unmeasured bounty; he thus quickly exhausted the two millions which his father had treasured up, and emptied the fullest coffer in Christendom. He had been educated with more than ordinary care; his father having given orders that both his elder brother and he should be well instructed : his brother, prince Arthur, dying at the age of eleven, he became heir to the crown.

One of the most conspicuous men of that age was cardinal Wolsey. He was of mean extraction, but possessed great parts, and had a wonderful dexterity in insinuating himself into favour. He had but a little time been introduced to the king before he

I

obtained an entire ascendancy over him; for fifteen years he continued to be the most absolute favourite ever known in England. He saw that Henry was much set on pleasure, and had a great aversion to business, so he undertook to free him from the trouble of government, and give him leisure to follow his appetites. This was the chief cause of that unbounded influence which Wolsey so soon acquired over a sovereign quite as ambitious as himself.

Wolsey soon became master of all offices at home and treaties abroad, so that affairs went as he directed them. He soon became obnoxious to parliaments, and therefore tried but one, when the supply granted was so scanty that afterwards he chose rather to raise money by loans and benevolences. After a time he became scandalous for his ill life, and a disgrace to his profession: for he not only served the king, but also shared with him in his pleasures, and became a prey to distempers arising from a sensual life. He was first made bishop of Tournay in Flanders, then of Lincoln; after that he was promoted to the see of York, and had both the abbey of St. Alban's and the bishopric of Bath and Wells in commendam; the last he afterwards exchanged for Durham; upon Foxe's death he quitted Durham that he might take Winchester; and besides all this, the king, by a special grant, gave him power to dispose of all the ecclesiastical preferments in England; so that in effect he was the pope of England. He had all the qualities necessary for a great minister, and all the vices common to a great favourite.

The immunity of churchmen for crimes, till first

degraded by the spirituality, occasioned the only contest that occurred in the beginning of this reign between the secular and ecclesiastical courts. Henry VII. had passed a law, that convicted clerks should be burnt in the hand. The abbot of Winchelsea preached severely against this, as being contrary to the laws of God and the liberties of the church. Afterwards he published a book to prove that all clerks, even of the lower orders, were sacred, and could not be judged by the temporal courts. The temporal lords and commons, therefore, desired the king to repress the insolence of the clergy. Accordingly, a public hearing was appointed before his majesty and the judges. Dr. Standish, a Franciscan, argued against the immunity, and proved that judging clerks had in all times been practised in England; and that it was necessary, for the peace and safety of mankind, that all criminals should be punished. The abbot argued on the other side, and said it was contrary to a decree of the church, and was a sin of itself. Standish answered, that all decrees were not observed; for, notwithstanding the decree for residence, bishops did not reside at cathedrals. After they had argued the matter, the laity were of opinion that the friar had the best of the argument, and therefore moved the king and the bishops that the abbot might be ordered to preach a recantation sermon. But they refused, saying they were bound by their oaths to maintain his opinions. Standish was upon this much hated by the clergy, but the matter was allowed to fall, the clergy carrying the point.

Not long after this, Richard Hunne, a merchant in London, being sued by his parish priest in the

legate's court, was advised by his friends to sue the
priest in the temporal court for bringing a king's
subject before a foreign and illegal bar.   This enraged the clergy so much, that they contrived his
destruction.   Accordingly, hearing that he had
Wickliffe's Bible in his house, he was put into the
bishop's prison for heresy ; but being examined on
sundry articles, he confessed some things, and submitted himself to mercy.   On this they ought,
according to the law, to have enjoined him penance
and discharged him ; but he could not be prevailed
on to let his suit fall in the temporal court: so one
night his neck was broken with an iron chain, and
he was wounded in other parts of the body, and then
it was given out that he had hanged himself; but
the coroner's inquest, by examining the body, and
by other evidence, particularly by the confession of
the sumner, gave it as their verdict that he was
murdered by the bishop's chancellor, Dr. Horsey,
and the bellringer.   The spiritual court proceeded
against the dead body, and charged Hunne with all
the heresy in Wickliffe's preface to the Bible, because
that was found in his possession : he was condemned
thus as a heretic, and his body was burnt.

The indignation of the people was raised to the
highest pitch by these proceedings, in which they
implicated the whole body of the clergy, whom they
esteemed no longer as their pastors, but as barbarous
murderers.   The rage went so high, that the bishop
of London complained he was not safe in his own
house.   The bishops, the chancellor, and the sumner
were indicted as principals in the murder.   In parliament, an act was passed restoring Hunne's children ;
but a bill sent up by the commons concerning the

murder was laid aside by the lords, where the clergy were the majority. The clergy looked on the opposition by Standish as that which gave rise to Hunne's first suit; and the convocation cited him to answer for his conduct; but he claimed the king's protection, since he had done nothing, but only pleaded in the king's name. The clergy pretended that they did not prosecute him for his pleading, but for some of his divinity lectures, which were contrary to the liberty of the church, which the king was bound to maintain by his coronation oath; but the temporal lords, the judges, and commons prayed the king also to maintain the laws according to his coronation oath, and to give Standish his protection. The king being in great perplexity, required Vevsey, afterwards bishop of Exeter, to declare upon his conscience the truth in that matter. His opinion was against the immunity; so another public hearing being appointed, Standish was accused of teaching—that the inferior orders were not sacred; that their exemption was not founded on a divine right, but that the laity might punish them; that the canons of the church did not bind till they were received; and that the study of the canon law was useless. Of these opinions, he denied some and justified others. Vevsey being required to give his opinion, alleged —that the laws of the church did only oblige where they were received; so the exemption of the clerks, not being received, did not bind in England. The judges gave as their opinion, that those who prosecuted Standish were wrong. So the court broke up. But in another hearing, in the presence of parliament, the cardinal said, in the name of the clergy, that though they intended to do nothing against the king's prerogative, yet the trying of clerks seemed to be contrary to the liberty of the church, which they were bound by their oaths to maintain. So they prayed that the matter might be referred to the pope.

The king said, that he thought Standish had answered them fully ; the bishop of Winchester replied, he would not stand to his opinion at his peril. Standish, upon that, asked, "What can one poor friar do against all the clergy of England ?" The archbishop of Canterbury answered, "Some of the fathers of the church have suffered martyrdom upon that account;" but the chief justice replied, "Many holy kings have maintained that law, and many holy bishops have obeyed it." In conclusion, the king declared that he would maintain his rights, and would not submit them to the decrees of the church, otherwise than as his ancestors had done. Horsey was appointed to be brought to his trial for Hunne's murder; and upon his pleading not guilty, no evidence was brought, and so he was discharged. The discontent of the people greatly increased at this, and very much disposed them for the pulling down of the ecclesiastical tyranny.

This was the first disturbance in this reign, till the suit for the divorce commenced. In all other points Henry was always in the pope's interests, who sent him the common compliments of roses, and such other trifles, by which that see had treated princes so long as children. But no compliment wrought so much on the king's vanity as the title of "Defender of the Faith," sent him by pope Leo for the book which he wrote against Luther. This book, besides the aforesaid title, drew upon the king all that flattery could invent to extol it; whilst Luther, not daunted with such an antagonist, answered it, and treated Henry as much below the respect due to a king as his flatterers had raised him above it. Tyndal's translation of the New Testament, with notes, drew a severe condemnation from the clergy, they being anxious to keep that book from the people. This may show the state of affairs both in church and state, when the process of the king's divorce was first set on foot. From this event began the rise of Cranmer and the decline of Wolsey. The great seal was taken from the latter and given to Sir Thomas More; and he was sued for having held legatine courts by an authority foreign to the laws of England. Wolsey confessed the endictment, pleaded ignorance, and submitted himself to the king's mercy: so judgment passed on him; when his rich palace and furniture were seized for the royal use. Yet the king restored to him the temporalities of the sees of York and Winchester, and about £6,000 in plate and other goods; at which he was so transported, that it is said he fell down on his knees in a kennel before the messenger who brought him the news. Articles were put in against him in the house of lords for a bill of attainder, where he had but few friends: in the house of commons, Cromwell, who had been his secretary, so managed the matter, that it came to nothing. This failing, his enemies had him sent into Yorkshire; thither he went in great state, with 160 horses and 72 carts in his train, and there he lived some time. But the king being informed that he was practising with the pope and the emperor, he sent the earl of Northumberland to arrest him for high treason, and bring him to London. On the way he sickened and died at Leicester, making great protestations of his constant fidelity to the king, particularly in the matter of the divorce : and wishing he had served God as faithfully as he had done the king, for then He would not have cast him off in his grey hairs: words that declining favourites are apt to reflect on in adversity, though they seldom remember them in the height of their fortune.

The archbishopric of Canterbury having become vacant by the decease of Warham, Cranmer, who was then in Germany, was fixed on by the king as his successor; he accordingly sent him word, that he might make haste to return. But such a promotion had not its common effect on him; he had a true sense of so great a charge, and, instead of aspiring to it, was afraid of it; he therefore returned very slowly to England, and endeavoured to be excused from the advancement. Bulls were sent for to Rome for his consecration, which the pope granted. On the 13th of March Cranmer was consecrated by the bishops of Lincoln, Exeter, and St. Asaph. The oath to the pope was of hard digestion to one "almost persuaded" to be a protestant; he therefore made a protestation before he took it, that he conceived himself not bound by it in anything that was contrary to his duty to God, to his king, or country ; and this he repeated when he took it.

The convocation had at this time two questions before them; the first was concerning the lawfulness of the king's marriage, and the validity of the pope's dispensation; the other was a curious question of fact, whether Prince Arthur had consummated the marriage. For the first, the judgments of nineteen universities were read ; and after a long debate, there being twenty-three only in the lower house, fourteen were against the marriage, seven for it, and two voted dubiously.   In the upper house, Stokesly, bishop of London, and Fisher, bishop of Rochester, maintained the debate at great length, the one for the affirmative, and the other for the negative.   At last it was carried without opposition against the marriage, 216 being present.   The other matter was referred to the canonists : and they all, except five or six, reported that the presumptions were very strong ; and these, in a matter not capable of plain proof, were received as legally conclusive.

The convocation having thus judged in the matter, the ceremony of pronouncing the divorce judicially was now the only thing wanting.   The new queen was reported to have been in a promising condition for the future monarchy.   On Easter Eve she was declared queen of England ; and soon after, Cranmer, with Gardiner, who had succeeded Wolsey as bishop of Winchester, and the bishops of London, Lincoln, Bath, and Wells, with many divines and canonists, went to Dunstable: queen Katharine living then near it, at Ampthill.   The king and queen were cited ; he appeared by proxy, but the queen refused to take any notice of the court : so, after three citations she was declared contumacious, and all the merits of the cause formerly mentioned were examined.   At last, on the 23rd of May, sentence was given, declaring the marriage to have been null from the beginning.

At Rome the cardinals of the imperial faction complained of the attempt made on the pope's power, and urged him to proceed to censures.   But there was only sentence given, annulling all that the archbishop of Canterbury had done; and the king was required under pain of excommunication, to place things again as they were formerly: this decree was brought for publication to Dunkirk. The king sent a great embassy to the French monarch, who was then setting out to Marseilles to meet the pope; they were to dissuade him from the journey, unless the pope would give the king satisfaction. Francis said, he was engaged in honour to go on; but assured them, he would mind the king's concerns with as much zeal as if they were his own. In September the queen brought forth a daughter, the renowned Elizabeth; and the king having, therefore, declared Lady Mary princess of Wales, did now the same for the infant: though since a son might exclude her from it, she could not be heir apparent, but only heir presumptive to the crown. The eventful moment was nigh at hand when the incident should take place that would cause the separation of England from the church of Rome.

There was a secret agreement between the pope and Francis, that if Henry would refer his cause to the consistory, excepting only to the cardinals of the imperial faction, as partial, and would in all other things return to his obedience to the see of Rome, the sentence should be given in his favour. When Francis returned to Paris, he sent over the bishop of that city to the king, to tell what he had obtained of the pope in his favour, and the terms on which it was promised. This wrought so much on the king, that he consented to them; on which the bishop of Paris, though it was the middle of winter, went to Rome with the welcome tidings. On his arrival there, the matter seemed agreed; for it was promised that, upon the king's sending a consent under his hand to place things in their former state, and his ordering a proxy to appear for him, judges should be sent to Cambray for making the process, and then sentence should be given. Upon the notice given of this, and of a day that was prefixed for the return of the courier, the king despatched him with all possible haste; and now the business seemed at an end. But the courier had a sea and the Alps to pass, and in winter it was not easy to observe a limited day so exactly. The appointed day came, and no courier arrived; upon which the imperialists gave out that the king was abusing the pope's easiness, and pressed him vehemently to proceed to a sentence, the bishop of Paris requesting only a delay of six days. The design of the imperialists was to hinder a reconciliation; for if the king had been set right with the pope, there would have been so powerful a league formed against the emperor as would have frustrated all his measures, and therefore it was necessary for his politics to embroil them. Seduced by the artifice of this intriguing prince, the pope, without consulting his ordinary prudence, brought in the matter to the consistory; and there the imperialists being the greater number, it was driven on with so much precipitation, that they did in one day, that which, according to form, should have extended at least to three.

They gave the final sentence, declared the king's marriage with queen Katharine good, and required him to live with her as his wife, otherwise they would proceed to censures. Two days after this the courier came with the king's submission in due form; he also brought earnest letters from Francis

in the king's favour. This brought on the in-
different cardinals, as well as those of the French
faction, so that they prayed the pope to recall what
was done. A new consistory was called, but the
imperialists urged, with greater vehemence than
ever, that they would not give such scandal to the
world as to recall a definitive sentence of the
validity of a marriage, and give heretics such
advantage by their unsteadiness; it was therefore
carried that the former sentence should remain, and
the execution of it be committed to the emperor.
When this was known in England, it determined
the king in his resolutions of shaking off the pope's
yoke, in which he had made so great progress, that
the parliament had passed all the acts concerning it
before he received the news from Rome; for he
judged that the best way to secure his cause was to
let Rome see his power, and with what vigour he
could make war. All the rest of the world looked
on astonished to see the court of Rome throw off
England, as if it had been weary of the obedience
and profits of so great a kingdom.

Several sees, as Ravenna, Milan, and Aquilea,
pretended exemption from the papal authority.
Many English bishops had asserted that the popes
had no authority against the canons, and to that
day no canon made by the pope was binding till it
was received, which showed the pope's authority
was not believed to be founded on Divine authority;
and as laws had given them some power, and princes
had been forced in ignorant ages to submit to their
usurpations, so they might, as they saw cause,
change those laws, and resume their rights.

The next point inquired into was, the authority

that kings had in matters of religion and the church. In the New Testament, Christ himself was subject to the civil powers, and charged his disciples not to affect temporal dominion. The apostles also wrote to the churches to be subject to the higher powers, and to call them supreme; they charged every soul to be subject to them. In Scripture the king is called head and supreme, and every soul is said to be under him; which, joined with the other parts of their sage argument, brought the wise men of that day to the conclusion that he is supreme head over all persons. In the primitive church the bishops only made rules or canons, but pretended to no compulsive authority but what came from the civil magistrate. Upon the whole matter, they concluded that the pope had no power in England, and that the king had an entire dominion over all his subjects, which extended even to the regulating of ecclesiastical matters. These questions being fully discussed in many disputes, and published in several books, all the bishops, abbots, and friars of England, Fisher only excepted, were so far satisfied with them, that they resolved to comply with the changes the king was determined to make.

At the next meeting of parliament there were but seven bishops and twelve abbots present; the rest, it seems, were unwilling to concur in making this change, though they complied with it when made. Every Sunday during the session a bishop preached at St. Paul's, and declared that the pope had no authority in England; before this they had only said that a general council was above him, and that the exactions of that court, and appeals to it, were unlawful; but now they went a strain higher, to prepare the people for receiving the acts then in agitation. On the 9th of March the commons began the bill for taking away the pope's power, and sent it to the lords on the 14th, who passed it on the 20th without any dissent. In it they set forth the exaction of the court of Rome, grounded on the pope's power of dispensation; and that as none could dispense with the laws of God, so the king and parliament only had the authority of dispensing with the laws of the land; therefore, such licences as were formerly in use should be for the future granted by the two archbishops, to be confirmed under the great seal. It was, moreover, appointed that thereafter all commerce with Rome should cease. They also declared that they did not intend to alter any article of the catholic faith of Christendom, or that which was declared in the Scriptures necessary to salvation. They confirmed all the exemptions granted to monasteries by the popes, but subjected them to the king's visitation, and gave the king and his council power to examine and reform all indulgences and privileges granted by the pope. This act subjected the monasteries entirely to the king's authority. Those who loved the reformation rejoiced to see the pope's power rooted out, and the Scriptures made the standard of religion.

After this act another passed in both houses in six days' time without any opposition, settling the succession of the crown, confirming the sentence of divorce, and the king's marriage with queen Anne; and declaring all marriages within the degrees prohibited by Moses to be unlawful; all that had married within them were appointed to be divorced, and their issue illegitimatised; and the succession to the crown was settled upon the king's issue by the present queen, or in default of that, to the king's right heirs for ever. All were required to swear to maintain the contents of this act; and if any refused the oath, or should say anything to the slander of the king's marriage, he was to be judged guilty of treason and to be punished accordingly.

The convocation sent in a submission at the same time, by which they acknowledged that all convocations ought to be assembled by the king's writ; and promised, upon the word of priests, never to make nor execute any canons without the king's assent. They also desired, that since many of the received canons were contrary to the king's prerogative and the laws of the land, there might be a committee named by the king of thirty-two, the one half out of the houses of parliament, and the other from the clergy, empowered to abrogate or regulate them as they could see cause. This was confirmed in parliament, and the act against appeal to Rome was renewed; an appeal was also allowed from the archbishop to the king, upon which the lord chancellor was to grant a commission for a court of delegates.

Another act passed for regulating the election and consecration of bishops; condemning all bulls from Rome, and appointing that, upon a vacancy, the king should grant licence for an election, and should by a missive letter, signify the person whom he wished to be chosen; and within twelve days after these were delivered, the dean and chapter, or prior and convent, were required to return an election of the person named by the king under their seals.

The bishop elect was upon that to swear fealty, and a writ was to be issued for his consecration in the usual manner; after that he was to do homage to the king, upon which both the temporalities and spiritualities were to be restored, and bishops were to exercise their jurisdiction as they had done before. A private act was passed depriving cardinal Campeggio and Jerome de Gainuccii of the bishoprics of Salisbury and Worcester; the reasons given were, that they did not reside in the dioceses, but lived at the court of Rome, and drew £3000 a year out of the kingdom.

In winter parliament met again, and the first act that passed declared the king to be supreme head on earth of the church of England, which was ordered to be prefixed to his other titles; and it was enacted that he and his successors should have full authority to reform all heresies and abuses in the spiritual jurisdiction. By another act, parliament confirmed the oath of succession. They also gave the king the first-fruits and tenths of the ecclesiastical benefices, as being the supreme head of the church; for the king being put in the pope's room, it was thought reasonable to give him what the popes had formerly exacted. Another act passed declaring some things treason; one of these was denying the king any of his titles, or calling him heretic, schismatic, or usurper of the crown. By another act, provision was made for setting up twenty-six suffragan bishops over England, for the more speedy administration of the sacraments, and the better service of God. The supreme diocesan was to present two names to the king, and upon the king's declaring his choice, the archbishop was to consecrate the person, and then the bishop was to delegate such parts of his charge to his care as he thought fit, which was to continue during his pleasure. The great size of the dioceses in England made it difficult for one bishop to govern them; these were, therefore, appointed to assist them.

But now a new scene commenced: before we enter upon it, it is necessary to state the progress the new opinions had made in England during the king's suit of divorce. While Wolsey was a minister, the reformed preachers were gently used: and it is probable the king, when the pope began to use him ill, ordered the bishops to cease inquiring after them, for the progress of heresy was always reckoned at Rome among the mischiefs that would follow the pope's rejecting the king's suit. But Sir Thomas More coming into favour, thought the king's proceeding severely against heretics would be so meritorious at Rome, that it would work more effectually than all his threatenings had done. Upon this, a severe proclamation was issued, both against their books and persons, ordering all the laws against them to be put in execution. Tyndal and others at Antwerp were every year either translating or writing books against some of the received errors, and sending them over to England; but his translation of the New Testament gave the greatest wound, and was much complained of by the clergy, as full of errors. Tonstal, then bishop of London, being a man of great learning, returning from the treaty of Cambray, as he came through Antwerp, dealt with an English merchant, who was secretly a friend of Tyndal's, to procure him as many of his Testaments as could be had for money.

K

Tyndal gladly received this: for being engaged on a more correct edition, he found he should be better able to proceed if the copies of the old were sold off; he therefore gave the merchant all that he had, and Tonstal paying the price of them, got them over to England and burnt them in Cheapside. This was called a burning of the word of God; and it was said the clergy had reason to revenge themselves on it, for it had done them more mischief than all other books whatsoever. But a year after this, the second edition being finished, great numbers were sent over to England, when Constantine, one of Tyndal's partners, happened to be taken; believing that some of the London merchants furnished them with money, he was promised his liberty if he would discover who they were; when he told them the bishop of London did more than all the world beside, for he had bought up the greatest part of a faulty impression. The clergy, on their condemning Tyndal's translation, promised a new one; but a year after they said it was unnecessary to publish the Scriptures in English, and that the king did well not to set about it.

The pen being thought too gentle a tool, the clergy betook themselves to persecution. Many were imprisoned for teaching their children the Lord's Prayer in English, for harbouring the preachers, and for speaking against the corruptions in the worship, or the vices of the clergy; but these generally abjured and saved themselves from death. Others, more faithful, were honoured with martyrdom. One Hinton, formerly a curate, who had gone over to Tyndal, was seized on his way back with some books he was conveying to England, and was condemned by archbishop Warham. He was kept long in prison; but remaining firm to his cause, was at length burned at Maidstone.

## Martyrdom of Thomas Bilney.

But the most remarkable martyr of this day was Thomas Bilney, who was brought up at Cambridge from a child, and became a bold and uncompromising reformer. On leaving the university, he went into several places and preached; and in his sermons spoke with great boldness against the pride and insolence of the clergy. This was during the ministry of Wolsey, who caused him to be seized and imprisoned. Overcome with fear, Bilney abjured, was pardoned, and returned to Cambridge in the year 1530. Here he fell into great horror of mind in consequence of his denial of the truth. He became ashamed of himself, bitterly repented of his sin, and, growing strong in faith, resolved to make some atonement by a public avowal of his apostasy, and confession of his sentiments. To prepare himself for his task, he studied the Scriptures with deep attention for two years; at the expiration of which he again quitted the university, and went into Norfolk, where he was born, and preached up and down that country against idolatry and superstition; exhorting the people to live well, to give much alms, to believe in Christ, and to offer up their souls and wills to Him in the sacrament. He openly confessed his own sin of denying the faith; and using no precaution as he went about, was soon taken by the bishop's officers, condemned of a relapse, and degraded. Sir Thomas More not only

sent down the writ to burn him, but, in order to
make him suffer another way, affirmed that he had
abjured; but no paper signed by him was ever
shown, and little credit was due to the priests who
gave it out that he did it by word of mouth.
Parker, afterwards archbishop, was an eye-witness
of his sufferings. He bore all his hardships with
great fortitude and resignation, and continued cheerful after his sentence. He ate the poor provisions
that were brought him heartily, saying, he must
keep up a ruinous cottage till it fell. He had the
words of Isaiah often in his mouth, "When thou
walkest through the fire, thou shalt not be burned;"
and by burning his finger in the candle, he prepared
himself for the fire, and said it would only consume
the stubble of his body, while it would purify his
soul, and give it a swifter conveyance to the region
where Elijah was conveyed by another fiery chariot.

On the 10th of November he was brought to the
stake, where he repeated the Creed, as a proof that
he was a true Christian. He then, with the deepest
feeling, offered this prayer: "Enter not into judgment with thy servant, O Lord, for in thy sight
no flesh living can be justified." Dr. Warner
embraced him, shedding many tears, and wishing
he might die in as good a frame as Bilney then was.
The friars requested him to inform the people, that
they were not instrumental to his death; which he
did, so that the last act of his life was full of charity,
even to those who put him to death.

The officers then put the reeds and fagots about
his body, and set fire to the first, which made a
great flame and disfigured his face; he held up
his hands, and often struck his breast, crying

FRITH IN PRISON, PREPARING HIS ANSWER TO SIR THOMAS MORE.

sometimes, "Jesus!" sometimes "Creda!" But the flame was blown away from him several times, the wind being very high, till at length the wood taking fire, the flame was stronger, and he yielded up his spirit to God who gave it.

As his body shrunk up, it leaned down on the chain, till one of the officers with his halbert struck out the staple of the chain behind him, on which it fell down into the bottom of the fire, when they heaped up wood upon it and consumed it. The sufferings, the confession, and the heroic death of this martyr, inspired and animated others with the same fortitude.

### Story and Martyrdom of Frith.

Frith was a young man famed for learning, and was the first in England who wrote against the corporeal presence in the sacrament. His book was answered by Sir Thomas More; but Frith never saw his publication till he was in prison, and then, though he was loaded with irons and had no books allowed him, he replied.

For these offences he was seized in May, 1533, and charged with not believing in purgatory and transubstantiation. He gave the reasons that determined him to look on neither of these as articles of faith. The bishops seemed unwilling to proceed to sentence; but he continuing resolute, Stokesley pronounced it, and delivered him to the secular power, at the same time desiring that his punishment might be moderated: a piece of hypocrisy which deceived no one.

Frith, with a fellow-martyr named Hewitt, was

brought to the stake at Smithfield on July 4th,
1533. On arriving there he expressed great joy,
and even embraced the fagots. A priest named
Cook, who stood by, told the people not to pray for
them more than they would for a dog. At this
Frith smiled, and said, "God forgive you." The
fire was then kindled, and the martyrs burned to
ashes.

## Martyrdom of John Lambert.

John Lambert, a teacher of languages in London,
who had drawn up ten arguments against the tenets
of Dr. Taylor on the above subject, as delivered in
a sermon at St. Peter's church, and presented them
to the doctor, was brought before the archbishop's
court to defend his writings. Having appealed to
the king, the royal theologian, who was proud of
displaying his talents and learning, resolved to hear
him in person. He therefore issued a commission,
ordering his nobility and bishops to repair to
London, to assist him against heretics.

A day was appointed for the disputation, when a
great number of persons of all ranks assembled, and
Lambert was brought from his prison by a guard,
and placed directly opposite the king. Henry
being seated on his throne, and surrounded by the
peers, bishops, and judges, regarded the prisoner
with a stern countenance, and then commanded
Day, bishop of Chichester, to state the occasion of
the present assembly. The bishop made a long
oration, stating that, although the king had abol-
ished the papal authority in England, it was not to
be supposed that he would allow heretics with impunity to disturb and trouble the church of which

he was the head. He had, therefore, determined to punish all schismatics : and being willing to have the advice of his bishops and counsellors on so great an occasion, had assembled them to hear the arguments in the case.

The oration being concluded, the king ordered Lambert to declare his opinion as to the sacrament of the Lord's Supper, which he did, by denying it to be the body of Christ. The king then commanded Cranmer to refute this assertion, which the latter attempted, but was interrupted by Gardiner, who vehemently interposed, and, being unable to bring argument to his aid, sought by abuse and virulence to overpower his antagonist. Tonstal and Stokesley followed them in the same course ; and Lambert, beginning to answer them, was silenced by the king. The other bishops then each made a speech in confutation of one of Lambert's arguments, till the whole ten were answered, or rather railed against, for he was not permitted to defend them, however misrepresented.

At last, when the day was passed, and torches began to be lighted, the king, desiring to break up this pretended disputation, said to Lambert, " What sayest thou now, after these great labours which thou hast taken upon thee, and all the reasons and instructions of these learned men ? Art thou not yet satisfied ? Wilt thou live or die ? What sayest thou ? Thou hast yet free choice."

Lambert answered, " I yield and submit myself wholly unto the will of your majesty." " Then," said the king, " commit thyself unto the hands of God, and not unto mine."

Lambert replied, " I commend my soul unto the

hands of God, but my body I wholly yield and submit unto your clemency." To which the king answered, "If you do commit yourself unto my judgment, you must die, for I will not be a patron to heretics;" and, turning to Cromwell, he said, "Read the sentence of condemnation against him," which he accordingly did.

On the day appointed for this holy martyr to suffer, he was brought from the prison at eight o'clock in the morning to the house of Cromwell, where, it is said, Cromwell desired his forgiveness for what he had done. Lambert being at last admonished that the hour of his death was at hand, and being brought into the hall, saluted the gentlemen present, and sat down to breakfast with them, showing neither sadness nor fear. When breakfast was ended, he was carried straight to the place of execution at Smithfield.

The manner of his death was dreadful; for after his legs were burned up to the stumps, and but a small fire was left under him, two of the inhuman monsters who stood on each side of him, pierced him with their halberts, and lifted him up as far as the chain would reach: while he, raising his half-consumed hands, cried unto the people in these words, "None but Christ, none but Christ!" and so, being let down again from their halberts, fell into the fire, and there ended his life.

The popish party greatly triumphed at this event, and endeavoured to improve it. They persuaded the king of the good effects it would have on his people, who would in this see his zeal for the faith; and they forgot not to magnify all that he had said, as if it had been uttered by an oracle, which proved

him to be both " Defender of the Faith and Supreme
Head of the Church." All this wrought so much on
the king, that he resolved to call a parliament for
the contradictory purposes of suppressing the still
remaining monasteries, and extirpating the "new
opinions."

## Sufferings and Martyrdom of Dr. Robert Barnes.

Dr. Barnes was educated in the university of Lou-
vain, in Brabant. On his return to England he
went to Cambridge, where he was made prior of the
order of Augustines, and steward of their house.
The darkest ignorance pervaded the university, excepting with a few persons whose learning was unknown to the rest. Dr. Barnes, zealous to promote
knowledge and truth, soon began to instruct the
students in classic languages, and, with the assistance of Parnel, he soon caused learning to flourish,
and the university to bear a very different aspect.
These foundations laid, he began to read openly the
epistles of St. Paul, and to teach in greater purity
the doctrine of Christ. He preached and disputed
with great warmth against the luxuries of the higher
clergy, particularly against cardinal Wolsey, and the
lamentable hypocrisy of the times. But still he remained ignorant of the great cause of these evils,
namely, the idolatry and superstition of the church;
and while he declaimed against the stream, he himself drank at the spring, and kept it running for
others. At length, becoming acquainted with Bilney,
he was converted to Christ. In the first reformed
sermon he preached, he commented on the epistle
for the day, following the Scripture and Luther's

exposition. For that sermon he was accused of
heresy by two fellows of the King's Hall. Dr.
Nottoris, a bitter enemy to Christ, then moved him
to recant; but he refused, as appears in his book
which he wrote to king Henry, confuting the judgment of cardinal Wolsey, and the residue of the
popish bishops. They continued in Cambridge, one
preaching against another, till within six days of
Shrovetide, when suddenly a sergeant-at-arms was
sent down to arrest Dr. Barnes openly in the convo-
cation-house. On Wednesday he arrived in London, and lay at Mr. Parnel's house. Next morning
he was taken before cardinal Wolsey at Westminster, and spake with him in his chamber of
state, kneeling.

"What! Mr. Doctor," said Wolsey, "had you
not a sufficient scope in the Scriptures to teach the
people, but that my golden shoes, my poll-axes, my
pillars, my cushions, my crosses, did so offend you,
that you make us ridiculous among the people, who
that day laughed us to scorn? Verily it was a sermon fitter to be preached on a stage than in a pulpit;
for at last, you said I wear a pair of red gloves, ' I
should say bloody gloves,' quoth you, that I should
not be cold in the midst of my ceremonies." To
this banter Dr. Barnes answered, "I spake nothing
but the truth out of the Scriptures, according to my
conscience, and according to the ancient doctors."
He then delivered him six sheets of paper, written to
corroborate his sentiments.

The cardinal received them smiling, saying,
"We perceive then that you intend to stand to
your articles, and show your learning." To which
Barnes replied, "Yea, that I do, by God's grace,

with your lordship's favour. " The cardinal now became angry, and said, "Such as you bear us little favour, and the catholic church less. I will ask you whether you think it more necessary that I should have all this royalty, because I represent the king's majesty in all the high courts of this realm; or to be as simple as you would have us, to sell all these things, and give them to the poor, who shortly will cast them in the dirt; and to pull away this princely dignity, which is a terror to the wicked, and to follow your counsel ?"

"I think," said Barnes, "it should be sold and given to the poor. All this is not becoming your calling; nor is the king's majesty maintained by your pomp and your poll-axes, but by God, who saith, 'Kings reign by me.'" Turning to the attendants, the cardinal then satirically said, "Lo, Master Doctors, he is the learned and wise man that you told me of!" Then they kneeled down, and said, "We desire your grace to be good unto him, for he will reform." The cardinal mildly said, "Stand you up; for your sakes and the university, we will be good unto him." Turning to Barnes, he added, "How say you, Master Doctor; do you not know that I am able to dispense in all matters concerning religion in this realm, as the pope himself?" Barnes meekly said, "I know it be so." The cardinal then asked, "Will you be ruled by us? and we will do all things for your honesty, and for the honesty of the university." Barnes answered, "I thank your grace for your goodwill; I will adhere to the holy Scripture, as God's book, according to the simple talent that God hath lent me." The cardinal ended the dialogue by saying, "Well, thou shalt have thy learning tried to the uttermost, and thou shalt have the law."

Next morning he was brought by the sargeant-at-arms into the chapter-house, before the bishops, and Islip, the abbot of Westminster. These asked the sergeant-at-arms what was his errand. He said he had brought Dr. Barnes on a charge of heresy, and then presented both his articles and his accusers. Dr. Barnes was asked whether he would subscribe to his articles? He subscribed willingly, when they committed him and young Parnel to the Fleet.

On the Saturday following he was again brought before them in the chapter-house. After long disputation, they asked whether he would abjure or burn. He was greatly agitated, and felt inclined rather to burn than abjure. But he then again had the counsel of Gardiner and Fox, who persuaded him to abjure, because, they pleaded, he might in future be silent; urging other reasons to save his life and check his heresy. Upon that, kneeling down, he consented to abjure; yet they would scarcely receive him into the bosom of the church, as they termed it. Then they put him to an oath, and charged him to fulfil all they commanded him; which he promised.

On this they commanded the warden of the Fleet to keep him in close prison, and in the morning to provide five fagots for Dr. Barnes and four other men charged with heresy, the fifth man being ordered to have a taper of five pounds' weight provided for him, to offer to the rood of Northen in Paul's, and in these things to be ready by eight on the following morning; and that he, with all he could make with bills and glaves, and the knight-marshal with all his tipstaves that he could make, should bring them to Paul's and conduct them home again. Accordingly, in the morning they were all ready by the appointed hour in St. Paul's church, which was crowded. The cardinal had a scaffold on the top of the stairs for himself, with six and thirty abbots, mitred priors, and bishops, and in his whole pomp mitred, sat there enthroned, his chaplains and spiritual doctors in gowns of damask and satin, and he himself in purple. There was also a new pulpit erected on the top of the stairs, for the bishop of Rochester to preach against Luther and Barnes; and great baskets full of books standing before them within the rails, which were commanded, after the great fire was made before the rood of Northen, there to be burned, and these heretics after the sermon to go thrice about the fire and cast in their fagots.

During the sermon Dr. Barnes and the men were made to kneel down and ask forgiveness of God and the catholic church and the cardinal's grace; after the sermon he was commanded to declare that he was used more charitably than he deserved, his heresies being so horrible and detestable: once more he kneeled, desiring of the people forgiveness, and to pray for him. This farce being ended, the cardinal departed under a canopy, with his mitred men with him, till he came to the second gate of Paul's, when he took his mule, and the mitred men came back again. Then the prisoners being commanded to come down from the stage, whereon the sweepers used to stand when they swept the church, the bishops sat them down again, and commanded the knight-marshal and the warden of the Fleet, with their company, to carry them about the fire; they were then brought to the bishops, and kneeled down for absolution. The bishop of Rochester, standing up, declared to the people how many days' pardon and forgiveness of sins they had for being at that sermon; and Dr. Barnes, with the others, was received into the church again. This done, they were taken to the Fleet again, there to remain till the cardinal's pleasure was known.

Dr. Barnes having remained here half a year, was delivered to be a free prisoner at the Austin friars in London. But here, being watched, new complaints of him were made to the cardinal, on which he was removed to the Austin friars of Northampton, there to be burnt; of which intention, however, he was ignorant. At length Mr. Horne, who was his particular friend, gaining intelligence of the writ which was shortly to be sent down to burn him, advised him to feign himself to be in a state of despair, and to write a letter to the cardinal and leave it on his table where he lay, with a paper to declare whither he was gone to drown himself, and to leave his clothes in the same place; and another letter to be left to the mayor of the town to search for him in the water, because he had a letter written in parchment about his neck, closed in wax, for the cardinal, which should teach all men to beware of him. This scheme he accordingly put in execution, and they were seven days searching for him : but he was conveyed to London in poor man's apparel, and from thence took shipping and went to Antwerp, where he found Luther.

Dr. Barnes now became learned in the word of God, and strong in Christ, and was in great esteem with all men whose esteem was honourable, particularly Luther, Melancthon, the duke of Saxony, and king of Denmark, the last of whom, in the time of More, sent him with the Lubecks as ambassador to king Henry the Eighth. Sir Thomas More, who succeeded Wolsey as chancellor, would fain have entrapped him; but the king would not let him, and Cromwell was his great friend. Before he left, the Lubecks and he disputed with the bishops of England in defence of the truth, and he was allowed to depart without restraint. After going to Wittenberg, to the duke of Saxony and Luther, he remained there to forward his works in print which he had begun, after which he returned again in the beginning of the reign of queen Anne, as others did, and continued a faithful preacher in London, being all her time well entertained and promoted. After that, he was sent ambassador by Henry to the duke of Cleves upon the business of the marriage between the Lady Anne of Cleves and the king. He gave great satisfaction in every duty which was entrusted to him.

Not long after this Dr. Barnes, with his brethren, was apprehended and carried before the king at Hampton Court. The king being desirous to bring about an agreement between him and Gardiner, at the request of the latter gave him leave to go home with the bishop to confer with him. But they not agreeing, Gardiner and his co-partners sought to entrap Barnes and his friends into further danger, which not long after was brought to pass. By certain complaints made to the king of them, they

L

were enjoined to preach three sermons the following Easter at the Spittle: at which sermons, besides other reporters which were sent thither, Gardiner himself was present, sitting with the mayor, either to bear record of their recantation, or else, as the Pharisees came to Christ, to ensnare them in their talk, if they should speak anything amiss. Barnes preached first, and at the conclusion of his sermon requested Gardiner, if he thought he had said nothing contradictory to truth, to hold up his hand in the face of all present, upon which Gardiner immediately held up his finger. Notwithstanding this, they were all three, by means of the reporters, sent for to Hampton Court, whence they were conducted to the Tower, where they remained till they were brought out to death.

Mr. Garret was a London curate. About the year 1526 he came to Oxford, and brought with him books in Latin, treating of the Scriptures, and Tyndal's first translation of the New Testament in English, which he sold to scholars in Oxford. After he had disposed of them, news came from London that he was searched for through all that city, as a heretic, and for selling heretical publications, as they were termed. It was not unknown to cardinal Wolsey, the bishop of London, and others, that Mr. Garret had a great number of those books, and that he was gone to Oxford to sell them. Wherefore they determined to make a secret search through all Oxford, to burn all his books, and him, too, if they could. But happily, one of the proctors, Mr. Cole, of Magdalen College, being well acquainted with Mr. Garret, gave warning of the search, and advised that he should, as secretly as possible, depart from Oxford.

A curacy being provided for him by Dalabar, another friend, Mr. Garret departed for Dorsetshire. How far he went, and by what occasion he soon returned, was not known.    But the following Friday night he came to Radley's house, where he lay before, and after midnight, in the privy search which was then made for him, he was taken by the two proctors, and on the Saturday morning delivered to Dr. Cottisford, master of Lincoln College, who kept him prisoner in his own chamber.    At this there was great rejoicing among the papists, and especially with Dr. Loudon, warden of the New College, and Dr. Higdon, dean of Frideswide, who immediately sent letters post-haste to the cardinal, to inform him of the apprehension of this notable heretic, for which they were well assured of receiving great thanks. But of all this sudden hurly-burly, Dalabar was utterly ignorant; he neither knew of Mr. Garret's return, nor that he was taken, until he came into his chamber; and as soon as he saw him, he said he was undone, for he was taken.    He spake thus unadvisedly in the presence of a young man.    When the young man was departed, Dalabar asked him what he was, and what acquaintance he had with him.    He said he knew him not; but that he had been to see a monk of his acquaintance in that college, and therefore desired his servant to conduct him to his brother.    He then declared how he was returned and taken in the privy search.

Delabar then said to him, "Alas! Mr. Garret, by your uncircumspect coming, and speaking before this young man, you have disclosed yourself, and utterly undone me."    He asked him why he went not to his brother with his letters.    He answered that after he was gone a day's journey and a half, he was so fearful, that his heart suggested that he must needs return to Oxford; and accordingly he came again on Friday at night, and was taken. But now, with tears, he prayed Dalabar to help him away, and then cast off his hood and gown wherein he came, and desired a coat with sleeves, saying he would if possible disguise himself, go into Wales, and thence into Germany. Dalabar then put on him a sleeved coat of his own. He would also have had another kind of cap, but there was no one to be found for him.

Then they both kneeled down, and lifting up their hearts to God, desired him to prosper him in his journey, that he might escape his enemies, to the glory of his holy name, if his good pleasure so were. They then embraced, and could scarcely bid adieu for sorrow; at length, disguised in his brother's garments, he departed. But his escape soon becoming known, he was pursued, and taken at a place called Hinksey, a little beyond Oxford, and being brought back again was committed to ward; that done he was brought before Dr. Loudon and Dr. Higdon, in St. Mary's church, convicted as a heretic, and afterwards compelled to carry a fagot in open procession from St. Mary's church to the place whence he came. After this, flying from place to place, he escaped their tyranny, until he was again apprehended with Dr. Barnes.

William Jerome was vicar of Stepney, and, convinced of the errors of the church of Rome, and the consequences that flowed from them, preached with great zeal the pure and simple doctrines of the gospel instead of the traditions of men. He soon became known to the enemies of the truth, who watched him with malignant jealousy. It was not long before, in a sermon preached in St. Paul's, wherein he dwelt upon justification by faith, he gave such offence, that he was summoned before the king at Westminster, accused of heresy.

It was urged against him, that he had said, according to St. Paul in the epistles to the Galatians —That the children of Sara—allegorically used for the children of the promise—were all born free; and, independently of baptism or of penance, were, through faith, made heirs of God. Dr. Wilson strongly opposed this doctrine. But Jerome defended it with all the force of truth, and said, that although good works were the means of salvation, yet they followed as a consequence of faith, whose fruits they were, and which discovered their root, even as good fruit proves a good tree. But so inveterate were his enemies, and so deluded was the king, that Jerome was committed to the Tower, in company with the other two good soldiers of Christ, with them to suffer for his faith.

Here they remained while a process was issuing against them by the king's council in parliament, by whom, without hearing or knowledge of their fate, they were attainted of heresy, and sentenced to the flames. On the 30th of the following June they were brought from the Tower to Smithfield, where they were permitted to address the people. Dr. Barnes first spoke, as follows :—" I am come hither to be burned as a heretic, and you shall hear my belief, whereby you may perceive what erroneous opinion I hold. I take God to record, I never to my knowledge taught any erroneous doctrine, but

only those things which Scripture led me into;
neither in my sermons have I ever given occasion
for insurrection; but with all diligence did I study
to set forth the glory of God, obedience to our sovereign lord the king, and the true and sincere religion of Christ; and now hearken to my faith:

"I believe in the holy and blessed Trinity, three
persons in one God, who created and made the
world; and that this blessed Trinity sent down the
second person, Jesus Christ, into the womb of the
most blessed and pure Virgin Mary. I believe that
he was conceived by the Holy Ghost, and took
flesh of her; and that he suffered hunger, thirst,
cold, and other passions of our body, sin excepted,
according to the saying, 'He was made in all things
like his brethren, except sin.' And I believe that
this his death and passion was a sufficient ransom
for sin. And I believe that through his death he
overcame sin, death, and hell, and that there is
none other satisfaction unto the Father, but his
death and passion only; and that no work of man
does deserve anything of God, but Christ's passion
only, as touching our justification, for I know the
best work that ever I performed is impure and
imperfect." With this he cast abroad his hands,
and desired God to forgive him his trespasses.
"Wherefore, I beseech thee, O Lord, not to enter
into judgment with me, according to the saying of
the prophet David. Wherefore, I trust in no good
work that ever I did, but only in the death of
Christ. I do not doubt but through him to inherit
the kingdom of heaven. But imagine not that I
speak against good works, for they are to be done;
and verily they that do them not shall never come

into the kingdom of God. We must do them, because they are commanded us of God, to show and set forth our profession, not to deserve or merit; but that is only by the death of Christ."

One then asked his opinion on praying to saints. "Now, of saints," said he, "I believe they are in heaven with God, and that they are worthy of all the honour that Scripture willeth them to have; but we are not commanded in Scripture to pray to them. Therefore I neither can nor will preach that saints ought to be prayed to; for then should I preach to you a doctrine of mine own head. As to whether they pray for us or no, that I refer to God. If saints do pray for us, then I trust to pray for you within this half-hour, Mr. Sheriff, and for every Christian living in the faith. Wherefore, if the dead may pray for the quick I will surely pray for you."

Then said he to the sheriff, "Have ye any articles against me for what I am condemned?" The sheriff answered, "No." Then said Barnes, "Is there here any man else that knoweth wherefore I die, or that by my preaching hath been led into error? Let him now speak and I will answer." But no man answered. Then said he, "Well, I am condemned by the law to die, and, as I understand, by an act of parliament; but wherefore I cannot tell; perhaps it is for heresy, for we are likely to suffer under this charge, cruel as it is. But they that have been the occasion of it, I pray God forgive them, as I would be forgiven myself. And Doctor Stephen, bishop of Winchester, if he have sought or wrought this my death, either by word or deed, I pray God to forgive him, as heartily, as freely, as charitably, and as sincerely as Christ forgave them that put him to death. I beseech you all to pray for the king's grace, as I have done ever since I was in prison, and do now, that God may give him prosperity, and that he may long reign among you; and after him that godly prince Edward, that he may finish those things that his father hath begun."

After this admirable address, Dr. Barnes desired, if he had offended any, or given any occasion of evil, that they would pardon him, and amend that evil they took of him, and to bear him witness that he detested and abhorred all evil opinions and doctrines against the word of God, and that he died in the faith of Jesus Christ, by whom he doubted not but to be saved. With these words he entreated them all to pray for him; and then he put off his clothes and prepared himself for death.

Jerome then addressed himself as follows: "I say unto you, good brethren, that Christ hath bought us with no small price, neither with gold nor silver, or other such things of small value, but with his most precious blood. Be not unthankful, therefore, to him; but fulfil his commandments—that is, love your brethren. Love hurteth no man : love fulfilleth all things. If God hath sent thee plenty, help thy neighbour that hath need. Give him good counsel. If he lack, consider if you were in necessity, you would gladly be refreshed. And again, bear your cross with Christ. Consider what reproof, slander, and reproach he suffered, and how patiently he suffered. Consider, that all Christ did was of his mere goodness, and not for our deserving. If we could merit our own salvation, Christ would not have died for us. Let Christians, therefore, put no trust or confidence in their works, but in the blood of Christ alone, to whom I commit my soul, beseeching you all to pray to God for me, and for my brethren here present with me, that our souls, leaving these wretched bodies, may depart in the true faith of Christ."

After he had concluded, Garret thus spoke: " I also detest all heresies and errors, and if I have taught any, I am sorry for it, and ask God's mercy. Or if I have been rash in preaching, whereby any person hath taken offence, or evil opinion, I desire his forgiveness. Notwithstanding, to my remembrance, I have never preached willingly anything against God's holy word, or contrary to the true faith; but have ever endeavoured, with the little learning and wisdom I have, to set forth the honour of God, and right obedience to his laws, and also the king's. If I could have done better, I would. Wherefore, Lord, if I have taken in hand to do that thing which I could not perfectly perform, I desire thy pardon for my bold presumption. And I pray God to give the king good counsel to his honour, and the increase of virtue in this realm. And thus do I yield my soul up unto Almighty God, trusting and believing that he, of his infinite mercy, according to his promise made in the blood of his Son Jesus Christ, will take it and pardon all my sins, of which I ask him mercy, and desire you all to pray with me and for me, that I may patiently suffer this pain, and die in true faith, hope, and charity."

The three martyrs then took each other by the hand, and after embracing, submitted themselves to the tormentors, who, fastening them to the stake, soon lighted the fagots, and terminated their mortal life and care.

## Martyrdom of Patrick Hamilton.

Patrick Hamilton was highly descended, and was bred up with the design of being advanced to clerical dignity. He went over to Germany to study; and there becoming acquainted with Luther and Melancthon, he became convinced of the truth of their doctrines.

After preaching some time to his countrymen, he was invited to St. Andrew's, to confer upon the points in question. But his enemies, finding themselves defeated in argument, resolved on revenge. Hamilton was accordingly imprisoned. Articles were exhibited against him, and upon his refusing to abjure, Beaton, archbishop of St. Andrew's, with the archbishop of Glasgow, three bishops, and five abbots, condemned him as an obstinate heretic, delivered him to the secular power, and ordered his execution that very afternoon. When tied to the stake, he expressed great joy in his suffering, since he was thus to enter into everlasting life. A friar, named Campbell, was very officious. Hamilton answered, that he knew he was not a heretic, and had confessed it to him in private, and charged him to answer for that at the throne of Almighty God. By this time the gunpowder was brought, and the fire being kindled, he died, after repeating these words, "Lord Jesus, receive my soul." His relentless persecutor, Campbell, soon after became deranged, and died without recovering his reason.

Henry Forest, a young man of Lithquow, was

the next victim. His first offence was saying that
Patrick Hamilton died a martyr, and that his
articles were true. For which he was apprehended
and put in prison by Beaton. He shortly after
caused a certain friar, named Walter Laing, to hear
his confession. When Forest had declared that he
thought Hamilton a good man, and wrongfully put
to death, and that his articles were true and not
heretical, the friar informed the bishop. His confession being brought as evidence against him, he
was summoned before the clergy and doctors, and
by them delivered to the secular power to be put
to death.

When the day came he was brought before the
clergy on a green between the castle of St. Andrew's
and a place called Monymaill. As soon as he saw
the faces of the clergy he cried with a loud voice,
" Fie on falsehood! fie on false friars, revealers of
confession! after this day let no man trust any
friars, contemners of God's word and deceivers of
men." After his degradation they condemned him
as a heretic equal to Hamilton; and he suffered
death for his faithful testimony to the truth of
Christ.

## Testwood and his Companions.

Robert Testwood, of London, had, by his knowledge in music, attained so great a name, that the
musicians in Windsor college thought him worthy
to have a place among them. He was so well liked,
both for his voice and skill, that he was settled in
Windsor, with his household, and held in estima-
tion by the dean and canons. One day dining
with Dr. Rawson, one of the canons, one of king

Edward's four chantry priests, named Ely, was present. Mr. Ely began to rail against laymen who took upon them to meddle with the Scriptures, and to be better learned, knowing only the English tongue, than scholars from Oxford and Cambridge. Testwood, perceiving he meant that for him, said, "Mr. Ely, by your patience, I think it be no hurt for a layman, as I am, to read and know the Scriptures."

A dispute then arose about the pope, whose supremacy was not known to be so far in question in parliament as it was. Ely demanded of Testwood whether the pope ought not to be the head of the church. Testwood said, "Every king, in his own realm, ought to be the head of the church under Christ." At this, Ely rose from the table in a great fume, calling Testwood a heretic. Testwood was sorry to see the old man act such a part, and after dinner, finding him walking in the church, thought to have talked with him charitably; but Ely shunned him, saying to others that walked by, "Beware of this fellow, for he is the greatest heretic that ever came into Windsor."

After this Testwood suffered much persecution; and although the king's supremacy passed in parliament, yet Testwood's enemies seemed bent on his ruin. He was afraid to leave his house; and once, when he did venture to the chapter-house, one of his enemies drew a dagger, and would have stabbed him, had not Ward, a justice of the peace, prevented him.

Anthony Pearson frequently went to Windsor, about the year 1540, preaching, and was greatly esteemed among the people, who flocked so much to his sermons that priests of the castle, with other papists in the town, especially Simons, were offended. Simons, at last, began to take down his sermons, and to mark his auditors; whereof ensued the death of many honest men. About a year after, Dr. Loudon, warden of the New College in Oxford, was admitted one of the prebendaries of Windsor, who, at his first coming, began to show his aversion to the Lutheran doctrine.

At his first residence dinner, his whole talk to two gentlemen, strangers at his board, was nothing else but of heretics, and what desolation they would bring the realm to, if they were suffered. "And by St. Mary, masters," said he, "there goeth a shrewd report of this house." Some made answer, it was undeserved. "I pray God it be. I am but a stranger among you; but I have heard it said, that there be some in this house that will neither have prayer nor fasting."

Then Testwood said, "By my troth, sir, I think that was spoken in malice; for prayer, as you know better than I, was one of the first lessons that Christ taught us." "Yea, sir," quoth he, "but the heretics will have no invocation to saints, which all the old fathers do allow." "What the old fathers do allow," quoth Testwood, "I cannot tell; but Scripture doth appoint us to go to the Father, and to ask our petitions of him in Christ's name." "Then you will have no mediator between you and God," quoth the doctor. "Yes, sir," quoth Testwood, "our mediator is Christ, as St. Paul said, 'There is one mediator between God and man, even Jesus Christ.'" "Give us water," quoth the enraged doctor, as though he were rendered impure by heretical company. Water being set on the board, he said grace, and washed, and so falling into other communication with the strangers, the clerks took their leave and departed.

When this haughty prebendary had been a while at Windsor, and learned what Testwood was, and what sort of heretics were in the town, and how they increased daily, through a priest called Anthony Pearson, he was almost infernally bent on doing them injury. Dr. Loudon went to work in earnest. Bishop Gardiner was his most important auxiliary, for he persuaded the king to grant permission to have the law put in operation. Soon after Robert Benet, Henry Filmer, John Marbeck, and Robert Testwood were apprehended for books and writings against the six articles found in their houses; they were kept till Monday after, and then fetched up to the council, excepting Testwood, who was ill of the gout. The other three were committed to prison: Filmer and Benet to the bishop of London's gaol, and Marbeck to the Marshalsea. They were most rigorously examined, but remaining unshaken, were condemned to death. Marbeck, through the bishop of Sarum, was pardoned, but his companions suffered, as is here set forth.

On Saturday morning two of the canons of the college came into the prison, the one called Dr. Blithe, and the other Mr. Arch, who were sent as confessors. Mr. Arch asked, if they would be confessed? They said, " Yea." Then he asked, if they would receive the sacrament? " Yea," said they, " with all our hearts." " I am glad," quoth Arch, " to hear you say so; but the law is, that it may not be ministered to any condemned of heresy;

however, it is enough for you that ye desire it."
And so he had them up to the hall to hear their
confessions, because the prison was full of people.
Dr. Blithe took Anthony Pearson to confess, and
Mr. Arch the other two. The doctor, howsoever,
was not long with Anthony before he came down
again, saying, " I will have no more of his doctrine."
Soon after the other two came down also. Then
Anthony began to say the Lord's Prayer, continuing
till the officer came to fetch them away; then taking
leave of Marbeck, they praised God for his deliverance, wishing him an increase of godliness and virtue,
and beseeching him to help them with his prayers,
so that they might be strong in their afflictions.

As they passed through the street, they desired
the people to pray for them, and to stand fast in the
truth of the gospel, not moved at their afflictions,
for it was the happiest thing that ever came to them.
And as Dr. Blithe and Arch would persuade them
to turn to their holy mother church—"Away,"
would Anthony cry; "away with your Romish
doctrine and your trumpery, for we will have no
more of it." When Filmer came to his brother's
door, he called for him; but he could not be seen,
for Dr. Loudon had kept him out of sight. When
he came not, he said, " And will he not come?
Then God forgive him, and make him a good man."
Thus they came to the place of execution, where
Anthony Pearson, with a cheerful countenance,
embraced the post in his arms, and kissing it, said,
" Now welcome, mine own sweet wife; for this day
shalt thou and I be married together in the love and
peace of God."

When they were all three bound to the post, a

young man of Filmer's acquaintance asked if he would drink. "Yea," quoth Filmer, "I thank you. And now, my brother, I desire you in the name of the Lord to stand fast in the truth of the gospel which you have received;" and so taking the cup into his hand, asked his brother Anthony if he would drink. "Yea, brother Filmer," quoth he; "I pledge you in the Lord."

When he had drunk, he gave the cup to Anthony, and Anthony gave it to Testwood; of which their adversaries made a jest, saying that they were all drunk, and knew not what they said; though they were no otherwise drunk than the apostles were, when the people said they were full of new wine; for when Anthony and Testwood had both drunk, Filmer, rejoicing in the Lord, said, "Be merry, my brethren, and lift up your hearts and hands unto God, for after this sharp breakfast I trust we shall have a good dinner in the kingdom of Christ, our Lord and Redeemer." At these words Testwood, lifting up his hands and eyes to heaven, desired the Lord to receive his spirit. Anthony Pearson, pulling the straw towards him, laid a good deal on his head, saying, "Now I am dressed like a true soldier of Christ, by whose merits only I trust this day to enter his joy." Thus yielded they up their souls in the faith of Jesus Christ, with such humility and steadfastness, that many who saw their patient suffering confessed that they could have found in their hearts to have died with them.

## Martyrdom of Adam Damlip.

About the same time Adam Damlip was martyred at Calais, then belonging to the English. The spot is still shown, just without the city, where he and others endured the fiery trial. Adam Damlip, otherwise George Bucker, went to Calais in the year 1539. He had been a zealous papist, and chaplain to Fisher, bishop of Rochester. After the death of the bishop he travelled through France, Holland, and Italy, conferring with learned men about matters of religion; and thence proceeded to Rome, where he expected to have found all godliness and sincerity; but instead of this, he found, as he said, such blasphemy of God, contempt of Christ's truth, looseness of life, and impurities, that he was unable to remain. Cardinal Pole wished him to read three lectures in the week in his house: but he preferred returning home by way of Calais. As he was waiting for a passage to England, he was seen by William Stevens and Thomas Lancaster to be a learned man, and well affected; and that, having been a zealous papist, he was now turned to a knowledge of true religion; they therefore entreated him to stay at Calais awhile, that he might do some good in the city. To this he gladly consented, if he could be licensed by those in authority.

Whereupon Stevens brought him to lord Lisle, the king's deputy, to whom he declared what conference had been between Damlip and him. The lord deputy then desired Damlip to stay there and preach, saying that he should both have his licence and that of Sir John Butler, his commissary. Having preached three or four times, he was so liked, both for his learning, his utterance, and the truth of his doctrine, that not only the soldiers and commoners, but the lord deputy and a great part of the council, gave him great praise and thanks for it.

M

The lord deputy also offered him a chamber in his
own house, and a place at his own mess, a man or
two of his to wait on him, and whatsoever he lacked,
if it were to be had for money; he also offered him
his purse to buy books, or otherwise, so that he
would remain with them, and preach only so long
as it should seem good for himself. Damlip refused
with much gratitude these liberal offers of his lordship, requesting him to be so good as to appoint him
only some quiet place where he might be able to
give himself to his books, and he would daily, forenoon and afternoon, preach among them as God
might enable him. On this the lord deputy sent for
William Stevens, whom he requested to lodge Damlip in his house, promising whatever he should
demand, to see it paid.

This godly man, for twenty days or more,
preached very learnedly and plainly the truth of
the blessed sacrament of Christ's body and blood,
inveighing against transubstantiation, and the propitiatory sacrifice of the mass.

Thus he continued awhile reading in the chapter-
house of the White Friars, but the place not being
large enough, he was desired to read in the pulpit,
and so proceeded to declare how the world was
deceived by the Roman bishops, who had set forth
the doctrine of transubstantiation, and the real
presence in the sacrament. He came at length to
speak against the picture of the resurrection in St.
Nicholas' church, declaring it to be idolatry, and
an illusion of the French, which the English should
remove. The consequence was there came a commission from the king to the lord deputy, that
search should be made whether there were three

hosts lying upon a marble stone besprinkled with blood; and if they found it so, that it should be plucked up. In searching, as they brake up a stone in the corner of the tomb, they found soldered, in the cross of marble lying under the sepulchre, three plain white counters, which had been painted like hosts, and a bone; all this trumpery Damlip showed to the people the Sunday following from the pulpit; after that they were sent by the deputy to the king.

Very soon, however, a prior of the White Friars, named Dove, with Buttoll, chaplain to lord Lisle, began to speak against him. Yet, after Adam had in three or four sermons confuted the erroneous doctrine of the mass, the friar outwardly seemed to give place, yet secretly impeached him by letters sent to the clergy in England. Within eight or ten days after Damlip was summoned before the archbishop of Canterbury, the bishops of Winchester and Chichester, and divers others, before whom he defended the doctrine he had taught, answering, confuting, and solving the objections; so that his adversaries, among whom was the learned and pious Cranmer, marvelled at it, and said plainly, that the Scriptures knew not such a term as transubstantiation. Then began the other bishops to threaten him with fire and fagot if he would still stand to what he had spoken. To this he answered that he would the next day deliver to them fully as much in writing as he had said, whereunto also he would stand; and so he was dismissed. The next day, when they looked to have apprehended him, he came not; for he had secret intimation from the archbishop of Canterbury, that if he appeared he would not likely escape a cruel death. On this he sent them four sheets of paper, written in Latin, containing his faith, by a friend of his. He then, with a little money given him, fled into the west country, where he taught a school a year or two, after which he was apprehended by the inquisition of the six articles, and brought to London. Gardiner commanded him into the Marshalsea, and there he lay other two years.

During his confinement John Marbeck was committed to the same prison, and conversing with him, learned who he was, what he had been, what troubles he had sustained, and how long he had lain in prison. "And now," said Damlip, "because I think they have forgotten me, I will make my humble suit to the bishop of Winchester, declaring mine obedience, humble submission, and earnest desire to come to examination. I know the worst: I can but lose my life, which I had rather do than not be suffered to use my talent to God's glory; wherefore, God willing, I will put it to the proof."

Damlip, for his goodly behaviour, was beloved of all the house; but especially by the keeper, whose name was Massy; and being suffered to go within the premises whither he would, he did much good among the dissolute sort of prisoners, rebuking vice and sin, thus keeping them in such good order, that the gaoler thought him a great treasure. Marbeck also found great comfort from him. For notwithstanding the strict command of the bishop of Winchester, that he should not speak with any, yet he often found means to comfort his companion.

When he had drawn out his epistle, he gave it to the keeper, desiring him to deliver it at the court to the bishop of Winchester. The keeper having done it, came home at night very late, when the prisoners, who had waited supper for his coming, seeing him look sad, deemed something to be amiss. At last, casting his eyes on Damlip, he said, "O George, I can tell thee tidings." "What is that, master?" quoth he. "Upon Monday next thou and I must go to Calais." "To Calais! what to do?" "I know not," quoth the keeper, and pulled out of his purse a piece of wax, with a little label of parchment hanging out thereat. When Damlip saw it, he said, "Well, master, now I know what the matter is." "What?" quoth the keeper. "Truly, master, I shall die in Calais." "Nay," quoth the keeper, "I trust it will not be so." "Yes, master, it is most true; and I praise God for his goodness." So the keeper, with Damlip and Marbeck, went to supper, with heavy cheer for Sir George, as they used to call him. He, notwithstanding, was merry himself: insomuch that some told him they marvelled how he could eat so well, knowing he was so near his death. "Ah, masters," quoth he, "do you think that I have been God's prisoner so long in the Marshalsea, and have not yet learned to die? Yes, yes! and I doubt not but God will strengthen me therein."

On Monday morning, the keeper, with three others of the knight-marshal's servants, conveyed Adam Damlip to Calais, and committed him to the Mayor's prison. On the same day John Butler, the commissary aforesaid, and Sir Daniel, the curate of St. Peter's, were committed to the same prison, and order given for no man to speak with Butler especially, nor generally to the rest.

The following Saturday was the day of execution

for Damlip. He was charged with heresy; but, by
reason of an act of parliament, all such offences done
by a certain day were pardoned. Through this act
he could not be burdened with anything he had
preached or taught before; yet for receiving a
French crown of cardinal Pole, to assist him in his
travelling expenses, he was condemned for treason,
and cruelly put to death, being hung, drawn and
quartered.

The day before his execution came unto him one
Mr. Mote, parson of Our Lady's church in Calais,
saying, "Your four quarters shall be hanged at four
parts of the town." "And where shall my head
be?" said Damlip. "Upon the Lantern-gate," said
Mote. "Then," answered Damlip, "shall I not
need to provide for my burial." At his death Sir
R. Ellerker, the knight-marshal, would not suffer
him to declare his faith or the cause he died for; but
said to the executioner, "Despatch the knave—have
done!" Mote was appointed to preach, and declared
that Damlip had been a sower of seditious doctrine;
and although he was for that absolved by the general
pardon, yet he was condemned as a traitor against
the king. To which, when Damlip would have replied, Ellerker commanded him to be had away.
Thus most meekly, patiently, and joyfully, this innocent martyr took his death.

## Martyrdom of George Wishart.

George Wishart was by birth a Scotchman, but
received his education at Cambridge. The year before his death (in 1546) he returned to Scotland, and
on his way preached in many places against idolatry.

He foretold several extraordinary things, particularly his own sufferings, and the spread of the reformation over the land.    He preached last in Lothian, where the earl of Bothwell took him, but promised that no harm should be done him; yet he delivered him to the cardinal, who brought him to St. Andrew's, and called a meeting of bishops to destroy him.

.   While imprisoned in the castle the dean of St. Andrew's was sent to summon him before the judge on the following morning, on account of his seditious and heretical doctrine, as they termed it.   Wishart answered, " What need my lord cardinal to summon me, when I am thus in his power and bound in irons? "   He was several times brought before his enemies, but he maintained his religious views and principles. At length he was condemned to be burnt as a heretic.   When the fire and gallows were made ready, the cardinal, fearing lest Wishart should be rescued by his friends, commanded his gunners to stand ready beside their guns, until such time as he was burned.   They then bound the martyr's hands behind him, and led him forth to the place of execution.   When he came to the fire he thrice repeated these words: " O thou Saviour of the world, have mercy on me.   Father of heaven, I commend my spirit into thy holy hands."   Then he turned to the people, and said, " I beseech you, Christian brethren and sisters, be not offended with the word of God on account of the affliction which ye see prepared for me; but love the word of God, and endure patiently.   Remember, that I suffer this fire for Christ's sake.   Consider and behold my visage: ye shall not see me change my colour.   This grim fire I fear not.   If any persecution come to you for the

word's sake, do not fear them that slay the body,
but have no power to slay the soul. Some have said
that I taught that the soul of man should sleep until
the last day; but I know surely that I shall sup with
my Saviour Christ this night. I beseech Christ to
forgive them that have condemned me to death this
day ignorantly. If they will not turn from their
wicked error, the wrath of God shall come on them,
and they shall not escape."

Many other faithful words said he, taking no heed
of the cruel torments which were prepared for him.
At last the hangman fell upon his knees, and said—
"I pray you forgive me, for I am not guilty of your
death." He answered—"Come hither to me." He
then kissed his cheek, and said, "Lo! there is a
token that I forgive thee. My heart, do thine office;"
he was then burnt to ashes, while, from a window,
the cardinal looked on. The people beheld this glorious exit of this triumphant martyr with sentiments
of mingled wonder, sorrow, and indignation.

The clergy rejoiced at his death, and extolled the
courage of the cardinal, for proceeding in it against
the order of the governor. But the people looked on
Wishart as a martyr and a prophet. It was also said
that his death was nothing less than a murder, since
no writ had been obtained for it; and the clergy
had no right to burn any one without a warrant
from the secular power. It was therefore inferred
that the cardinal deserved death for his presumption.
His insolence had rendered him generally hateful;
and twelve persons entered into an engagement to
kill him privately in his own house. On the 30th
of May, they surprised the gate early in the morning; and though there were a hundred men in the

MARTYRDOM OF GEORGE WISHART.

castle, yet being all asleep, they came on them one
by one, and either turned them out or shut them up.
Having made all sure, they proceeded to the cardinal's chamber; who, perceiving they had a design
upon his life, exclaimed, "Fie! fie! slay me not; I
am a priest:" but, paying as little regard to him as
he had done to Wishart, they immediately slew him,
and laid out his body in the same window from
which he had looked on Wishart's execution. Some
justified this act, as the killing of a robber and a
murderer; but it was generally condemned.

## Martyrdom of Kerby and Roger Clarke.

Towards the end of the reign of Henry VIII.
Kerby and Roger Clarke were apprehended at Ips-
wich, and brought before lord Wentworth, with
other commissioners appointed to sit upon their examinations. Kerby and Clarke being in the house
of the gaoler, whose name was Bird, there came in
a Mr. Robert Wingfield, who said to Kerby, "Remember, the fire is hot; take heed of thine enterprise, that thou take no more upon thee than thou
shalt be able to perform. The pain will be extreme,
and life is sweet. Better it were betimes to stick to
mercy, than rashly to begin and then to shrink."
Kerby answered—"Ah, Wingfield, be at my burning, and you shall say, There standeth a Christian
soldier in the fire: for I know that fire and water,
sword, and all other things are in the hands of God,
and he will suffer no more to be laid on us than he
will give us strength to bear." "Ah, Kerby," said
Wingfield, "if thou be at that point, I bid thee
farewell: for I am not so strong that I can burn."

When Kerby and Clarke came to the judgment-seat, they lifted up their eyes and hands to heaven, praying earnestly to God. That done, their articles were declared to them; and then it was demanded whether they believed that in the sacrament, after the words spoken by the priest, there were not the very body and blood of Christ, flesh, blood and bone, as he was born of the Virgin Mary, and no bread after? To this sweeping question they answered, "No! we do not so believe; but we believe the sacrament which Jesus Christ instituted was only to put his disciples in remembrance of his precious death and blood-shedding for the remission of sins." Then with much persuasions, both with fair means and threats, were they beset; yet they both continued faithful, choosing rather to die than live, and so continued to the end.

Sentence was then given upon them; Kerby to be burnt in the said town on the next Saturday, and Clarke at Bury on the Monday after. On Saturday, about ten o'clock, Kerby was brought to the market-place, where a stake with wood and straw was ready. He put off his clothes to his shirt, and was then fastened to the stake with irons; there being on the gallery Lord Wentworth, with some of the justices, where they might see his execution, and also hear what Kerby had to say; there was also a great number of people. Upon the gallery also stood Dr. Rugham, having on a surplice and a stole about his neck. Then silence was proclaimed, and the doctor began to excuse himself, as not meet to declare the Holy Scriptures, being unprovided because the time was so short, but he hoped in God's assistance it should come well to pass.

While the executioners were preparing their irons, fagots, and straw, the martyr, nothing changed in cheer or countenance, but with a most meek spirit, glorified God. Dr. Rugham at last entered into the sixth chapter of St. John, and so often as he alleged the Scriptures, and applied them rightly, Kerby told the people that he said true, and bade them believe him. But when he did otherwise, he told him again, "You say not true; believe him not, good people." Whereupon, as the voice of the people was, they judged Dr. Rugham a false prophet. When he had ended his collation, he said to Kerby, "Thou good man, dost thou not believe that the blessed sacrament of the altar is the very flesh and blood of Christ, and no bread, even as he was born of the Virgin Mary?" Kerby answered, "I do not so believe." "How dost thou believe?" said the doctor. Kerby said, "I believe that in the sacrament which Jesus Christ instituted at his last supper, his death and passion, and blood-shedding for the redemption of the world is to be remembered; and, as I said before, yet bread, and more than bread, for that it is consecrated to a holy use."

The under-sheriff then demanded of Kerby whether he had anything more to say. "Yea, sir," said he, "if you will give me leave." "Say on then," said the sheriff. The martyr, summoning all his fortitude, and lifting up his hands, repeated the *Te Deum*, and the Belief, with other prayers, in the English tongue. Lord Wentworth, while Kerby was thus engaged, concealed himself behind one of the posts of the gallery and wept, and so did many others. Then said Kerby, "I have done: you may execute your office, good.

sheriff." On this fire was set to the wood, while
with a loud voice he called on God, striking his
breast and holding up his hands ; and so ended his
life, the people giving shouts and praising God for
his constancy.

On the following Monday, about ten o'clock,
Roger Clarke, of Mendlesham, was brought out of
prison, and led on foot to Southgate, in Bury. By
the way the procession met them ; but he would
not bow, and with vehement words rebuked their
superstition. Without the gate, the stake being
ready, and the wood lying by, he kneeled down
and said *Magnificat* in the English tongue, making,
as it were, a paraphrase upon the same, wherein he
declared that the blessed Virgin Mary, who might
as well rejoice in pureness as any other, yet humbled
herself to our Saviour. "And what sayest thou,
John Baptist," said he, "the greatest of all children?
'Behold the Lamb of God, that taketh away the
sins of the world!'" Thus, with a loud voice, he
cried unto the people, while they were fastening
him to the stake, and then the fire was set to him.
His sufferings were dreadful, for the wood was
green, and would not burn, so that he was choked
with smoke ; and moreover, being set in a pitch
barrel with some pitch still by the sides, he was
therewith sore pained, till he got his feet out of the
barrel. At length one standing by took a fagot-
stick, and striking at the ring of iron about his
neck and then upon his head, he shrank down on
one side of the fire, and so was destroyed.

The reformation now appeared to go back instead
of forward for a time. In the month of December
following, the king came into the parliament house

to give his royal assent to such acts as were passed; where, after an eloquent oration made to him by the speaker, he answered him in an artful speech composed by himself.

He at first eloquently declared his grateful heart to his subjects for their grants and supplies offered unto him. In the second part he exhorted them to concord, peace, and unity; but had he sought the right way to work charity, and to help innocency amongst his subjects, he would have taken away the impious law of the six articles. By this law—known also as the bloody statute—burning or hanging was made the punishment of all who should deny that the bread and wine of the sacrament was the natural body and blood of the Saviour; or that the communion in both kinds was not necessary to salvation; or that the priests may not marry; or that vows of chastity ought to be observed; or that the mass was agreeable to God's law; or that auricular confession is expedient and necessary. Now, what is it to the purpose to exhort to charity in words, and at the same time to put a weapon into the murderer's hand to run upon his naked brother, who hath no power to defend himself? The mischief and misery produced by this law never was more fully shown than in its operation against two or three martyrs at this time upon whom it was put in force. Of these the most memorable was Anne Askew, whose bitter persecution and merciless death tended to show the sanguinary spirit of the times, while they also showed the firmness which a female can attain when aided by the power of religion and truth.

## Martyrdom of Anne Askew.

This lady was descended from a good family,
and had received an accomplished education. Her
first examination was in the year of our Lord 1545,
in the month of March. Christopher Dare examined her at Sadler's Hall. Her answers to the
several questions he put to her were such as com-
pletely astonished and silenced him.

After the chancellor and the bishop of London
had examined her, without being able to shake her
firmness, came her cousin, Britain, with divers
others, among whom was a Mr. Hall, of Gray's-inn.

The bishop inquired what her faith and belief
was touching the sacrament. She answered him,
"I believe as the Scripture doth teach me." On
this he inquired, "What if the Scripture doth say
that it is the body of Christ?" "I believe," she
said, "as the Scripture doth teach." Then he
asked again, "What if the Scripture doth say that
it is not the body of Christ?" Her answer was
still, "I believe all the Scripture informeth me."
On this argument he tarried a great while, to have
driven her to have made him an answer to his
mind. Howbeit, she would not, but concluded thus
with him, "I believe therein, and in all other things,
as Christ and his apostles did leave them."

There were certain priests who tempted her much
to know her mind. She answered them always
thus: "What I have said to my lord of London I
have said." Then Dr. Standish desired the bishop
to bid her speak her mind concerning the text of
St. Paul's learning, probably to betray her, that she
being a woman should interpret the Scriptures in

the presence of so many wise and learned men.
The bishop then quickly said, "I am informed that
one has asked you if you would receive the sacrament at Easter, and you made a mock of it." To
this she calmly and meekly replied, "I desire that
my accuser might come forth," which he would not
allow. But he said again to her, "I sent one to
give you good counsel, and at the first word you
called him papist." "I deny not that," she said,
"for I perceived he was no less, and I made him no
other reply." Then he rebuked her, and said that
she had reported there were sent against her threescore priests at Lincoln. "Indeed," she answered,
"I said so; for my friends told me if I did come
to Lincoln the priests would assault me and put me
to great trouble; and when I heard it I went
thither, not being afraid, because I knew my matter
to be good. Moreover, I remained there nine days,
to see what would be said to me; and as I was in
the minster, reading the Bible, they resorted unto me
by two and two, and by greater numbers, minding
to have spoken to me, yet went their ways again
without speaking." The bishop asked if there was
not one who had spoken to her. She answered,
"Yes, there was one of them which did speak; but
his words were of small effect, so that I do not now
remember them." Then said the bishop, "There
are many that read and know the Scripture, and
yet follow it not, nor live thereafter." She said
again, "My lord, I would wish that all men knew
my conversation and living in all points; for I am
sure myself this hour that there are none able to
prove any dishonesty against me."

This pious and gifted lady was, notwithstanding,

N

deemed a heretic, and doomed to undergo further suffering. In a few days she was sent from Newgate to the sign of the Crown, where Mr. Rich and the bishop of London, with all their power and flattering words, went about to persuade her from God; but she did not esteem their glossing pretences. After them either came one Nicholas Shaxton, who counselled her to recant as others had done. She said to him, "It had been good for you never to have been born;" with many other like words, chiefly from Scripture. She was then sent to the Tower, where she remained till three o'clock, when Rich came, and one of the council, charging her upon her obedience, to show unto them if she knew any man or woman of her sect. Her answer was, "I know none." Then they asked her of lady Suffolk, lady Sussex, lady Hertford, lady Denny, and lady Fitzwilliam. Of whom she answered, "If I should pronounce anything against them, I should not be able to prove it." Then said they unto her, "The king is informed that you could name, if you would, a great number of your sect." She answered that, "The king was as well deceived in that behalf, as he was dissembled with by them in other matters."

At length they put her on the rack, because she had confessed no ladies or gentlemen to be of her opinion, and thereon they kept her a long time; and because she lay still and did not cry, the lord chancellor and Mr. Rich took pains to rack her with their own hands till she was nigh dead—an instance of unusual cruelty even for that age. The lieutenant then caused her to be loosed from the rack, when she immediately swooned, and then recovered again.

Then she was brought to a house and laid on a bed, with as weary and painful bones as ever had patient Job, yet expressing her thanks to God. Then the lord chancellor sent her word, if she would leave her opinion she should want for nothing; if she would not, she should be burned. She sent him word that she would rather die than break her faith—praying that God would open his eyes.

Being born of such stock and kindred as would have enabled her to live in great wealth and prosperity, if she had chosen rather to have followed the world than Christ, she had now been so tormented, that she could neither live long in such great distress, nor yet by her adversaries be suffered to die in secret; the day of her execution being appointed, she was brought to Smithfield in a chair, because she could not walk, from the cruel effects of the torments. When she was brought to the stake, she was fastened to it by the middle with a chain that held up her body. Three others were brought to suffer with her, and for the same offence; these were Nicholas Belenian, a priest of Shropshire; John Adams, a tailor; and John Lacel, gentleman of the court and household of king Henry. The martyrs being chained to the stake, and all things ready for the fire, Dr. Shaxton, then appointed to preach, began his sermon. Anne Askew hearing and answering him : where he said well, she approved; where he said amiss, expressing firmly her dissent, saying, "He speaketh without the book."

The sermon being finished, the martyrs, standing at their several stakes, began their prayers. The multitude of the people was exceedingly great, the place where they stood being railed about to keep out the press. Upon the bench, under St. Bartholomew's church, sat Wriothesley, the chancellor of England, the old duke of Norfolk, the old earl of Bedford, the lord mayor, and others. Before the fire was kindled, one of the bench hearing that they had gunpowder about them, began to be afraid; but the earl of Bedford said that the gunpowder was not laid under the fagots, but only about the bodies of the martyrs, to rid them of their pain, so that there was no danger.

The lord chancellor then sent to Anne Askew, offering her the king's pardon if she would recant; a letter said to be written by the king was put into her hand; but she, refusing to look upon it, made answer, "I come not hither to deny my Lord and Master." Then were letters offered to the others, who in like manner refused even to look on them: continuing to cheer and exhort each other by the hope of the glory they were about to enter; whereon the lord mayor, commanding fire to be put to them, cried with a loud voice, "*Fiat justitia.*" Thus were these holy martyrs compassed in with flames of fire, as holy sacrifices to God and his truth.

## Life and Martyrdom of William Tyndal.

We shall now rehearse the story and martyrdom of William Tyndal, who, although he did not suffer in England, ought to be ranked with the martyrs of our country, of which, from his great zeal, perseverance, and dispersing of truth, he may properly be esteemed the apostle.

He was born on the borders of Wales, and brought up in the university of Oxford. He afterwards removed to Cambridge, and then to Gloucestershire, and was engaged by a knight, named Welch, as tutor to his children.   To this gentleman's table several abbots, deans, and others used to resort, with whom Tyndal conversed of learned men—particularly of Luther and Erasmus—and of questions relative to the Scriptures.

In course of time it happened that the bishop's chancellor held a court, to which the priests—and Tyndal among them—were summoned.   The latter feared that a conspiracy had been formed against him ; and on his way thither earnestly prayed that God would enable him to bear witness to the truth. The chancellor reviled him grievously ; but as nothing definite could be proved against him, he escaped out of their hands.

Not far off there dwelt a doctor, named Munmouth, who had been an old acquaintance of Tyndal's.   To him Tyndal went to disclose his heart.   After some discourse the doctor said—

" Do you not know that the pope is the very anti-christ whom the Scripture speaketh of ?   But beware what you say, for if you be known to be of that opinion it will cost you your life.   I have been an officer of his ; but I have given it up, and defy him and all his works."

Not long after Tyndal met a certain divine, and in disputing with him, pressed him so hard that the doctor burst out into these blasphemous words : " We had better be without God's laws than the pope's."   Tyndal, full of godly zeal, replied, "I defy the pope and all his laws ; " and added that if God spared him, ere many years he would cause a plough-boy to know more of the Scriptures than he did."

Being now much molested by the priests, he was obliged to leave Mr. Welch's service. On coming to London he was recommended to Bishop Tonstall; but God, who orders all things according to his own will, saw that this course was neither for the profit of Tyndal nor of his church, and therefore gave him no favour in the bishop's eyes. He remained in London almost a year, greatly distressed with the pomp, pride, and ignorance of the clergy, insomuch that he perceived not only no room in the bishop's house for him to translate the New Testament, but also that there was no place for him to do so in all England.

He therefore went to Germany, after which he moved to the Netherlands, and resided principally at Antwerp. Having finished a portion of his translation, he sailed to Hamburg, intending there to print it, when a mysterious providence prevented. On his voyage he was wrecked, and lost all his manuscripts, and almost all he possessed. However, with true moral heroism, he proceeded to Hamburg, and in 1529 began the work anew, in company with Mr. Coverdale. When the translation of the New Testament was first issued, the English prelates were filled with wrath, and did not rest until they had persuaded the king to take hostile proceedings in the matter. A proclamation was issued, under authority, which condemned and prohibited it. But not content with this, they studied how they might entangle and destroy its author.

Accordingly, after some stratagem and the employment of treachery, Tyndal was betrayed at Antwerp, by one Phillips, and conveyed to the castle of Filford, eighteen miles distant, where he remained until his death. At last, after the lapse of a year and a half, and much fruitless disputation, he was condemned. When he was tied to the stake he cried with a loud and earnest voice, "Lord, open the king of England's eyes!" He was then strangled, and his remains burnt to ashes. Such was the power and excellence of this truly good man, that during his imprisonment he converted his keeper, with his daughter, and others of his attendants. Several of those who came in contact with him said that if he were not a good Christian they did not know whom to trust. Yet he was offered up by those modern priests as a victim to ignorance and superstition.

## Martyrdom of Thomas Benet.

Thomas Benet was born at Cambridge, and by order of the university was made M.A. The more he increased in the knowledge of God and his holy word, the more he disliked the corrupt state of religion; and, therefore, thinking his own country to be no safe place for him, he went into Devonshire, in the year 1524, and resided at Torrington, unknown to all who were there. For the better maintenance of himself and his wife he kept a school for young children. But that town not serving his expectation, he removed to Exeter, and there resumed his teaching.

But daily seeing God to be so blasphemed, idolatrous religion so maintained, and the usurped power of the bishop of Rome so extolled, he was so troubled in spirit as to be unable to be quiet.

Wherefore he told certain of his friends that he could no longer endure, but must needs utter his conscience, and that, for the defence of God's true religion, he would yield himself most patiently, as God would give him grace, to die, alleging that his death would be more profitable to the church of God than his life could be. He gave away such books as he had, and shortly after wrote on certain scrolls of paper, which privately he fixed to the doors of the cathedral church of the city, these words—" The pope is anti-christ; and we ought to worship God only, and no saints."

These bills being found, there was no little search made for the heretic who had set them up. Orders were given that the doctors should haste to the pulpit every day, and confute this heresy. Nevertheless, Benet keeping his doings to himself, went the Sunday following to the cathedral church to the sermon, and by chance sat down by two men who had been the busiest in all the city in seeking for heretics; and they beholding Benet, said one to the other, " Surely this fellow is the heretic that set up the bills, and it were good to examine him." Nevertheless, when they saw his quiet and sober behaviour, his attentiveness to the preacher, his godliness in the church, being always occupied in his book, which was a Testament in the Latin tongue, they had no power to speak to him, but departed, leaving him reading his book. At last the priests found out a toy to curse him, whatsoever he were, with book, bell, and candle; which curse at that day was thought most terrible. The manner of the curse was after this sort :—

One of the priests, apparelled in white, ascended

the pulpit. The other rabble, with certain of the
two orders of friars, and some superstitious monks
of St. Nicholas standing round about, and the cross
being holden up, with holy candles of wax fixed to
the same, he began his sermon with this theme of
Joshua:—There is a curse in the camp. On this
he made a long protestation, but not so long as
tedious and superstitious; and concluded that the
foul and abominable heretic who had put up the
bill was for that his blasphemy damnably cursed,
and besought God, Our Lady, St. Peter, patron of
that church, with all the holy company of martyrs,
confessors, and virgins, that it might be known what
heretic had done the accursed thing! Then followed
the curse, uttered by the priest in these words:—

"By the authority of God the Father Almighty,
and of the blessed Virgin Mary, of St. Peter and
Paul, and of the holy saints, we excommunicate,
we utterly curse and ban, commit and deliver to
the devil of hell, him or her, whatsoever he or she
be, that have in spite of God and of St. Peter,
whose church this is, in spite of all holy saints, and
in spite of our most holy father the pope, God's
vicar here on earth, and in spite of the reverend
father in God, John our diocesan, and the worshipful canons, masters, and priests, and clerks, which
serve God daily in this cathedral church, fixed
up with wax such cursed and heretical bill, full
of blasphemy, upon the doors of this and other
holy churches within this city. Excommunicate
plainly, be he or she penally, or they, and delivered over to the devil, as perpetual malefactors
and schismatics. Accursed may they be, and given
body and soul to the devil. Cursed be they, he, or

she, in cities and towns, in fields, in ways, in paths,
in houses, out of houses, and in all other places,
standing, lying, rising, walking, running, waking,
sleeping, eating, drinking, and whatsoever thing they
do besides.   We separate them, him, or her, from the
threshold, and from all the good prayers of the
church, from the participation of the holy mass, from
all sacraments, chapels, and altars, from holy bread
and holy water, from all the merits of God's priests
and religious men, and from all their cloisters, all
their pardons, privileges, grants, immunities, which
all the holy fathers, popes of Rome, have granted to
them. We give them over utterly to the power of the
fiend, and let us quench their souls, if they be dead,
this night in the pains of hell-fire, as this candle is
now quenched and put out "—with that he put out
one of the candles. "And let us pray to God, if they
be alive, that their eyes may be put out as this candle
is "—then he put out the other candle; "and let us
pray to God, and to Our Lady, and to St. Peter and
Paul, and all holy saints, that all the senses of their
bodies may fail them, and that they may have no
feeling, as now the light of this candle is gone "—
putting out the third candle—" except they, he, or
she, come openly now and confess their blasphemy,
and by repentance make satisfaction unto God, Our
Lady, St. Peter, and the worshipful company of this
cathedral church ; and as this holy cross staff now
falleth down, so may they, except they repent and
show themselves ! "   Here, one first taking away
the cross, the staff fell down; and then what a shout
and noise was there ! what terrible fear ! what holding up of hands to heaven, to hear this terrible de-
nunciation !

This foolish fantasy being played, Benet could not forbear, but fell into laughter, and could not cease, by which thing the poor man was discovered. For those next to him, wondering at the curse, and believing that it could not but light on one or other, asked Benet why he laughed. "My friend," said he, "who can forbear, hearing such merry conceits!" Straightway a cry was raised, "Here is the heretic! here is the heretic! Hold him fast!" He was committed to prison.

On the morrow the canons and heads of the city began to examine him. Finding both their threats and persuasions useless, they proceeded to judgment, and condemned him to the flames; the writ which they had procured being brought from London, they delivered him the 15th of January, 1531, to Sir Thomas Denis, sheriff of Devonshire, to be burnt. The martyr, rejoicing that his end was so near, as the sheep before the shearer yielded himself, with all humbleness, to abide and suffer the cross of persecution. Being brought to his execution, in a place called a liverydole, without Exeter, he made his prayer to Almighty God, and requested the people to do the like for him; so exhorting them to seek the true honouring of God, and the true knowledge of him, as to leave the imaginations of man's inventions, that the hearers were in great admiration, insomuch that most of them confessed that he was God's servant, and a good man.

Two esquires, namely, Thomas Carew and John Barnehouse, standing at the stake by him, first with goodly words, and at length with threatenings, required him to revoke his errors, and to call to Our Lady and the saints. To them he with all meekness

answered, "No, no; it is God only upon whose
name we must call, and we have no advocate with
him but Jesus Christ, who died for us, and now
sitteth at the right hand of the Father to intercede
for us.   By him must we offer our prayers to God, if
we will have them to be heard."   With this answer
Barnehouse was so enraged, that he took a furze-
brush on a pike, and thrust it into his face, saying,
"Heretic, pray to Our Lady, or by God's wounds I
will make thee do it."   To whom, with an humble
and meek spirit, he most patiently answered, "Alas!
sir, trouble me not."   And holding up his hands,
he said, "Father, forgive them."   Whereon the
wood and furze were set on fire, and therewith this
goodly man lifted up his eyes and hands to heaven,
saying, "Lord, receive my spirit!"   And so, continuing in prayer, most patiently he endured the
fire until his life was ended.

## Martyrdom of Six Persons in Scotland.

In 1543 the archbishop of St. Andrew's making
a visitation into various parts of his diocese,
several persons were accused at Perth of heresy.
Among these the six following were condemned to
die: William Anderson, Robert Lamb, James Fin-
layson, James Hunter, James Raveleson, and Helen
Stark.

The accusations laid against them were to the
following effect:

The first four were accused of having hung up the
image of St. Francis, nailing rams' horns on his
head, and fastening a cow's tail to his rump; but the
principal matter on which they were condemned

was, having regaled themselves with a goose on
Allhallows' Eve, a fast-day, according to the Roman
superstition.   James Raveleson was accused of having ornamented his house with the three-crowned
diadem of Peter, carved in wood, which the archbishop conceived to be done in mockery to his cardinal's hat.   Helen Stark was accused of not having
accustomed herself to pray to the Virgin Mary.  On
these accusations they were found guilty, and received sentence of death : the four for eating a goose,
to be hanged; James Raveleson, to be burnt; and
the woman, with her sucking infant, to be put into
a sack and drowned.   The four men, with the
woman and child, suffered at the same time; but
James Raveleson was not executed till some days
after.

On the day appointed for the execution of the
former they were conducted, under a proper guard,
to the place, attended by a prodigious number of
spectators.   As soon as they arrived, they all prayed
fervently; after which Robert Lamb addressed himself to the spectators, exhorting them to fear God,
and quit the practice of papistical abominations.
The four men were hanged on the same gibbet: and
the woman, with her sucking child, was conducted
to a river adjoining, and being fastened in a large
sack, was thrown into it and drowned.

They suffered their fate with fortitude and resignation, committing their departing spirits to that
Redeemer who they hoped would receive them into
everlasting bliss.

When we reflect on their sufferings we are apt to
lament their fate, and to drop the tear of commise-
ration.   The putting to death four men, for little

other reason than that of eating an article of food
sent by Providence for that very purpose, merely
because it was on a day prohibited by bigotry and
superstition, is shocking indeed ; but the fate of the
harmless woman, and her still more harmless infant,
makes one tremble at the thought of what mankind
may become when incited by bigotry to the most
diabolical cruelty.

Besides the above-mentioned persons, many others
were cruelly persecuted during the archbishop's
stay at Perth, some being banished, and others confined in loathsome dungeons.   In particular, John
Rogers, a pious and learned man, was, by the archbishop's orders, murdered in prison, and his body
thrown over the walls into the street; after which
the archbishop caused a report to be spread, that he
had met with his death in an attempt to make his
escape.

# CHAPTER X.

### ACCESSION OF QUEEN MARY, AND PERSECUTIONS DURING HER REIGN.

ROMAN CATHOLICS assert that " Those who suffered death during the reign of queen Mary had been guilty of high treason, in desiring the succession of lady Jane Grey to the crown." To disprove this, however, is easy. Whoever heard of any one being burnt alive for treason? Even supposing that those men and women from the poorer classes who suffered torture and death had been guilty of attempting to deprive Mary of her legal rights, the punishment the law ordained was hanging or beheading, and not those horrible tortures the perusal of which makes our very blood run cold. If traitors, why were they taken before bishops to be examined, who certainly were not the usual judges in such cases? And if high treason was their crime, how was it that it was never even mentioned on their trials? Having said thus much, by way of introduction, we shall proceed with the Acts and Monuments of the British Martyrs.

On the death of king Edward the crown devolved by law on his elder sister, Mary, who was within half a day's journey of London. She had notice given her by the earl of Arundel of her brother's death, and of the patent for lady Jane's succession. On this she retired to Framlingham, in Suffolk, to be near the sea, that she might escape to Flanders if necessary. On the 9th July she wrote to the council, telling them that "she understood that her brother was dead, by which she succeeded to the crown, but wondered that she heard not from them; she well understood the treasonable consultation they were engaged in, but would pardon all such as would return to their allegiance and proclaim her title to the crown."

It was now found that the king's death could be no longer kept a secret; accordingly some of the privy council went to lady Jane and acknowledged her as their queen. The news of the king's death afflicted her much, and her being raised to the throne rather increased than lessened her trouble. She was a person of extraordinary abilities, acquirements, and virtues. She was mistress both of the Greek and Latin tongues, and delighted much in study. As she was not tainted with the levities which usually accompany her age and station, so she was not exalted with the prospect of a crown, and as little cast down when her palace was made her prison. The only passion she showed was in the concern she expressed for her father and her husband, who fell with her, and seemingly on her account, though, in reality, Northumberland's ambition and her father's weakness ruined her.

She rejected the crown when it was first offered her; she said she knew that of right it belonged to the late king's sisters, and therefore she could not with a good conscience assume it; but she was told that both the judges and privy councillors had declared that it fell to her according to law. This, joined with the importunities of her husband, her father, and father-in-law, made her submit. Upon this twenty-one privy councillors set their hands to a letter to Mary, telling her that queen Jane was now their sovereign, and that as the marriage between her father and mother had been declared null, so she could not succeed to the crown; they therefore required her to submit to the settlement now made, and, if she gave a ready obedience, promised her much favour. The day after this they proclaimed Jane.

Northumberland's known enmity to the late duke of Somerset, and the suspicions of his being the author of Edward's untimely death, begot a great aversion in the people to him and his family, and disposed them to favour Mary; who, in the meantime, was very active in raising forces to support her claim. To attach the protestants to her cause she promised not to make any change in the reformed worship as established under her brother; and on this assurance a large body of the men of Suffolk joined her standard.

Northumberland was now perplexed between his wish to assume the command of an army raised to oppose Mary, and his fear of leaving London to the government of the council, of whose fidelity he entertained great doubts. He was, however, at length obliged to adopt the latter course; and before his departure from the metropolis, he adjured the members of the council, and all persons in authority, to be steadfast in the cause of queen Jane, on whose success, he assured them, depended the continuance of the protestant religion in England. They promised all he required, and he departed encouraged by their protestations and apparent zeal.

Mary's party in the meantime continued daily to increase. Hastings went over to her with 4,000 men out of Buckinghamshire, and she was proclaimed queen in many places. At length the privy council began to see their danger; and besides fears for their personal safety, other motives operated with many of the members. To make their escape from the Tower, where they were detained, ostensibly to give dignity to the court of queen Jane, but really as prisoners, they pretended it was necessary to give an audience to the foreign ambassadors, and the earl of Pembroke's house was appointed for the purpose.

There they resolved to declare for queen Mary. They sent for the lord mayor and aldermen, and gaining their concurrence, Mary was proclaimed queen on the 19th of July. They then sent to the Tower, requiring the duke of Suffolk to quit the government of that place, and the lady Jane to lay down the title of queen. To this she submitted with much greatness of mind, and her father with abjectness.

The council next sent orders to Northumberland to submit to the queen. On this, he disbanded his forces, went to the market-place at Cambridge, and proclaimed Mary as queen. The earl of Arundel was sent to apprehend him: when Northumberland was brought before him, he fell at his feet to beg his favour. He was sent to the Tower, with three of his sons and sir Thomas Palmer.

Every one now flocked to implore the queen's favour, and Ridley among the rest, but he also was committed to the Tower; the queen being resolved to put Bonner again into the see of London. Some of the judges, and several noblemen, were also sent thither, among the rest the duke of Suffolk; who was, however, three days after set at liberty.

Mary came to London on the 3rd of August. On her way she was met by her sister Elizabeth, with a thousand horse she had raised to assist her. Thus Mary was seated on the throne of England. She was crowned at Westminster in the usual form; but dreadful were the consequences that followed. The first thing she did was to wreak her vengeance upon all those who had supported the title of lady Jane Grey. The duke of Northumberland was beheaded on Tower Hill, and died unpitied. The other executions that followed were numerous. The parliament was pliant enough to comply with all the queen's requests, and an act was passed establishing the popish religion. This was what she wished. Power being now put into her hands, she proceeded to exercise it in the most arbitrary manner. It soon appeared that she was destitute of human compassion, and could without the least reluctance tyrannize over the consciences of men.

### Rebellion of Wyatt—Lady Jane Grey's Conduct and Execution.

The first month of 1554 commenced with persecution. Dr. Crome was committed to the Fleet for preaching without licence on Christmas Day; and Thomas Wotton, Esq., on account of religion.

The publication of Mary's intended marriage with Philip of Spain was very ill received by the people and several of the nobility; and it was not long before a rebellion broke out, of which Sir Thomas Wyatt was one of the ringleaders. He said that the queen and council would, by this marriage, bring upon the realm that slavery and despotism, religious and civil, which is one of the natural results of developed popery.

As soon as intelligence was received in London of the insurrection in Kent, and of the duke of Suffolk having fled into Warwickshire and Leicestershire to raise forces in those counties, the queen caused them both, with the Carews of Devonshire, to be proclaimed traitors: she also sent some forces, under Thomas, duke of Norfolk, into Kent; but on reaching Rochester Bridge he found himself so deserted that he had to return to London.

Suffolk having fled into Warwickshire, the earl of Huntingdon was sent against him, who, entering Coventry before the duke, frustrated his designs. In his distress the duke confided in one of his servants in Astley Park; but being betrayed, he was apprehended, sent up to London, and committed to the Tower. Early in February Wyatt advanced towards London, when the queen repaired to Guildhall, and made a vehement oration against him.

At the conclusion of her speech Gardiner exclaimed aloud, with great admiration, "Oh, how happy are we, to whom God hath given so wise and learned a queen."

On the 3rd of February lord Cobham was committed to the Tower. Wyatt, with 4,000 forces, came to Southwark, but could not force the bridge of London. He was informed the city would rise if he came to its aid; but he could not find boats to take him into Essex, so he was forced to go to the bridge of Kingston. On the 4th of February he got there, but found it broken; his men, however, mended it, and he reached Hyde Park next morning.

His troops were weary and disheartened, and did not now amount to more than 500: so that though the queen's forces could have easily dispersed them, yet they let them advance that they might cast themselves into their hands. Wyatt accordingly marched through the Strand and Ludgate Hill. Returning from thence, he was opposed at Temple Bar, and there surrendered himself to sir Clement Parson, who brought him to court. With him the remains of his army were also taken, about 100 having been killed. A great number were hanged, and Wyatt was executed on Tower Hill.

It was soon after resolved to proceed against lady Jane Grey and her husband. She had lived six months in the daily prospect of death, so she was not much surprised at the reality. Fecknam, who was sent to prepare her, acknowledged that he was astonished at her calm behaviour, her great knowledge, and the extraordinary sense she had of religion. The following is part of their conversation :—

*Fecknam :* Madam, I lament your heavy case, and yet I doubt not but that you bear this sorrow with a constant and patient mind.

*Jane :* You are welcome, sir, if your coming be to give Christian exhortation. As for my heavy case, I thank God I do so little lament it that I rather account it a more manifest declaration of God's favour towards me than ever he showed me before. Therefore, there is no cause why any who bear me good-will should be grieved with a thing so profitable for my soul's health.

*Fecknam :* I am come to you from the queen and her council to instruct you in the right faith, although I have so great confidence in you that I shall have, I trust, little need to travel with you much therein.

*Jane :* Forsooth, I heartily thank the queen's highness, who is not unmindful of her humble subject; and I hope, likewise, that you will no less do your duty therein truly and faithfully.

*Fecknam :* What is, then, required of a Christian man ?

*Jane :* That he should believe in God the Father, the Son, and the Holy Ghost; three Persons and one God.

*Fecknam :* What! is there nothing else to be required in a Christian but to believe in him ?

*Jane :* Yes; we must love him with all our heart, with all our soul, and with all our mind : and our neighbour as our self.

*Fecknam :* Why, then, faith neither justifieth nor saveth ?

*Jane :* Yes, verily ; faith, as St. Paul saith, alone justifieth.

*Fecknam :* But St. Paul saith, " If I have all faith without love, it is nothing."

*Jane :* True it is, for how can I love him whom I trust not? or how can I trust him whom I love not? Faith and love go both together, and yet love is comprehended in faith.

*Fecknam :* How many sacraments are there ?

*Jane :* Two: the one the sacrament of baptism, and the other the sacrament of the Lord's supper.

*Fecknam :* There are seven sacraments.

*Jane :* By what scripture find you that ?

*Feckman :* Well, we will talk of that hereafter. But what is signified by your two sacraments ?

*Jane:* By the sacrament of baptism I am washed with water, and regenerated by the Spirit; and that washing is a token to me that I am a child of God. The sacrament of the Lord's supper, offered unto me and received in faith, is a sure seal and testimony that I am, by the blood of Christ, which he shed for me on the cross, made partaker of the everlasting kingdom.

*Fecknam:* Why, what do you receive in that sacrament? Do you not receive the very body and blood of Christ?

*Jane:* No, surely; I believe not so. I think that at the supper I neither receive flesh nor blood, but bread and wine; which bread when broken, and which wine when drank, putteth me in remembrance that for my sins the body of Christ was broken, and his blood shed on the cross; and with that bread and wine I receive the benefits that come by the breaking of his body and shedding of his blood.

*Fecknam:* Why, doth not Christ speak these words, " Take, eat, this is my body ?" Require you any plainer words? Doth he not say it is his body?

*Jane:* I grant he doth: and so he saith, " I am the vine," " I am the door; " but he is never the more the door, nor the vine. Doth not St. Paul say, " He calleth things that are not as though they were?" God forbid that I should say that I eat the very natural body and blood of Christ, for then either I should pluck away my redemption, or else there were two bodies or two Christs. One body was tormented on the cross, and if they did eat another body, then he had two bodies; or if his body were eaten, then was it not broken upon the cross; or if it were broken upon the cross, it was not eaten of his disciples.

Thus vainly did he strive to pervert her faith. They reasoned at great length; but she, being built upon the sure foundation, remained proof against his sophistry.

She was at first much affected when she saw her husband, lord Guildford Dudley, led out to execution, but recovered herself when she considered how soon she was to follow him; and when he desired that they might take leave of one another, she declined it, for she thought it would increase their grief. She now continued so perfectly calm that when she saw the lifeless body of her husband conveyed to the chapel in the Tower, she expressed no emotion thereat.

On mounting the scaffold she addressed the spectators thus:—"Good people, I am come hither to die, and by a law I am condemned to the same. The fact against the queen's highness was unlawful, and the consenting thereunto by me; but touching the procurement and desire thereof by me, or on my behalf, I do wash my hands in innocency before God and the face of you, good Christian people, this day. I pray you all to bear me witness that I die a true Christian woman, and that I do look to be saved only by the mercy of God in the blood of his only Son, Jesus Christ. I confess that when I did know the word of God, I neglected the same, loved myself and the world, and therefore this plague and punishment has worthily happened to me for my sins. Yet I thank God that of his goodness he hath given me time and respite to repent. And now, good people, while I am alive, I pray you assist me with your prayers." Then, kneeling down, she turned to Fecknam, saying, "Shall I say this psalm?" and he said, "Yea."

Then she repeated the 51st psalm in English most devoutly. She then stood up, and gave her maid her gloves and handkerchief, and her book to Mr. Burges. After this she untied her gown, when the executioner pressed forward to help her, but she, desiring him to let her alone, turning towards her two gentlewomen, who helped her off with it, and also with her frowes, paaft, and neckerchief, giving to her a fair handkerchief to bind round her eyes.

Then the executioner knelt down and asked her forgiveness, which she willingly granted. He then desired her to stand upon the straw, when she saw the block, whereon she said, "I pray you despatch me quickly." She then kneeled, saying, "Will you take it off before I lay me down?" The executioner said, "No, madam." She then tied the handkerchief about her eyes, and feeling for the block, she said, "What shall I do? Where is it? where is it?" One of the bystanders guiding her thereunto, she laid her head down upon it, and then stretching forth her body, said, "Lord, into thy hands I commend my spirit!" Thus this noble, learned, and saintly lady finished her life on the 12th February, 1554, about the seventeenth year of her age.

Her death was as much lamented as her life had been admired. It affected judge Morgan, who had pronounced the sentence, so much, that he went mad, and thought she still followed him. The queen herself was troubled at it, it having been rather reasons of state than private resentment that induced her to enact the tragedy.

Her father, the duke of Suffolk, was soon after tried by his peers, condemned, and executed. He was the less pitied, because it was by his means that his daughter was brought to her untimely end.

## Martyrdom of John Rogers and Laurence Saunders.

John Rogers, vicar of St. Sepulchre, and reader at St. Paul's, received his education in the university of Cambridge, and at length was chosen chaplain to the English factory at Antwerp. There he became acquainted with Mr. Tyndal, whom he assisted in his translation of the New Testament; and with Miles Coverdale, who had been driven from England on account of the five articles, in the latter end of the reign of Henry VIII. By conversing with these undaunted and pious servants of God, Mr. Rogers became learned in the Scriptures; and, finding from these sacred oracles that marriage was honourable in all, he entered into that state, and went with his wife to Wittenberg, in Saxony. There, through study and application, he in a short time attained such a knowledge of the Dutch language as to be capable of taking charge of a Christian congregation in that part of Europe.

When Edward ascended the throne of England Mr. Rogers returned to this country to preach the gospel; and having laboured with great success, Dr. Ridley, then bishop of London, gave him a prebend in his cathedral church of St. Paul's. He was afterwards chosen by the dean and chapter one of the divinity lecturers in that church.

When Mary was in the Tower of London, imbibing Gardiner's pernicious counsels, Mr. Rogers preached at Paul's Cross, confirming those doctrines which he and others had taught in king Edward's days, and exhorting the people to continue steadfast in the same, and to beware of the false tenets about to be introduced. For this sermon the preacher was summoned before the council, when he pleaded his own cause in so pious and bold, yet prudent a manner, as to obviate their displeasure for that time. He was accordingly dismissed. But after Mary's proclamation against the doctrines of the reformed religion Mr. Rogers was again summoned before a council of bishops, who ordered him to keep close prisoner in his own house. There he remained a considerable time, till, at the instigation of the sanguinary Bonner, bishop of London, he was removed to Newgate, and placed among felons.

After Mr. Rogers had been long imprisoned in Newgate amongst thieves, often examined, very uncharitably treated, and at length unjustly and most cruelly condemned by Gardiner, he was, on February 4th, warned suddenly by the wife of the keeper of Newgate to prepare himself for the fire. He was found asleep, and was, with great difficulty, awoke. At length being roused, he was led down first to Bonner to be degraded; which done, he craved of him one petition—that he might speak a few words with his wife before his burning. But that was denied him. "Thus," said he, "you show your charity, of what sort it is."

When the time came that he should be brought to Smithfield the sheriff came to him, and asked

him if he would revoke his abominable doctrines.
To whom Mr. Rogers said, "That which I have
preached I will seal with my blood!" Then said
the sheriff, "Thou art a heretic." "That shall be
known," said Rogers, "at the day of judgment."
"Well," quoth the sheriff, "I will never pray for
thee." "But I will pray for *you*," replied Rogers.
He was brought the same day, which was Monday,
the 4th of February, towards Smithfield, saying
the psalm "*Miserere*" by the way, the people rejoicing at his constancy. There, in the presence of
Rochester, comptroller of the queen's household, sir
Richard Southwell, both the sheriffs, and many
people, the fire was kindled. When it had taken
hold upon his legs and shoulders, he, as one feeling
no smart, washed his hands in the flame, as though
it had been cold water. After lifting up his hands
unto heaven, not removing the same until such time
as the devouring fire had consumed them, most
mildly this happy martyr yielded up his spirit into
the hands of his heavenly Father. A little before
his burning pardon was offered if he would recant;
but he utterly refused. He was the first of all the
martyrs that suffered in the reign of queen Mary,
those who had previously been put to death having
suffered as traitors. His wife and children met him
as he went to Smithfield. But this sorrowful sight
did not move him; he cheerfully yielded his life in
defence of the gospel of Christ.

Then followed the Rev. Laurence Saunders. He
was martyred at Coventry the next month. He
was a man of good parentage, and was placed early
at Eton School, whence, at a proper age, he went
to King's College, Cambridge. There he continued

three years, and profited in knowledge and learning very much; shortly after he quitted the university, and, by the advice of his parents, became a merchant. Coming up to London, he was bound apprentice to sir William Chester, who chanced afterwards to be sheriff of London when Saunders was burnt at Coventry.

It happened that the master, being a good man, and hearing Saunders mourning in his secret prayers, called him to know the cause of his solitariness and lamentations. Finding him not to fancy that kind of life, and perceiving also that he was bent on study and spiritual contemplation, he wrote to his friends, and, giving him his indentures, set him free. Thus Mr. Saunders, being ravished with the love of learning, and especially with the reading of God's word, tarried not long in the traffic of merchandize, but returned to Cambridge, where he began to add to the knowledge of the Latin that of the Greek tongue, in which he soon made great progress. To this he joined the study of the Hebrew. Then he gave himself wholly to the Scriptures, that he might be fitted for the office of a preacher.

In the beginning of king Edward's reign he began to preach, and was so liked by those in authority, that they appointed him to read a divinity lecture in the college of Fotheringhay, where, by doctrine and life, he edified the pious, drew many ignorant to the true knowledge of God, and stopped the mouths of adversaries. He married about that time, and led a life unblameable before all men. The college of Fotheringhay being dissolved, he was appointed a reader in the minster at

Lichfield, where he so behaved himself in teaching and living, that even his adversaries bore testimony to his learning and piety. After a time he went to a benefice in Leicestershire, called Churchlanton, where he taught diligently, and kept a liberal house. From thence he was called to Allhallows, Bread Street, in the city of London. He then wished to resign his cure in the country; and after he had taken possession of his benefice in London, he returned to Churchlanton to discharge himself thereof.

On Sunday, October 15th, in the forenoon, he delivered a sermon in his parish, treating on those words of St. Paul to the Corinthians, "I have coupled you to one man, that ye should make yourselves chaste virgins unto Christ. But I fear lest it come to pass, that as the serpent beguiled Eve, even so your wits should be corrupt from the singleness which ye had towards Christ." In the afternoon he was ready in his church to have given another exhortation to his people. But the bishop of London interposed, by sending an officer for him. This officer charged him upon pain of contumacy forthwith to come to the bishop. And thus was Saunders brought before Bonner, who laid to his charge treason for breaking the queen's proclamation, and heresy and sedition for his sermon.

After much talk the bishop desired him to write what he believed of transubstantiation. Saunders did so, and this writing the bishop kept for his purpose. Bonner sent him to the lord chancellor, who, unable to resist his arguments, cried, "Carry away this frenzy-fool to prison." Here Saunders continued a year and three months, during which time he wrote affecting letters to Cranmer, Ridley, and Latimer, also to his wife and others.

After his examination the officers led him out of the court, and stayed for the rest of his fellow-prisoners, that they might have them all together to prison. Mr. Saunders, standing among the officers, seeing a great multitude of people, spoke freely, warning them of that which, by their falling from Christ to anti-christ, they deserved. This faithful procedure did not, of course, produce either a diminution of his adversaries' cruelty or a delay of his mortal suffering. It rather augmented the one and accelerated the other. Almost immediately he was delivered over to the secular power, and was brought by the sheriffs of London to the Compter, a prisoner in his own parish of Bread Street. At this he rejoiced greatly, both because he found there a fellow-prisoner, Mr. Cardmaker, with whom he had much Christian and comfortable discourse; and because out of prison, as before out of a pulpit, he might have an opportunity of preaching to his parishioners.

On the 4th day of February Bonner came to the prison to degrade him, which when he had done, Mr. Saunders said to him, "I thank God I am not of your church." The day following, in the morning, the sheriff of London delivered him to certain of the queen's guard, which were appointed to carry him to Coventry, there to be burned. On his arrival there a poor shoemaker, who used to serve him, came to him and said, "O my good master, God strengthen and comfort you." "Good shoemaker," replied he, "I desire thee to pray for me, for I am the most unfit man for this high office that ever was appointed to it: but my gracious God and dear Father is able to make me strong enough." The same night he was put into the common gaol among other prisoners, where he slept little, but spent the night in prayer and instructing others.

The next day, being the 8th of February, he was led to the place of execution in the park, without the city, clad in an old gown and shirt, bare-footed, and oftentimes falling on the ground for prayer. When he was come to the place the officer said to Mr. Saunders that he was one of them who marred the queen's realm with false doctrine and heresy, wherefore he deserved death; but yet if he would revoke his heresies, the queen would pardon him; if not, yonder fire was prepared for him. To whom Mr. Saunders answered, "It is not I, nor my fellow-preachers of God's truth, that have hurt the queen's realm; but it is yourself, and such as you are, who have resisted God's holy word; it is you who mar the queen's realm. I hold no heresies, but the doctrine of God, the blessed gospel of Christ; that hold I, that believe I, that have I taught, and that will I never revoke." With that his tormentor cried, "Away with him." And away from him went Mr. Saunders, with a cheerful courage, to the fire. He fell to the ground once more and prayed: he then took the stake to which he should be chained in his arms, and kissed it, saying, "Welcome the cross of Christ, welcome everlasting life:" and being fastened to the stake, and fire put to him, he sweetly slept in the Lord.

## Martyrdom of John Hooper, Bishop of Worcester and Gloucester.

John Hooper, student and graduate in the university of Oxford, in the time of Henry VIII., fell under the displeasure of certain doctors in Oxford, who soon discovered their enmity to him, till at length, through Dr. Smith, he was compelled to quit the university.

Not long after this, as malice is always working mischief, intelligence was given to Mr. Hooper, to see to himself, for there was danger; whereon he took his journey to the seaside, to go to France. Mr. Hooper arrived at Paris, but soon returned to England, and was retained by Mr. Sentlow till he was again molested and sought for: when he was compelled, under pretence of being captain of a ship going to Ireland, to take to the seas, and so escaped through France to the higher parts of Germany. There, becoming acquainted with learned men, he was by them lovingly entertained, both at Basil and Zurich: at the latter place in particular by Mr. Bullinger. Here also he married, and applied very diligently to the study of the Hebrew tongue.

At length, when God saw it good to end the bloody persecution which arose from the six articles, and to raise king Edward to reign over this realm, among other English exiles who then returned home was Mr. Hooper, who thought it his duty to forward the cause of God in his native country.

Having taken an affectionate farewell of Mr. Bullinger and his friends in Zurich, he returned to England in the reign of Edward the Sixth; and

P

coming to London, used to preach, most times twice, and at least once every day. In his discourses, as was his custom, he reproved sin, and sharply inveighed against the iniquity of the world, and the corrupt abuses of the church.

He was at length called to preach before the king, and soon after made bishop of Gloucester by his majesty's commands. In that office he continued two years, and behaved himself so well that his very enemies could find no fault in him, except after the way of the foes of Daniel, "concerning the law of his God." After two years he received, in connection with Gloucester, the bishopric of the neighbouring city of Worcester.

But sinister contention concerning the ordering and consecration of bishops, and of their apparel, with other like trifles, began to disturb the good beginning of this bishop. For, notwithstanding that godly reformation of religion that arose in the church of England, besides other ceremonies more ambitious than profitable or tending to edification, they used to wear such garments and apparel as the popish bishops were wont to do; first a chymere, and under that a white rochet; then a mathematical cap with four angles, indicative of dividing the world into four parts. These trifles, as tending more to superstition than otherwise, he could never abide, so in nowise could he be persuaded to wear them. For this cause he made supplication to the king, most humbly desiring his highness either to discharge him of the bishopric, or else to dispense with him for such ceremonial orders; which petition the king granted immediately, writing to the archbishop in his behalf.

The earl of Warwick seconded this request of his majesty by addressing another letter to the archbishop, begging that he would dispense with Mr. Hooper's being burdened by the oath commonly used in the consecration of bishops. But these letters availed not; the bishops stood earnestly in defence of the ceremonies. This being the case, Mr. Hooper at length agreed, that sometimes he should in his sermons show himself apparelled as the other bishops were. Accordingly, being appointed to preach before the king, he appeared in the objectionable habiliments. But this private contumely and reproach in respect to the public profit of the church, he suffered patiently. Then also very soon these differences vanished amidst the rage of persecution; and the trifling shades of opinion were lost in their unanimity of essential truths; so that, while they were in prison, several affectionate letters passed between them.

After this discord, and not a little vexation, about vestures, at length Mr. Hooper, entering into his diocese, there employed his time, under king Edward's reign, with such diligence and as may be an example to all bishops. So careful was he in his cure, that he left neither pains untaken, nor ways unsought, how to train up the flock of Christ in the true word of salvation. Everwhere he kept religion in one uniform doctrine and integrity: so that if you entered into the bishop's palace, you would suppose yourself to have entered some church or temple. In every corner there was the beauty of virtue, good example, honest conversation, and reading of the holy Scriptures. There was not to be seen in his house any courtly rioting or idleness; no pomp, no dishonest word, no swearing could there be heard. As to the revenues of his bishoprics, if anything surmounted thereof, he saved nothing, but bestowed it in hospitality.

After this, in the reign of queen Mary, religion being subverted and changed, this good bishop was one of the first who was sent for by a pursuivant to London. Two reasons were assigned for this step. The first, that he might answer to Dr. Heath, then re-appointed bishop of that diocese, who was deprived thereof in king Edward's days, why he continued in an office to which he had no right? And next, to render an account to Bonner, bisop of London, because he had in king Edward's time been one of his accusers. When he met the council Gardiner received him very opprobriously, railing at him, and accusing him of his religion. He freely answered, and cleared himself. But he was, notwithstanding, committed to prison, and it was declared to him that the cause of his imprisonment was only for certain sums of money, for which he was indebted to the queen, and not for religion.

The first examination of bishop Hooper was before five bishops as commissioners—of London, Durham, Winchester, Chichester, and Llandaff. On his entering their presence, Gardiner, bishop of Winchester and lord chancellor, asked whether he was married. To this the good man smilingly answered, "Yes, my lord, and will not be unmarried till death unmarry me. And this is not enough to deprive me, except you do it against the law." The subject of marriage was no more talked of then for some time; but all began to make great outcries, and laughed, and used such gestures as were unseemly for the place, and for such a matter.

After a clamorous and spiteful discussion they at length bade the notaries write that Hooper was married, and said that he would not go from his wife; and that he believed not the corporeal presence in the sacrament, for which he ought to be deprived of his bishopric.

His next examination at Winchester House was rather more private than the former, no doubt to prevent much of the noise made on that occasion. On the 22nd of January, 1555, Babington, the warden of the Fleet, was commanded to bring him before Gardiner and some other bishops; when the latter moved Hooper earnestly to forsake the evil and corrupt doctrine preached in the days of king Edward, to return to the unity of the catholic church, and to acknowledge the pope to be the head of the church, according to the determination of the parliament; promising, likewise, that as they, with their other brethren, had received the pope's blessing, and the queen's mercy, even so mercy would be showed to him, if he would submit with them to the pope.

Mr. Hooper answered that, forasmuch as the pope taught contrary to the doctrine of Christ, he was not worthy to be counted a member of Christ's church, much less to be the head thereof: wherefore he would in nowise condescend to any such usurped jurisdiction. Neither esteemed he the church whereof they call him head, to be the catholic church of Christ; for the church only heareth the voice of her spouse Christ, and flieth the strangers. "Howbeit," saith he, "if in any point, to me unknown, I have offended the queen's majesty, I shall most humbly submit myself to her mercy, if mercy may be had with safety of conscience, and without the displeasure of God." Answer was made that the queen would show no mercy to the pope's enemies. Whereupon Babington was commanded to carry him again to the Fleet. He did so, and shifted him from his former chamber into another, near to the warden's own chamber, where he remained six days; and, in the meantime, his former chamber was searched by Dr. Martin and others, for writings and books which Mr. Hooper was thought to have made; but none were found.

One more examination, or rather effort to make Hooper recant, occurred at the same place, and before the same crafty and cruel inquisitors. January 28th, the bishop of Winchester, and other commissioners, again sat in judgment at St. Mary Overy's, where Hooper appeared before them in the afternoon; and after much reasoning and disputation, the sheriffs were commanded, about four o'clock, to carry him to the Compter in Southwark, there to remain till the following day at nine o'clock, to see whether he would come home again to the catholic church.

By the way the sheriff said to Mr. Hooper, "I wonder that ye were so hasty and quick with my lord chancellor, and did use no more patience." He answered: "Master sheriff, I was nothing at all impatient, although I was earnest in my Master's cause; and it standeth me so in hand, for it goeth upon life and death: not the life and death of this world only, but also of the world to come." Then he was committed to the keeper of the Compter.

On the day following, January 29th, at the hour

appointed, he was brought up again by the sheriffs before Gardiner and the commissioners in the church. After long and earnest talk, when they perceived that Hooper would by no means condescend unto them, they condemned him to be degraded, and read to him his condemnation. He was then delivered to the secular power, the two sheriffs of London, who were ordered to carry him to the Clink, a prison not far from the bishop of Winchester's house, and there to remain till night. When it came dark, Hooper was led by one of the sheriffs, with many bills and weapons, through the bishop of Winchester's house, and over London bridge, through the city to Newgate, and by the way some of the sergeants were sent before to put out the costermongers' candles, who used to sit with lights in the streets; either fearing that the people would make some attempt to take him away from them by force, if they had seen him go to that prison, or else, being burdened with an evil conscience, they thought darkness to be a most fit season for such a business. But notwithstanding this device, the people had some knowledge of his coming, and many of them came forth to their doors with lights, and saluted him, praising God for his constancy in the true doctrine which he had taught them, and desiring God to strengthen him in the same to the end. The bishop requested the people to make their earnest prayers to God for him; and so went through Cheapside to the place appointed, and was delivered as close prisoner to the keeper of Newgate, where he remained six days, nobody being permitted to come to him, saving his keepers, and such as should be appointed therein.

During this time Bonner, bishop of London, and others at his appointment, as Fecknam, Chedsey, and Harpsfield, went several times to him, to try if they could persuade him to become a member of their church. All the ways they could devise they attempted: for, besides the disputations and allega-tions of testimonies of the Scriptures, and of ancient writers wrested to a wrong sense, according to their accustomed manner, they used also all out-ward gentleness and signs of friendship, with promises of worldly wealth; not omitting, at the same time, most grievous threatenings, if with gentleness they could not prevail: but they found him always the same, steadfast and immovable.

On the Monday following Bonner came to New-gate, and there degraded bishop Hooper. The same Monday, at night, his keeper gave Hooper a hint that he should be sent unto Gloucester to suffer death; whereat he rejoiced very much, lifting up his eyes and hands to heaven, and praising God that he saw it good to send him among the people over whom he was pastor, there to confirm with his death the truth which he had before taught them, not doubting but the Lord would give him strength to perform the same to his glory; and immediately he sent to his servant's house for his boots, spurs, and cloak, that he might be in readiness to ride when he should be called.

The day following, about four o'clock in the morning, the keeper, with others, came and searched him, and the bed whereon he lay, to see if he had written anything; after which he was led by the sheriffs of London and their officers from Newgate to a place not far from St. Dunstan's church in

Fleet Street, where six of the Queen's guard were
to conduct him to Gloucester, there to be delivered
unto the sheriff, who, with lord Chandos, Mr.
Wicks, and other commissioners, were to see the
execution done. The guard brought him to the
Angel, where he brake his fast with them, eating
his meat at that time more liberally than he had a
good while before. About break of day he leaped
cheerfully on horseback, having a hood on his head,
under his hat, that he should not be known, and so
took his journey towards Gloucester. By the way
the guard inquired of him where he was accustomed
to bait or lodge, but always carried him to another
than the one he named.

On the Thursday following he came to Cirencester,
fifteen miles from Gloucester, and there dined at a
woman's house who had always hated the truth,
and spoken all the evil she could of him. This
woman, perceiving the cause of his coming, showed
him all the friendship she could, and lamented his
case with tears, confessing that she had often before
reported that, if he were put to the trial, he
would not stand to his doctrines. After dinner he
resumed his journey, and came to Gloucester about
five o'clock.

Sir Anthony Kingston, formerly Hooper's good
friend, was appointed by the queen's letter to attend
at his execution. As soon as he saw the bishop he
burst into tears. Hooper did not know him at first:
the knight, therefore, addressing him, said, "Why,
my lord, do you not know me—an old friend of
yours, Anthony Kingston?" "Yes," answered
Hooper, "sir Anthony Kingston, I do know you
well, and am glad to see you in health, and praise

God for the same." " But I am sorry to see you, my lord, in this case," replied Kingston; " for, as I understand, you are come hither to die. But, alas! consider that life is sweet, and death is bitter. Therefore, seeing life may be had, desire to live; for life hereafter may do good." "Indeed, it is true, sir Anthony, I am come hither to end this life, and to suffer death, because I will not gainsay the truth that I have heretofore taught amongst you in this diocese and elsewhere : and I thank you for your friendly counsel, although it be not as I could wish. True it is, that death is bitter and life is sweet; but the death to come is more bitter, and the life to come is more sweet."

After these and other words they took leave of each other with tears. At his departure the bishop told him that all the trouble he had sustained in prison had not caused him to utter so much sorrow. Then the bishop was committed by the guard into the custody of the sheriffs of Gloucester.

The two sheriffs went aside to consult, and would have lodged him in the common gaol of the town, called Northgate, had not the guard made earnest intercession for him; declaring how quietly, mildly, and patiently he had behaved on the way; adding thereto, that any child might keep him well enough, and that they themselves would rather take pains to watch with him, than that he should be sent to the common prison. It was therefore determined that he should remain in Robert Ingram's house; and the sheriffs, the sergeants, and other officers, agreed to watch with him that night themselves. His desire was, that he might go to bed betime, saying that he had many things to remember: accordingly, he went at five o'clock, and slept one sleep soundly, then spent the rest of the night in prayer. After he got up in the morning he desired that no man should be suffered to come into the chamber, that he might be solitary till the hour of execution.

About eight o'clock came sir John Bridges, lord Chandos, with a great band of men, sir Anthony Kingston, sir Edmund Bridges, and other commissioners appointed to see the execution. At nine Hooper had himself in readiness, the time being now at hand. Immediately he was brought down from his chamber by the sheriffs, who were accompanied with bills and other weapons. When he saw the weapons, he said to the sheriffs, "I am no traitor, neither needed you to have made such a business to bring me to the place where I must suffer; for if you had suffered me, I would have gone alone to the stake, and troubled none of you." Afterwards, looking upon the multitude of people that were assembled, about 7,000, he spake unto those who were about him, saying, "Alas! why are these people come together? Peradventure they think to hear something of me now, as they have in times past: but alas! speech is prohibited me. Notwithstanding, the cause of my death is well known to them. When I was appointed to be their pastor, I preached to them true and sincere doctrine, and that out of the word of God; and because I will not now account the same to be heresy and untruth, this kind of death is prepared for me." Having said this, he went forward, led between the two sheriffs, in a gown of his host's, his hat upon his head, and a

staff in his hand to rest himself upon; for the pain
of the sciatica, which he had taken in prison, caused
him somewhat to halt.   All the way, being strictly
charged not to speak, he could not be perceived
once to open his mouth; but beholding the people,
who mourned bitterly for him, he would sometimes
lift up his eyes towards heaven, and look very
cheerfully upon such as he knew.   He was never
known, during the time of his being among them,
to look with so happy and ruddy a countenance as
he did then.

When he came to the place he smilingly beheld
the stake, which was near the great elm tree over
against the college of priests, where he had been
wont to preach.   The place round about the houses,
and the boughs of the trees, were filled with
spectators: and in the chamber over the gate stood
the priests of the college.   Then he kneeled down
(forasmuch as he was not suffered to speak to the
people) to prayer, and beckoned six or seven times
unto one whom he well knew, that he might hear
his prayer, and report faithfully the same.   When
this person came to the bishop, he poured tears on
his shoulders and in his bosom, and continued his
prayer for half an hour, which prayer was drawn
from the whole creed.   While at his prayer a box
was brought and laid before him upon a stool, with
his pardon from the queen if he would recant.   At
the sight of this he cried, " If you love my soul,
away with it."   The box being taken away, the
lord Chandos said, " Seeing there is no remedy,
despatch him quickly."   Hooper replied, " Good,
my lord, I trust your lordship will give me leave to
make an end to my prayers."

MARTYRDOM OF BISHOP HOOPER.

When he had risen from his last devotions in this world, he prepared himself for the stake. He had put off his host's gown, and delivered it to the sheriffs, requiring them to see it restored to its owner, and put off the rest of his apparel, unto his doublet and hose, wherein he would have burned. But the sheriffs would not permit that, unto whose pleasure he very obediently submitted himself; and his doublet, hose, and waistcoat were taken off. Thus, being in his shirt, he took a point from his hose himself, and trussed his shirt between his legs, where he had a pound of gunpowder in a bladder, and under each arm the like quantity, delivered him by the guard.

Command was now given that the fire should be kindled. But because there were not fewer green fagots than two horses could carry, it did not kindle speedily, but was some time before it took the reeds upon the fagot. At length it burned about him; but the wind having full strength in that place, and it being a lowering, cold morning, it blew the flame from him, so that he was in a manner little more than touched by the fire. Endeavours were then made to increase the flame, and then the bladders of gunpowder exploded, but did him little good, being so placed and the wind having such power. In this fire he prayed with a loud voice, "Lord Jesus, have mercy upon me! Lord Jesus, have mercy upon me! Lord Jesus, receive my spirit!" And these were the last words he was heard to utter. Yet he struck his breast with his hands, until by the renewing of the fire his strength was gone, and his hands stuck fast in striking the iron upon his breast. So immediately, bowing forwards,

he yielded up his spirit.   Thus lingering were his
last sufferings.   He was nearly three-quarters of an
hour or more in the fire, as a lamb, patiently bearing the extremity thereof, neither moving forwards,
backwards, nor to any side; but he died as quietly
as a child in his bed.

### Sufferings and Martyrdom of Dr. Rowland Taylor.

The town of Hadley was one of the first that
received the word of God in England, at the
preaching of Thomas Bilney.   Of this parish Dr.
Rowland Taylor was vicar, being doctor both in
the civil and canon laws.   In addition to eminent
learning, his known attachment to the pure principles of Christianity recommended him to the
favour and friendship of Cranmer, with whom he
lived, till through his interest he obtained the
vicarage of Hadley.

Dr. Taylor promoted the interest of the great
Redeemer, and the souls of men, both by his
preaching and example during the reign of king
Edward; but on his demise, and the succession of
Mary to the throne, he could not escape the cloud
that burst on the protestant community.   Two of
his parishioners, Foster, an attorney, and Clark, a
tradesman, out of blind zeal, resolved that mass
should be celebrated, in all its superstitious forms,
in the parish church at Hadley on the Monday
before Easter.   Taylor being employed in his
study, was alarmed by the ringing of bells at an
unusual time, and went to the church to inquire the
cause.   He found the great doors fast, but, lifting
up the latch of the chancel door, he entered, and

was surprised to see a priest in his habit prepared
to celebrate mass, and guarded by a party of men
under arms, to prevent interruption.

Being vicar of the parish, he demanded of the
priest the cause of such proceedings without his
knowledge or consent; and how he dared profane
the temple of God with abominable idolatries.
Foster, the lawyer, insolently replied, " Thou
traitor, how darest thou to intercept the execution
of the queen's orders?" But the doctor undauntedly denied the charge of traitor, and asserted his
mission as a minister of Jesus Christ to that portion
of his flock, commanding the priest, as a wolf in
sheep's clothing, to depart, nor infect the pure
church of God with popish idolatry. A violent
altercation then ensued between Foster and Dr.
Taylor, the former asserting the queen's prerogative, and the other the authority of the canon law,
which commanded that no mass be said but at a
consecrated altar. Meanwhile the priest, intimi-
dated by the intrepid behaviour of the protestant
minister, would have departed without saying mass,
but Clark said to him, " Fear not, you have a *super
altare;*" which is a consecrated stone, commonly
about a foot square, which the popish priests carry
instead of an altar when they say mass in gentlemen's houses. Clark then ordered him to proceed
in his duty. They then forced the doctor out of
the church, celebrated mass, and immediately informed the bishop of Winchester, who summoned
him to answer the complaints brought against him.

Dr. Taylor, on receipt of the summons, cheerfully
prepared to obey the same. On some of his friends
advising him to fly beyond sea in order to avoid

Q

the cruelty of his enemies, he told them that he was
determined to go to the bishop.  He accordingly
repaired to London, and waited on him.

Gardiner reviled him in the most shocking manner, calling him a traitor and an heretic; all which
our pious martyr patiently submitted to.  In the
opinion of Gardiner he might have been an heretic;
but according to law he could not have been a
traitor.  Dr. Taylor answered his accuser with
becoming firmness; he told him that he was the
persecutor of God's people, and that he himself had
adhered to our Saviour and his word; he put the
bishop in mind of the oath he had taken in the
beginning of king Edward's reign, to maintain the
protestant religion and oppose the papal supremacy; but Gardiner answered that the oath had
been extorted, so that he was not obliged to abide
by it.  Dr. Taylor defended himself so boldly that
Gardiner was greatly exasperated, and at last called
his men, and said, " Have this fellow to the King's
Bench, and see that he be straitly kept."  Then
Taylor knelt, and held up both his hands, and said,
" Good Lord, I thank thee! and from the tyranny
of the bishop of Rome, and all his detestable errors,
idolatries, and abominations, good Lord deliver us!
and God be praised for good king Edward."  They
carried him to prison to the King's Bench, where
he was confined almost two years.

In January, 1555, Dr. Taylor, Mr. Bradford, and
Mr. Saunders were again called to appear before
the bishops of Winchester, Norwich, London, Salisbury, and Durham, and being again charged with
heresy and schism, a determinate answer was required, whether they would submit themselves to

the Roman bishop, and abjure their errors, or hear their condemnation. Dr. Taylor and his fellows answered boldly that they would not depart from the truth which they preached in king Edward's days, neither would they submit to the Romish anti-christ; but they thanked God for so great mercy, that he would count them worthy to suffer for his word. When the bishops saw them so unmovably fixed in the truth, they read the sentence of death; which, when they heard, they most joyfully gave God thanks, and said to the bishops, "We doubt not but God, the righteous judge, will require our blood at your hands; and the proudest of you all shall repent this receiving again of anti-christ, and your tyranny that ye now show against the flock of Christ."

When Dr. Taylor had lain in the Compter, in the Poultry, about a week, on the 4th February, 1555, bishop Bonner, with others, came to degrade him, bringing with them such ornaments as do appertain to their massing mummery. He called for Taylor to be brought; the bishop being then in the chamber where the keeper of the Compter and his wife lay. Dr. Taylor was accordingly brought down to Bonner. "I wish you would remember yourself, and turn to your holy mother church, so may you do well enough, and I will sue for your pardon," said Bonner. Dr. Taylor answered, "I wish that you and your fellows would turn to Christ. As for me, I will not turn to anti-christ." Said the bishop, "I am come to degrade you; therefore, put on these vestures." Dr. Taylor said, resolutely, "I will not." "Wilt thou not? I shall make thee ere I go," replied Bonner. "You shall not, by the grace of God," said Taylor. Again Bonner charged him upon his obedience to do it, but he would not. Upon this he ordered another to put them upon his back; and being thoroughly furnished therewith, he set his hands to his side, walking up and down, and said, "How say you, my lord: am not I a goodly fool? How say you, my masters: if I were in Cheapside, should I not have the boys to laugh at these apish toys and trumpery?" At this Bonner was so enraged that he would have given Dr. Taylor a stroke on the breast with his crozier-staff, when his chaplain said, "My lord, strike him not, for he will certainly strike again." The bishop then laid his curse upon him, but struck him not. Dr. Taylor said, "Though you curse me, yet God doth bless me."

The night after his degradation his wife, his son, and his servant came to him, and were, by the keepers, permitted to sup with him; at their coming, they kneeled down and prayed. After supper, walking up and down, he gave God thanks for his grace that had so called him, and given him strength to abide by his holy word.

On the following morning the sheriff of London, with his officers, came by two o'clock, and brought him forth, and, without any light, led him to the Woolpack, an inn without Aldgate. Mrs. Taylor, suspecting that her husband would that night be carried away, watched in St. Botolph's church porch, without Aldgate, having her two children— the one named Elizabeth, an orphan, whom the doctor had adopted at three years old; the other Mary, his own daughter. When the sheriff and his

company came against St. Botolph's church, the
grateful little Elizabeth cried, " O my dear father!
Mother, mother, here is my father led away!"
" Rowland," said his wife, " where art thou?" for
it was so dark a morning that the one could not
see the other.   " Dear wife, I am here," said the
doctor, and stopped.   The sheriff's men would have
forced him on, but the sheriff said, " Stay a little, I
pray you, and let him speak to his wife."

She then came to him, when he took his daughter
Mary in his arms, while he, his wife, and Elizabeth,
kneeled down and prayed.   At which sight the
sheriff wept much, as did several others of the
company.   The prayer finished, Taylor rose up and
kissed his wife, and pressing her hand, said, " Farewell, my dear wife; be of good comfort, for I am
quiet in my conscience.   God shall raise up a father
for my children."   And then he kissed his daughter
Mary, and said, " God bless thee, and make thee
his servant;" and kissing Elizabeth, he said, " God
bless thee.   I pray you all, stand strong and steadfast unto Christ and his word, and beware of
idolatry."   Then said his wife unto him, " God be
with thee, my dear Rowland: I will, with God's
grace, meet thee at Hadley."

He was led on, while his wife followed him.   As
soon as he came to the Woolpack he was put into a
chamber, wherein he was kept with four yeomen of
the guard, and the sheriff's men.   As soon as he
entered the chamber he fell on his knees, and gave
himself wholly to prayer.   The sheriff then seeing
Mrs. Taylor there, would in no case grant her to
speak any more with her husband, but gently
desired her to go to his house and use it as her own,

promising her that she should lack nothing, and sending two officers to conduct her thither. Notwithstanding this, she desired to go to her mother's, whither the officers led her, and charged her mother to keep her there till they came again. Meanwhile the journey to Hadley was delayed. Dr. Taylor was confined at the Woolpack by the sheriff and his company till eleven o'clock, by which time the sheriff of Essex was ready to receive him; when they set him on horseback within the inn, the gates being shut.

On coming out of the gates his servant, John Hull, stood at the rails with young Taylor. When the doctor saw them he called them, saying, "Come hither, my son Thomas." John Hull lifted the child up, and set him on the horse before the father; who then took off his hat, and said to the people, "Good people, this is mine own son, begotten in lawful matrimony; and God be blessed for lawful matrimony." Then he lifted up his eyes towards heaven and prayed for his child, placing his hat upon his head. After blessing him, he delivered him to his faithful servant, whom he took by the hand, and said, "Farewell, John Hull, the most faithful servant ever man had." After this they rode forth, the sheriff of Essex and four yeomen of the guard, and the sheriff's men leading them.

All the way Dr. Taylor was joyful and merry, as one that accounted himself going to a most pleasant banquet or bridal. He spake many notable things to the sheriff and yeomen of the guard that conducted him, and often moved them to weep through his much earnest calling on them to repent, and turn to the true religion. Of these yeomen of the guard, three used him very tenderly; but the fourth, named Holmes, treated him most unkindly. The party supped and slept at Chelmsford.

At Chelmsford he was delivered to the sheriff of Suffolk, and by him conducted to Hadley. On their arrival at Lavenham, the sheriff stayed there two days; and thither came to him great numbers of gentlemen and justices, who were appointed to aid him. These endeavoured very much to seduce the doctor to the Romish religion, promising him his pardon, which they said they had for him. They also promised him great promotion, even a bishopric, if he would take it; but all their labour and flattery were vain.

When they came to Hadley, and were passing the bridge, there waited a poor man with five children, who, when they saw Dr. Taylor, fell down upon their knees, and holding up their hands, cried with a loud voice, "O dear father and good shepherd! God help and succour thee, as thou hast many a time succoured us!"

At last, coming to Aldham Common, and seeing a great multitude, he asked, "What place is this, and what meaneth it that so much people are gathered hither?" It was answered, "It is Aldham Common, the place where you must suffer; and the people are come to see you." Then said he, "God be thanked, I am even at home;" and so alighted from his horse, and with both his hands rent the hood from his head. When the people saw him they cried, "God save thee, good Dr. Taylor! Jesus Christ strengthen thee: the Holy Ghost comfort thee;" with such other like godly wishes. Dr. Taylor then asked leave of the sheriff to speak; but he denied it him. Perceiving that he could not be suffered to speak, he sat down, and seeing one named Soyce, he called him, and said, "Soyce, I pray thee come pull off my boots, and take them for thy labour: thou hast long looked for them, now take them." Then he rose up and put off his clothes unto his shirt, and gave them away. Which done, he said, with a loud voice, "Good people, I have taught you nothing but God's holy word, and those lessons that I have taken out of God's blessed book, the Holy Bible; and I am come hither this day to seal it with my blood."

On hearing his voice, the yeoman of the guard who had used him cruelly all the way, gave him a blow on the head, and said, "Is that keeping thy promise, thou heretic?" Then, seeing they would not permit him to speak, he kneeled down and prayed, and a poor woman, who was among the people, stepped in and prayed with him: they endeavoured to thrust her away, and threatened to tread her down with their horses: notwithstanding this she would not move, but remained and prayed with him. When he had finished his devotions he went to the stake and kissed it, and set himself into a pitch-barrel, which they had brought for him to stand in, and thus stood with his back upright against the stake, his hands folded together, and his eyes towards heaven, and continually prayed. Then they bound a chain around him; and the sheriff called Richard Donningham, a butcher, and commanded him to set up the fagots; but the man refused, and said, "I am lame, sir, and not able to lift a fagot." The sheriff on this threatened to send him to prison: still he would not do it. The sheriff then compelled several worthless fellows of the multitude to set up the fagots and make the fire, which they most diligently did; and one of them cruelly cast a fagot at the martyr, which struck him on the face, and the blood ran down. He meekly said, " O friend, I have suffered enough: what needed that?"

Sir John Shelton standing by, as Dr. Taylor was speaking and saying the psalm *Miserere* in English, struck him on the lips: "You knave," he said, "speak Latin, or I will make thee." At last they kindled the fire: when the martyr, holding up his hands, called upon God, and said, "Merciful Father of heaven, for Jesus Christ my Saviour's sake, receive my soul into thy hands." He then remained still, without either crying or moving, with his hands folded together, till Soyce, with an halberd, struck him on the head so violently that his brains fell out, and the dead corpse fell down into the fire. Thus rendered he his soul into the hands of his merciful Father, and to his most dear and certain Saviour Jesus Christ, whom he most entirely loved, faithfully and earnestly preached, obediently followed in living, and glorified in death.

### Martyrdom of Numerous Persons in Various Parts of England.

The names of six prisoners brought before Bonner, the 8th February, were Tomkins, Pygot, Knight, Haukes, Lawrence, and Hunter. Thomas Tomkins, a weaver by occupation, and an honest

Christian, living in Shoreditch, was kept in prison
six months, and treated with the utmost cruelty.
So great was Bonner's rage against him that he
beat him about the face, and plucked off a piece of
his beard with his own hands; yet was Tomkins so
endued with God's mighty Spirit, and so firmly
planted in the knowledge of God's truth, that by no
means could he be removed therefrom. On another
occasion, Bonner, having a lighted taper in his
hand, held the flame under Tomkins' hand until
the veins shrunk and the sinews burst; but Tomkins never shrunk, but continued steadfast and
unmovable.

When he had been half a year in prison he was
brought with several others before bishop Bonner
in his consistory to be examined. Against him
first was brought forth a certain bill or schedule
subscribed with his own hand, the fifth day of the
same month, containing these words following:
"Thomas Tomkins, of Shoreditch, and of the
diocese of London, hath believed and doth believe,
that in the sacrament of the altar, under the forms
of bread and wine, there is not the very blood and
body of our Saviour Jesus Christ in substance, but
only a token in remembrance thereof, the very
body and blood of Christ being only in heaven, and
nowhere else. By me, Thomas Tomkins."

On this being read, he was asked whether he
did acknowledge the same subscription to be of his
own hand. He granted it so to be.

The next day Tomkins was again brought before
the bishop and his assistants, and pressed to recant
his errors and return to the mother-church; but he
maintained his fidelity, nor would swerve in the

least from the articles he had signed. Having
therefore declared him an obstinate and damnable
heretic, they delivered him to the secular power,
and he was burned in Smithfield, March 6th, 1555,
triumphing in the midst of the flames, and adding
to the noble company of martyrs who had preceded
him through the path of fiery trial to the realms
of immortal glory.

The next of this noble band of intrepid saints
was an apprentice of only nineteen years of age.
His name was William Hunter. He had been
trained in the doctrine of the reformation from
his earliest youth, being descended from religious
parents, who had carefully instructed him.

When queen Mary succeeded to the crown,
orders were issued to the priest of every parish
to summon their parishioners to receive the communion at mass the Easter after her accession,
and Hunter, refusing to obey the summons, was
threatened to be brought before the bishop.

A neighbouring justice, named Brown, having
heard that he maintained heretical principles, sent
for his father, and inquired of him concerning his
son. The old man assured him that he had left
him, that he knew not whither he had gone; and
on the justice threatening to imprison him, he
said, with tears in his eyes, " Would you have
me seek out my son to be burned?" The old
man, however, was obliged to seek him, and by
accident meeting him, with tears said that it was
by command of the justice, who threatened to
imprison him. The son, to prevent his father
incurring danger, said that he was ready to
accompany him home; on which they returned

together. The following day he was taken and kept in the stocks four-and-twenty hours, and then brought before the justice, who called for a Bible, and turning to the sixth chapter of St. John, desired his opinion as to the meaning of it as it related to the sacrament of the altar. He fearlessly denied the corporeal presence. The justice then upbraided him with damnable heresy, and wrote to the bishop of London, to whom this valiant young martyr was soon conducted.

After Bonner had read the letter, he caused William to be brought into a chamber, where he began to reason with him in this manner: "I understand, William Hunter, by Mr. Brown's letter, that you have denied the blessed sacrament of the altar; whereupon Mr. Brown sent for you to bring you to the catholic faith, from which, he saith, you have departed. Howbeit, if you will be ruled by me, you shall have no harm for anything said or done in this matter." To this William answered, "I am not fallen from the catholic faith of Christ, I am sure; but do believe it, and confess it, with all my heart."

Said the bishop, "How sayest thou to the blessed sacrament of the altar? Wilt thou not recant thy saying before Mr. Brown, that Christ's body is not in the sacrament of the altar, the same that was born of the Virgin Mary?" No way daunted, William said, "My lord, I understand that Mr. Brown hath certified you of the talk which he and I had together, and thereby you know what I said to him, which I will not recant, by God's help." Then said the bishop, "I think thou art ashamed to bear a fagot, and recant openly; but if thou wilt recant privately, I promise that thou shalt not be put to open shame; even speak the word here now between me and thee, and I promise it shall go no farther, and thou shalt go home again without any hurt." To this cunning William replied, "My lord, if you let me alone, and leave me to my conscience, I will go to my father and dwell with him, or else with my master again; and if nobody disquiet my conscience, I will keep my conscience to myself."

Then the bishop commanded his men to put William in the stocks in his gatehouse, where he sat two days and two nights with only a crust of bread and a cup of water. At the two days' end the bishop came, and finding the crust and the water still by him, said to his men, "Take him out of the stocks, and let him break his fast with you." After breakfast Bonner sent for William, and demanded whether he would recant or no. But he made answer, how that he would never recant as concerning his faith in Christ. Then the bishop said that he was no Christian; but denied the faith in which he was baptized. But William answered, "I was baptized in the faith of the Holy Trinity, which I will not go from, God assisting me with his grace." Then the bishop sent him to the convict prison, and commanded the keepers to lay irons upon him, as many as he could bear; and, moreover, asked him how old he was. William said that he was nineteen years old. "Well," said the bishop, "you will be burned ere you be twenty years old, if you will not yield yourself better than you have done yet." William answered, "God strengthen me in his truth." And then they parted, the bishop allowing him a halfpenny a day to live on, in bread or drink. Thus he continued in prison three quarters of a year, in the which he was before the bishop five times, besides when he was condemned in the consistory in St. Paul's, the 9th day of February; at the which his brother, Robert Hunter (who continued with his brother William till his death, and sent the true report unto us), was present, and heard the bishop condemn him and the five others.

Then the bishop departed, and William and the other prisoners returned to Newgate. About a month after Hunter was sent to Brentwood, on the Saturday before the Annunciation of the Virgin Mary, that followed on the Monday after: he therefore remained till the Tuesday, because they would not put him to death then for the holiness of the day. In the meantime William's father and mother came to him, and desired heartily of God that he might continue as he had begun; his mother said to him that she was glad she ever bare such a child, who could find in his heart to lose his life for Christ's sake. To this he replied, "For the little pain I shall suffer, which will soon be at an end, Christ hath promised me, mother, a crown of joy; should not you be glad of that?" With that his mother kneeled down, saying, "I pray God strengthen thee, my son, to the end: yea, I think thee as well bestowed as any child I ever bore." His father, suppressing his tears, then said, "I was afraid of nothing but that my son would have been killed in the prison by hunger and cold;" a result, however, which the good parent had prevented as well as apprehended, for he was at the expense of the very best food and clothing he could send him, which the son gratefully acknowledged.

On Monday night William dreamed that he was at the place where the stake was pitched, at which he should be burned: he also thought that he met with his father, and there was a priest at the stake who wanted him to recant; to whom he said, "Away, false prophet!" and exhorted the people to beware of him, and such as he was: all which came to pass. In the morning he was commanded by the sheriff to prepare for his fate. At the same time the sheriff's son came to him, and embraced him, saying, "William, be not afraid of these men with bows and weapons prepared to bring you to the place where you shall be burned." "I thank God I am not afraid," said the undaunted youth, "for I have reckoned what it will cost me already." Then the sheriff's son could speak no more to him for weeping.

Hunter then took up his gown, and went forward cheerfully, the sheriff's servant taking him by one arm, and his brother by the other; and going along he met with his father, according to his dream, who said to him, weeping, "God be with thee, son William." He then went to the place where the stake stood, even according to his dream: where all things being not ready, he kneeled and read the 51st Psalm, till he came to these words: "The sacrifice of God is a contrite spirit; a contrite and a broken heart, O God, thou wilt not despise." As one was attempting to dispute the translation of his words the sheriff brought a letter from the queen, and said, "If thou wilt recant, thou shalt live; if not, thou shalt be burned." "I will not recant,

God willing," answered the noble youth ; on which he rose up and went to the stake, and stood upright against it. Addressing the justice, he said, " Mr. Brown, now you have that which you sought : and I pray God it be not laid to your charge in the last day; howbeit, I forgive you. If God forgive you, I shall not require my blood at your hands."

He then prayed : " Son of God, shine upon me!" and immediately the sun shone out of a dark cloud so full in his face that he was constrained to look another way ; whereat the people wondered, because it was so much obscured before. He then took up a fagot of broom, and embraced it. The priest whom he had dreamed of now came to his brother Robert with a popish book to carry to William, that he might recant ; which book his brother would not meddle with. Then William, seeing the priest, and perceiving how he would have showed him the book, said, "Away, thou false prophet! Beware of them, good people, and come away from their abominations, lest ye be partakers of their plagues." " Then," quoth the priest, " look how thou burnest here : so shalt thou burn in hell." William answered, " Thou liest, thou false prophet! Away, thou false prophet ; away ! " There was there a gentleman who said, " I pray God have mercy upon his soul." The people said, " Amen, Amen ! " Immediately after, the fire was made. Then William cast his psalter to his brother, who said, " William, think on the holy passion of Christ, and be not afraid of death." William answered, " I am not afraid." Then he lifted up his hands to heaven, and said, " Lord, Lord, Lord, receive my spirit ; " and casting down his head again into the smothering smoke, he yielded up his life for the truth, sealing it with his blood to the praise of God.

William Pygot and Stephen Knight suffered upon the 28th of March, and John Lawrence on the following day. At their examinations it was first demanded of them what their opinion was of the sacrament of the altar. Whereunto they severally answered, and also subscribed, that in the sacrament of the altar, under the forms of bread and wine, there is not the substance of the body and blood of our Saviour Jesus Christ, but a special partaking of the body and blood of Christ; the very body and blood of Christ being only in heaven, and nowhere else. The present examination ended, they were commanded to appear again the next day, being the 9th of February, at eight o'clock in the morning, and in the meanwhile to bethink themselves what they would do.

At length, finding that neither his flatterings nor his threatenings could prevail, the bishop gave them severally their judgments. And because John Lawrence had been one of their appointed priests, he was by the bishop there solemnly degraded. Their sentence of condemnation and this degradation ended, they were committed to the custody of the sheriffs of London, who sent them to Newgate, where they remained with joy together until they were carried into Essex; and there, on the 28th day of March, William Pygot was burned at Braintree, and Stephen Knight at Maldon.

The next day Mr. Lawrence was taken to Colchester. The irons he had worn in prison had so injured his limbs, and his body was so reduced by

R

want of food that he was taken to the fire in a chair, and so sitting, was consumed. An incident which is well worthy of remark occurred at his martyrdom. Several young children came about the fire, and cried, as well as they could speak, "Lord, strengthen thy servant, and keep thy promise: strengthen thy servant, according to thy promise." God answered their prayer, for Mr. Lawrence died as firmly and calmly as any one could wish to breathe his last.

Dr. Farrar, the venerable bishop of St. David's, was marked out by the bloodthirsty Gardiner as a victim. This excellent and learned prelate had been promoted to his bishopric by the lord protector in the reign of Edward; but after the fall of his patron, he also had come into disgrace through the malice of several enemies, among whom was George Constantine, his own servant. Articles, to the number of fifty-six, were preferred against him, in which he was charged with many negligences and contumacies of church government. These he answered and denied. But so bitter were his enemies, that they prevailed, and he was, in consequence, detained in prison till the death of king Edward, and the coming in of queen Mary and popish religion, whereby a new trouble rose upon him, being now accused and examined for his faith and doctrine. Whereupon he was called before the bishop of Winchester, with Mr. Hooper, Mr. Rogers, Mr. Bradford, Mr. Saunders, and others, on the 4th day of February. On the which day he should also with them have been condemned, but because leisure or list did not so well then serve the bishop, his condemnation was deferred, and he was sent to prison again, where he continued till the 14th day of the said month of February.

After this he was sent down to Wales, there to receive sentence of condemnation. Upon the 26th of February, in the church of Carmarthen, being brought by Griffith Leyson, Esq., sheriff of the county of Carmarthen, he was there personally presented before the new bishop of St. David's and Constantine the public notary, who did there and then discharge the said sheriff, and receive him into their own custody, further committing him to the keeping of Owen Jones; and thereupon declared to Dr. Farrar the great mercy and clemency that the king and queen offered to him; that if he would submit himself to the laws of the realm, and conform to the unity of the catholic church, he should be received and pardoned.

The new bishop of St. David's was one Henry Morgan, a furious papist, who now became the chief judge of his persecuted predecessor. This Morgan, sitting as a judge, ministered unto bishop Farrar certain articles and interrogatories in writing, which, being openly read unto him, Farrar refused to answer till he might see his lawful commission and authority. Whereupon Morgan pronounced him *contumax*, and for the punishment of this his contumacy committed him to the custody of Owen Jones until the 4th of March, then to be brought again into the same place between one and two.

The day and place appointed the bishop appeared again before his haughty successor, submitted himself as ready to answer to the articles

and positions above-mentioned, gently required a
copy of the articles, and a suitable time to be
assigned to him to answer for himself.    This being
granted, and the Thursday next being assigned to
him, between one and three, he was committed
again to custody.    On the appointed day he again
appeared and exhibited a bill in writing, containing in it his answer to the articles objected
and ministered unto him before.    Then Morgan
offered him the articles in this brief form: "That
he willed him, being a priest, to renounce matrimony; to grant the natural presence of Christ in
the sacrament, under the form of bread and wine;
to confess and allow that the mass is a propitiatory
sacrifice for the quick and the dead; that the
general councils lawfully congregated never die,
and never can err; that men are justified before
God, not by faith only, but that hope and charity
are also necessarily required to justification; and
that the catholic church only hath authority to
expound the Scriptures and to define controversies
of religion, and to ordain things appertaining to
public discipline.

To these articles he refused to subscribe, affirm-
ing that they were invented by man, and pertained
not to the catholic faith.    After this Morgan delivered unto him the copy of the articles, assigning
him Monday following to answer and subscribe to
them, either affirmatively or negatively.    The day
came, and he exhibited in a written paper his mind
and answer to the articles, which were as before.
The bishop assigned the next Wednesday, in the
forenoon, to hear his final and definite sentence.
On that day Morgan demanded of him whether he

would renounce his heresies, schisms, and errors, which hitherto he had maintained, and if he would subscribe to the catholic articles otherwise than he had done before.

On this Farrar exhibited a certain schedule written in English, and remaining in the acts, appealing from the bishop, as from an incompetent judge, to cardinal Pole, and other the highest authorities. This, however, did not avail him. Morgan, proceeding in his rage, pronounced sentence against him, condemning him as a heretic excommunicate, and to be given up forthwith to the secular power, namely, to the sheriff of the town of Carmarthen, Mr. Leyson. After which his degradation followed, of course.

Thus was this godly bishop condemned and degraded, and committed to the secular power, and not long after was brought to execution in the town of Carmarthen, where, in the market-place, on the south side of the cross, on the 30th of March, being Saturday before Passion Sunday, he most patiently sustained the torments of the fire. Among the incidents of this martyrdom worthy of mentioning is the following:—One Richard Jones, a young gentleman, and son of a knight, coming to Dr. Farrar a little before his death, seemed to lament the painfulness of what he had to suffer: unto whom the bishop answered that if he saw him once to stir in the pains of his burning, he should give no credit to his doctrine. And as he said, so he performed; for so patiently he stood that he never moved till one Richard Gravell, with a staff, struck him down, so that he fell amid the flames and expired, or rather rose to heaven to live for ever.

## Martyrdom of the Rev. George Marsh.

George Marsh was born in the parish of Deane, in the county of Lancaster, and having received a good education, his parents brought him up in the habits of trade and industry. About the 25th year of his age he married a young woman of the country, with whom he continued living upon a farm, having several children. His wife dying, he, having formed a proper establishment for his children, went to the university of Cambridge, where he studied, and much increased in learning, and was a minister of God's holy word and sacraments, and for awhile curate to the Rev. Laurence Saunders. In this situation he continued for a time, earnestly setting forth the true religion, to the weakening of false doctrine, by his godly readings and sermons, as well there and in the parish of Deane, as elsewhere in Lancashire. But such a zealous protestant could not be safe. He was at length apprehended, and kept close prisoner in Chester, by the bishop of that see, about four months.

He was afterwards sent to Lancaster Castle; and being brought with other prisoners to the sessions, he was made to hold up his hand with the malefactors.

While at Lancaster many came to talk with him, giving him such counsel as Peter gave Christ; but he answered that he could not follow their counsel, but that by God's grace he would live and die with a pure conscience, and as hitherto he had believed and professed.

Within a few days after Mr. Marsh was removed

from Lancaster; and coming to Chester, was sent for by Dr. Cotes, then bishop, to appear before him in his hall. Then he asked him certain questions concerning the sacrament, and Marsh made such answers as seemed to content the bishop, saying that he utterly denied transubstantiation, and allowed not the abuse of the mass, nor that the lay people should receive under one kind only, contrary to Christ's institution: in which points the bishop went about to persuade him, howbeit (God be thanked) all in vain. Much other talk he had with 'him to move him to submit to the church of Rome; and when he could not prevail he sent him again to prison. And after, being there, came to him many times one Massie, a fatherly old man, one Henshaw, the bishop's chaplain, and the achdeacon, with many more; who, with much philosophy, worldly wisdom, and deceitful vanity, after the tradition of men, but not after Christ, endeavoured to persuade him to submit himself to the church of Rome, to acknowledge the pope as its head, and to interpret the Scripture no otherwise than that church did.

To these Mr. Marsh answered that he did acknowledge and believe only one catholic and apostolic church, without which there was no salvation; and that this church is but one, because it hath ever confessed and shall ever confess and believe one only God, and one only Messiah, and in him only trust for salvation: which church also is ruled and led by one Spirit, one word, and one faith; and that this church is universal and catholic, because it hath been since the world's beginning, is, and shall endure to the world's end, comprehending

within it all nations, kindreds, and languages,
degrees, states, and conditions of men; and that
this church is built only upon the foundation of the
prophets and apostles, Jesus Christ himself being
the chief corner-stone, and not upon the Romish
laws and decrees, whose head the bishop of Rome
was. And where they said the church did stand in
ordinary succession of bishops, being ruled by
general councils, holy fathers, and the laws of the
holy church, and so had continued for the space of
fifteen hundred years and more; he replied that the
holy church, which is the body of Christ, and therefore most worthy to be called holy, was before any
succession of bishops, general councils, or Romish
decrees; neither was it bound to any time or place,
ordinary succession, or traditions of fathers; nor
had it any supremacy over empires and kingdoms;
but it was a poor simple flock, dispersed abroad, as
sheep without a shepherd in the midst of wolves;
or as a family of orphans and fatherless children;
and that this church was led and ruled by the word
of Christ, he being its supreme head, and assisting,
succouring, and defending it from all assaults,
errors, and persecutions, wherewith it is ever en-
compassed.

Mr. Marsh was afterwards examined several times
by the bishop and the chancellors, who tried every
means in their power to induce him to recant; but
all their efforts were ineffectual, for the noble
martyr resisted their persuasions and threats alike.

The bishop of Chester then began to read the
sentence of condemnation; but when he had proceeded half through it the chancellor called him,
and said, " Good, my lord; stay, stay! for if you

read any further, it will be too late to call it again."
The bishop accordingly stopped, when several
priests, and many of the ignorant people, called
upon Mr. Marsh, with many earnest words, to recant. They bade him kneel down and pray, and
they would pray for him; so they kneeled down,
and he desired them to pray for him, and he would
pray for them. When this was over the bishop
again asked him whether he would not have the
queen's mercy in time? He answered he gladly
desired the same, and loved her grace as faithfully
as any of them; but yet he durst not deny his
Saviour Christ, lest he lose his mercy everlasting,
and so win everlasting death.

The bishop then proceeded with the sentence for
about five or six lines, when again the chancellor,
with flattering words and smiling countenance,
stopped him and said, "Yet, good my lord, once
again stay, for if that word be spoken, all is past:
no relenting will then serve." Then, turning to
Mr. Marsh, he asked, "How sayest thou? wilt thou
recant?" Many of the priests and people again
exhorted him to recant and save his life. To
whom he answered, "I would as fain live as you, if
in so doing I should not deny my master Christ;
but then he would deny me before his Father in
heaven."

The bishop then read his sentence unto the end,
and afterwards said to him, "Now, I will no more
pray for thee than I will for a dog." Mr. Marsh
answered, that notwithstanding he would pray for
his lordship. He was then delivered to the sheriffs
of the city; when his late keeper, finding he should
lose him, said with tears, "Farewell, good George;"

which caused the officers to carry him to a prison at the north gate, where he was very strictly kept until he went to his death, during which time he had little comfort or relief of any creature. For being in the dungeon or dark prison, none that would do him good could speak with him, or at least durst attempt it, for fear of accusation; and some of the citizens who loved him for the gospel's sake, although they were never acquainted with him, did sometimes in the evening call and ask him how he did. He would answer them most cheerfully that he did well, and thanked God highly that he would vouchsafe of his mercy to appoint him to be a witness of his truth, and to suffer for the same, wherein he did most rejoice; beseeching that he would give him grace not to faint under the cross, but patiently bear the same, to his glory and to the comfort of his church.

The day of his martyrdom being come, the sheriffs of the city, with their officers, went to the Northgate, and brought him forth, with a lock upon his feet. As he came toward the place of execution some offered him money, and looked that he should have gone with a little purse in his hand to give unto a priest to say masses for him after his death; but Mr. Marsh said he would not be troubled to receive money, but desired some good man to take it if the people were disposed to give any, and give it to the prisoners or the poor. He went all the way reading intently, and many said, "This man goeth not unto his death as a thief, or as one that deserveth to die." On coming to the place of execution without the city, a deputy chamberlain of Chester showed Mr. Marsh a writing under a great seal, saying that it was a pardon for him if he would recant. He answered, forasmuch as it tended to pluck him from God, he would not receive it upon the condition.

He now began to address the people, showing the cause of his death, and would have exhorted them to be faithful to Christ, but one of the sheriffs told him there must be no sermoning now. He then, kneeling down, prayed earnestly, and was then chained to the post, having a number of fagots under him, and a barrel, with pitch and tar in it, over his head. The fire being unskilfully made, and the wind driving it to and fro, he suffered great extremity in his death, which notwithstanding he bore very patiently. When the spectators supposed he had been dead, suddenly he spread abroad his arms, saying, "Father of heaven, have mercy upon me," and so yielded his spirit into the hands of the Lord. Upon this, many of the people said he was a martyr, and died marvellously patient, which caused the bishop shortly after to make a sermon in the cathedral church, and therein to affirm that the said Marsh was a heretic, burnt as such, and was then a firebrand in hell.

## Martyrdom of William Flower.

William Flower was born at Snowhill, in the county of Cambridge. He was educated as a Roman catholic; and being brought up to the church, was admitted into orders, and became a monk in the abbey of Ely. After residing some time in the monastery, he became a secular priest, returned to the place of his birth, and officiated some years in a

clerical capacity.   After a time, on a review of the
sacred Scriptures, he began to doubt the doctrines
and practices of the Romish church; and on further
inspection, finding them wholly repugnant to the
word of God, he abjured them, and embraced the
doctrines of the reformation.   He then came to
London, and took up his residence at Lambeth,
where he married, and kept a school.   Going one
day to Westminster, he went into St. Margaret's
church at the time of mass.   As he refused to kneel
at the elevation of the host, he was reprimanded by
the priest; at which Flower was so irritated, that
he struck him on the head, the priest having in
his hand a chalice, containing some consecrated
wafers.

As his behaviour proceeded rather from rash zeal
than well-grounded knowledge, he submitted himself to the award of bishop Bonner, willing to
endure, for his folly, whatever punishment he
should think proper to inflict.   The bishop would
have mitigated his punishment if he would have
subscribed to the popish faith, but that he absolutely refused; he was therefore committed a
prisoner to the Gate-house.   Here the following
conversation took place between himself and a
fellow prisoner, Mr. Robert Smith, which, as it
explains his conduct, we give in full:—

*Smith.*   Friend, as I understand that you profess
the gospel, and have done so long, I am bold to
inquire of you regarding certain things by you
committed, to the astonishment of such as profess
the truth.

*Flower.*   I praise God for showing me the light
of his holy word; and give you hearty thanks for

your visit. I will declare the truth in all things that you shall lawfully demand of me.

*Smith.* Show me then the truth as to your deed, committed on John Cheltam, priest, in the church, as near as you can.

*Flower.* I came from my house at Lambeth, and entering into St. Margaret's church, and seeing the people falling down before a most detestable idol, being moved with zeal for my God, whom I saw dishonoured, I drew forth my hanger and struck the priest, whereupon I was immediately apprehended.

*Smith.* Did you not know the person that you struck? was there no evil will or hatred between you at any time?

*Flower.* No, verily: I never to my knowledge saw the person before, neither had evil will or malice.

*Smith.* Do you think that thing to be well done, and after the rule of the gospel.

*Flower.* I confess all flesh to be subject to the power of Almighty God, who maketh his ministers to do his will and pleasure; as for example, Moses, Aaron, Phineas, Joshua, Zimri, Jehu, with many others, not only changing decrees, but also planting zeals to his honour, against all order and respect of flesh and blood. For as St. Paul saith, "His works are past finding out:" by whose spirit I have also given my flesh to suffer as it shall please the good will of God to appoint.

*Smith.* Think you it right for me, or any other, to do the like by your example?

*Flower.* No, verily; neither do I know that I could do it again myself: when I came to St. Paul's church, I was no more able to do it, than now to undo that which is done; but being compelled by the Spirit, and being fully content to die for the Lord, I gave over my flesh willingly without fear. Wherefore I cannot teach you to do the like. First, Because I know not what is in you. Secondly, Because the rules of the gospel command us to suffer with patience all wrongs: yet nevertheless, if he makes you worthy who made me zealous, you shall not be hindered nor condemned: for he doth in his people unspeakable works in all ages, which no man can comprehend. I humbly beseech you to judge the best of the spirit, and condemn not God's doings; for I cannot express with my mouth the great mercies that God hath showed me in this thing, which I repent not.

*Smith.* Are you not sure to have to die for the act, and that with extremity?

*Flower.* I did, before the deed was committed, adjudge my body to die for the same: wherefore I carried about me, in writing, my opinion of God and the holy Scriptures; that if it had pleased God to have given them leave to have killed me in the church, they might, in the writing, have seen my hope which (I praise God) is laid up safe within my breast; being sure of everlasting life through Jesus Christ our Lord, and heartily sorry for all my sins, and trusting shortly, through his mercy, to cease from the same.

*Smith.* I need not speak with you of the hope you have any further: for I perceive (God be praised) you are in a good state; and therefore I beseech God to spread his wings over you, that, as for his love you have been zealous, even to the loss of this life, so he may give you his Holy Spirit to conduct you into a better life, which I think will be shortly.

*Flower.* I hunger for the same, dear friend, being assured that they can kill but the body, and that I shall receive life everlasting, and see death no more. Robert Smith then departed, leaving Flower in the dungeon.

After some time he was brought before the bishop, who administered to him, on oath, several articles. But not answering satisfactorily, he was committed to the Fleet prison, when he was brought before the warden, and found guilty of abusing a priest in the duty of his office, and also of maintaining damnable heresies. The bishop then asked him if he knew any cause why sentence should not be pronounced against him as a heretic? To which Flower answered, "I have nothing at all to say, for that I have already said I will not go from; and therefore do what you will."

The bishop then passed sentence on him as a heretic, and delivered him to the secular power.

On the 24th of April, 1555, he was led to the stake, at St. Margaret's churchyard, Westminster, amidst a prodigious number of spectators. There he knelt down and prayed as follows:—

"O eternal God, most mighty and merciful Father, who hast sent down thy Son upon the earth to save me and all mankind: who ascended up into heaven again, and left his blood upon the earth behind him for the redemption of our sins, have mercy upon me, for thy dear Son our Saviour Jesus Christ's sake, in whom only I confess to be all salvation and justification, and that there is no other way, nor holiness, in which, or by which, any man can be saved. This is my faith, which I beseech all men here to bear witness of."

He then repeated the Lord's Prayer; after which he prepared himself for undergoing his sentence. A Romish priest desired him to recant his heresy, and thereby save his life: to whom he said, " Sir, I beseech you, for God's sake, to be contented: for that I have said, I have said; and I trust in God that he will enable me to be steadfast to the end."

This done, he was chained to the stake, and his left hand fastened to his side. The other, with which he had struck the priest, was then held up, and cut off: this he bore without the least apparent emotion. The fagots were then piled round him, and being kindled, he cried out, " O thou Son of God, have mercy upon me; O thou Son of God, receive my soul." These words he repeated three times, when the smoke took away his speech; but he still showed the spectators that he was not deprived of life, by holding up the arm from whence the hand had been cut, with the other, as long as he was able. There not being a sufficiency of fagots he underwent great torture, the lower parts of his body being consumed a considerable time before the others were much affected. At length, however, the executioner finished his miseries by striking him a violent blow on the head, which brought the upper part of him into the fire; and in this dreadful manner he yielded up his life.

### Martyrdom of the Rev. John Bradford and John Leafe.

The first of these martyrs was born at Manchester, where he received a liberal education, having attained to a considerable knowledge of classical and mathematical literature. On arriving at years of maturity, having some distinguished friends, by their interest he became secretary to sir John Harrington, treasurer to Henry VIII. After a time, being of a studious turn, he quitted this office, and went to Cambridge, where, at the end of one year, he was made master of arts; soon after he was admitted to a fellowship in Pembroke College.

At this time Martin Bucer, a zealous advocate for the reformed religion, resided at Cambridge. Having a great regard for Mr. Bradford, he persuaded him to study for the work of the ministry. Mr. Bradford, being diffident, would have excused himself as not being sufficiently qualified; but Bucer gained his consent, and he was ordained a deacon by Dr. Ridley, bishop of London, who afterwards made him a prebendary of St. Paul's, where, in rotation, he preached, during three years, the true gospel of Christ.

After the accession of queen Mary Mr. Bradford continued his preaching till he was obstructed by the following incident. In the first year of the reign of that princess, Bonner, then bishop of London, ordered Mr. Bourn, afterwards bishop of Bath, to preach a sermon, wherein he took occasion, from the gospel appointed for the day, to justify Bonner, then restored to his bishopric, in preaching on the same text that very day four years, and enforcing doctrines for which, according to the preacher, he was thrown into the Marshalsea, and there kept prisoner during the time of king Edward VI. These words occasioned great murmurings among

s

the people; nay, so incensed were they that one of them threw a dagger at the preacher, and threatened to drag him from the pulpit. He therefore desired Mr. Bradford to endeavour to appease the people, who were so tumultuous that they could not be quelled even by the authority of the lord mayor. As soon as Mr. Bradford ascended the pulpit the people shouted, "God save thy life, Bradford!" and then quietly attended to his discourse, in which he reproved them for their disorderly behaviour, and exhorted them to quietness; on which, after he had finished, they peaceably dispersed. In the afternoon of the same day Mr. Bradford preached at Bow church, and rebuked the people for their tumultuous behaviour at St. Paul's in the morning.

Three days after he was summoned before the queen and her council, and there charged as being the cause of the riot, though he was the very person that stopped it. He was also accused for preaching at Bow church, though he then warmly exhorted the people to peace. But nothing that he could allege availed; and he was committed to the Tower on a charge of sedition. There he was confined above a year and six months, till the popish religion was restored by act of parliament. He then examined himself concerning his faith, because he could not speak against the doctrine of the church of Rome without danger; whereas, while the laws of king Edward were in force, he might speak freely according to his conscience.

The principal articles alleged against him were— his denying the doctrine of transubstantiation, or the bodily presence of Christ in the sacrament, and asserting that wicked men did not partake of

Christ's body in the sacrament. Several bishops and learned men conferred with him, but their arguments had no weight with him, not being founded on Scripture. As Mr. Bradford would not admit of any tenets but what was sanctioned by the word of God, he was first excommunicated, then condemned, and committed to the sheriffs of London, by whom he was conducted, the night before his execution, to Newgate; on the following day he was brought to the stake, with the martyr whose sufferings we are about to relate.

John Leafe was an apprentice to a tallow-chandler, and at the age of nineteen, being charged with heresy, he was committed to the Compter by the alderman of the ward in which he lived. After being some time confined he was brought before bishop Bonner, and examined concerning his faith in the sacrament of the altar, and other points; his answers gave little satisfaction to the bishop. A few days after he was examined again; but his answers being the same, he was condemned, and delivered to the secular power, for not believing that the bread and wine in the sacrament, by the words of consecration, are changed, really and substantially, into the body and blood of Christ.

After his condemnation the bishop sent two papers to him, the one containing a recantation, the other his confession. The messenger, after reading the former to him (for he could neither read nor write himself), asked if he would sign it; to which, without the least hesitation, he answered in the negative. He then read to him his confession, when he immediately took a pin, and pricking his hand, sprinkled the blood upon the paper, desiring the messenger to show the bishop that he had signed it with his blood.

When these two martyrs were conducted to the place of execution, in Smithfield, Mr. Bradford fell prostrate on one side of the stake, and Leafe on the other. In this position they continued for some minutes, till Mr. Bradford was desired by the sheriff to arise. On this they both arose, and after Mr. Bradford had made a short harangue to the people, they were fastened to the stake, and the reeds and fagots piled round them. Mr. Bradford then, lifting up his eyes and hands to heaven, exclaimed, "O England, England, repent thee of thy sins; beware of anti-christ, beware of idolatry; take heed they do not deceive you." Then turning to young Leafe, he said, "Be of good comfort, brother; the time of deliverance is at hand." The young man replied, "The Lord Jesus receive our spirits." The fire was then put to the fagots, and they both endured their sufferings with the utmost resignation, reposing unshaken confidence in that blessed Redeemer who died to save mankind.

## Martyrdom of Margaret Polley.

Such was the fury of bigoted zeal during the reign of Mary, that even the more tender sex did not escape persecution. Information being given against Margaret Polley to Maurice, bishop of Rochester, she was brought before him, when he, in solemn parade, harangued her as follows:—

"We, Maurice, by the sufferance of God, bishop of Rochester, proceeding in a cause of heresy against thee, Margaret Polley, of the parish of

Popingberry, in our diocese of Rochester, do lay against thee the ensuing articles. To these we require of thee a true, full, and plain answer, by virtue of thine oath thereupon to be given."

The oath being administered, the bishop demanded of the woman an answer to each of the following articles:

1. "Are not those heretics who maintain and hold other opinions than our holy mother and catholic church doth?"

To this she replied, "They are, indeed, heretics, and grossly deceived, who hold and maintain doctrines contrary to the word of God, which, I sincerely believe, was written by holy men taught by the Holy Ghost."

2. "Do you hold and maintain that in the sacrament of the altar, under the form of bread and wine, there is not the very body and blood of Christ, and that the said body is verily in heaven only, and not in the sacrament?"

She answered, "What I have learned from the holy Scriptures I steadfastly maintain, viz., that the very body which was crucified for the sins of all true believers ascended into heaven, is there at the right hand of the Majesty on high; that such body has ever since remained there, and cannot, according to my belief, be in the sacrament of the altar. I believe that the bread and wine in the sacrament are to be received as symbols and representatives of the body and blood of Christ, but not as his body really and substantially. I think, in my weak judgment, that it is not in the power of any man, by pronouncing words over the elements of bread and wine, to transubstantiate them into the real body and blood of Christ. In short, it is my belief that the eucharist is only a commemoration of the death of our Saviour, who said, 'As oft as ye do this, do it in remembrance of me.'"

These pertinent and frank replies provoked the haughty prelate, who, after much scurrilous language, told her she was a silly woman, and knew not what she said: and that it was the duty of every Christian to believe as the mother-church doth teach. He then asked her, "Will you recant the error which you maintain, be reconciled to the church, and receive the remission of sins?" To which she replied, "I cannot believe otherwise than I have spoken, because the practice of the church of Rome is contrary not only to reason, and my senses, but also to the word of God."

On this, the bishop pronounced sentence of condemnation; when she was carried back to prison, where she remained for upwards of a month. She was in the prime of life, pious, charitable, humane, learned in the Scriptures, and beloved by all who knew her. She was repeatedly exhorted to recant; but she refused all offers of life on such terms, choosing glory, honour, and immortality hereafter, rather than a few short years in this vale of grief, purchased at the expense of truth and conscience.

When the day for her execution arrived, which was in July, 1555, she was conducted to Tunbridge, where she was burned, sealing the truth with her blood, and showing that God can cause the meanest instruments to magnify the glories of his grace.

On the same day, one Christopher Wade, a weaver, of Dartford, in Kent, who had likewise been condemned by the bishop of Rochester, shared the same fate, and at the same place; but they were executed separately, he first submitting to the dreadful sentence.

About the same time, John Bland, John Frankesh, Nicholas Sheterden, and Humphrey Middleton were all burnt together at Canterbury. The two first were ministers and preachers of the gospel, the one being rector of Adesham, and the other vicar of Rolvindon, in Kent. They resigned themselves with Christian fortitude, fervently praying that God would receive them into his heavenly kingdom.

### Martyrdom of John Launder and Dirick Carver.

John Launder, of Godstone, in the county of Surrey, husbandman, and Dirick Carver, of Bright-helmstone, in the county of Sussex, brewer, were apprehended in the dwelling-house of the latter, as they were at prayers, and sent up to the council at London, where, not giving satisfactory answers to the questions proposed, they were sent to Newgate, to await the leisure and abide the determination of the cruel and arrogant Bonner.

Launder said, that, being at Brighthelmstone to transact some business for his father, and hearing that Mr. Carver was a promoter of the doctrines of the reformation, he went to his house to join in prayer with the pious Christians which resorted thither. He avowed his belief that "There is on earth one whole and universal catholic church, the members of which are dispersed throughout the world; that the same church doth set forth and teach only two sacraments, which are baptism and

the Lord's supper; and that to teach or use any
more sacraments, or other ceremonies, is contrary
to Scripture."

He further said that "All the service, sacrifices,
and ceremonies, now used in England are erroneous,
contrary to Christ's institution and the determination of Christ's catholic church, whereof he believed
himself to be a member. That in the sacrament
there is not really and truly contained, under the
forms of bread and wine, the very body and blood
of Christ in substance; but that when he did
receive the material bread, he received the same
in remembrance of Christ's death and passion, and
no otherwise.

"Moreover, that the mass is abominable, and
against God's word and his catholic church.
Lastly, that auricular confession is not necessary,
but that every person ought to confess his sins to
God alone." Having maintained these opinions
in the bishop's court and refused to recant, he was
condemned and delivered over to the secular power.

Dirick Carver, being examined by Bishop Bonner
concerning his faith in the sacrament of the altar,
the mass, auricular confession, and the religion
then taught in the church of England, made a
similar good confession. He also said that since
the queen's coronation he had had the bible and
psalter read in English, divers times, at his house
in Brighthelmstone; and that, for about twelve
months past, he had had the English litany said in
his house, with other prayers in English."

After this examination he was strongly persuaded
to recant, but this he refused, on which sentence of
condemnation was passed on him at the same time

as on Launder, and the time of his execution fixed for the 22nd of July, at Lewes, in Sussex.

On his arrival at the stake he kneeled down and prayed, and then addressed the spectators as follows :—" Dear brothers and sisters, bear witness that I am come. to seal with my blood the gospel of Christ, because I know that it is true. Many of you know that the gospel hath been truly preached to you here in Lewes, and now it is not so preached; and because I will not here deny God's gospel I am condemned to die."

On this the sheriff said, " If thou dost not believe in the pope thou art damned, body and soul." But our martyr pitied his blindness, and begged of God to forgive his errors. Being then fastened to the stake and the fire kindled round him, he patiently submitted, and expired calling out, " O Lord, have mercy upon me! Lord Jesus, receive my spirit."

His fellow-prisoner, John Launder, was burnt the following day at Steyning, where he cheerfully gave up his life to that God from whose hands he had received it.

### Martyrdom of John Denley, John Newman, and Patrick Packingham.

So perpetually were the popish emissaries in search of their prey in all parts of the kingdom that it was almost impossible long to escape them. As Mr. Denley and Mr. Newman were travelling into Essex on a visit to some friends, they were met by Mr. Tyrrel, a justice of the peace, who, suspecting them of heresy, apprehended them, and at the same time took from Mr. Denley a confession of his faith in writing.   He then sent them to London, with a letter to be presented to the council.   On being brought before the council, they were admonished to yield obedience to the queen's laws, but this advice proving ineffectual, their examination was referred to Bonner.

On the 28th of June, 1555, Denley and Newman, together with Patrick Packingham (who had been apprehended two days before), were brought before Bonner at his palace in London.   The bishop having examined the two former upon their confessions, and finding them inflexibly to adhere to the same, used his customary exhortation ; on which Denley said, "God save me from your counsel and keep me in the mind I am in, for that which you count heresy I take to be the truth."

On the 5th of July the bishop proceeded in the usual form against them in his consistory court at St. Paul's.   After the various articles and their answers had been read, they were exhorted to recant.   On their remaining steadfast, they were condemned as heretics and delivered to the sheriffs of London, who conducted them to Newgate, where they were kept till writs were issued for their execution.

Denley was ordered to be burned at Uxbridge. There he was chained to the stake, and expired in the midst of the flames singing a psalm to the praise of his Redeemer.   A popish priest who was present was so incensed at his singing that he ordered one of the attendants to throw a fagot at him, which was accordingly done, and he received a violent fracture in his skull, which, with the fire, soon deprived him both of speech and life.

A few days after Packingham suffered at the same place; but Newman was executed at Saffron Walden, in Essex. They both died with great fortitude, cheerfully resigning their souls into the hands of him who gave them, in full expectation of receiving crowns of glory in the heavenly mansions. Nor will their expectations be unfulfilled. He "who cannot lie" has declared that they who suffer for his sake on earth shall be amply rewarded in heaven. "Blessed are ye when men shall revile you, and persecute you, and shall say all manner of evil against you falsely, for my sake. Rejoice and be exceeding glad, for great is your reward in heaven; for so persecuted they the prophets which were before you."

# CHAPTER XI.

THE SUFFERINGS AND MARTYRDOM OF HUGH LATIMER, BISHOP OF
WORCESTER; NICHOLAS RIDLEY, BISHOP OF LONDON; AND OTHERS.

HUGH LATIMER was born at Thirkestone, in
Leicestershire, about the year 1475. He
received a good education, and was sent to Cambridge, where he was a zealous papist; but conversing frequently with Thomas Bilney, he saw the
errors of popery, and became a zealous protestant.
Latimer being thus converted, laboured to promote
the reformed opinions, and pressed the necessity
of a holy life in opposition to outward forms.
This rendered him obnoxious at Cambridge—then
the seat of ignorance, bigotry, and superstition.
However, the unaffected piety of Mr. Bilney, and
the cheerful and natural eloquence of Latimer,
wrought greatly upon the junior students, and also
increased the credit of the protestants, so that the
papist clergy were greatly alarmed and called aloud
for the secular arm.

Under this arm Bilney suffered at Norwich; but
this, far from shaking the reformation at Cambridge, inspired its leaders with new courage.
Latimer began to exert himself more than he had
yet done; and succeeded to that credit with his
party which Bilney had possessed so long. Among
other instances of his zeal and resolution there
was this: he had the courage to write to the king

(Henry VIII.) against a proclamation, forbidding the use of the Bible in English, and other books on religious subjects. He had preached before his majesty once or twice at Windsor, and had been favourably taken notice of by that monarch. But whatever hopes of preferment his sovereign's favour might have raised in him, he put all to hazard rather than omit what he thought his duty. His letter is the picture of an honest and sincere heart, and thus concludes: "Accept, gracious sovereign, without displeasure, what I have written. I thought it my duty to mention these things to your majesty. No personal quarrel, as God shall judge me, have I with any man; I wanted only to induce your majesty to consider well what kind of persons you have about you, and the ends for which they counsel. Indeed, great prince, many of them, or they are much slandered, have very private ends. God grant your majesty may see through all the designs of evil men, and be in all things equal to the high office with which you are entrusted. Wherefore, gracious king, remember yourself; have pity upon your own soul, and think that the day is at hand when you shall give account of your office and the blood which hath been shed by your sword; in the which day that your Grace may stand steadfastly and not be ashamed, but be clear and ready in your reckoning, and have your pardon sealed with the blood of our Saviour, Christ, which alone serveth at that day, is my daily prayer to him who suffered death for our sins. The Spirit of God preserve you."

Lord Cromwell was now in power, and being a favourer of the reformation, he obtained a benefice

in Wiltshire for Latimer, who immediately went
thither, discharging his duty very conscientiously,
though much persecuted by the Romish clergy,
who at length carried their malice so far as to
obtain an archiepiscopal citation for his appearance
in London.   His friends would have had him quit
England, but their persuasions were in vain.

He set out for London in the depth of winter,
and under a severe fit of the stone and colic, but
most distressed at leaving his parish exposed to
the popish clergy.   On his arrival he found a court
of bishops and canonists ready for him, where,
instead of being examined, as he expected, about
his sermons, a paper was put into his hands,
which he was ordered to subscribe, declaring his
belief in the efficacy of masses for the souls in
purgatory, of prayers to the dead saints, of pilgrim-
age to their sepulchres and relics, the pope's
power to forgive sins, the doctrine of merit, the
seven sacraments, and the worship of images,
which, when he refused to sign, the archbishop,
with a frown, ordered him to consider what he did.
"We intend not," said he, "Mr. Latimer, to be
hard upon you; we dismiss you for the present.
Take a copy of the articles, examine them carefully,
and God grant that at our next meeting we may
find each other in better temper."

At the next and several succeeding meetings the
same scene was acted over again.   He continued
inflexible, and they continued to distress him.
Tired out with this usage, when he was again
summoned, instead of going he sent a letter to the
archbishop, in which he told him " That the treatment he had lately met with had brought him into

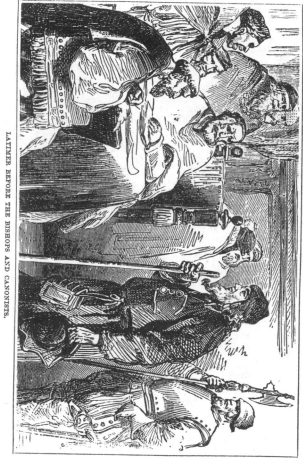

LATIMER BEFORE THE BISHOPS AND CANONISTS.

such a disorder as rendered him unfit to attend that day; that in the meantime he could not help taking this opportunity to expostulate with his grace for detaining him so long from his duty; that it seemed to him most unaccountable that they who never preached themselves should hinder others; that as for their examination of him, he really could not imagine what they aimed at: they pretended one thing in the beginning and another in the progress; that if his sermons gave offence, although he persuaded himself they were neither contrary to the truth nor to any canon of the church, he was ready to answer whatever might be thought exceptionable in them; that he wished a little more regard might be had to the judgment of the people, and that a distinction might be made between the ordinances of God and man; and if some abuses in religion did prevail, as was then commonly supposed, he thought preaching was the best means to discountenance them; that he wished all pastors might be obliged to perform their duty, but that, however, liberty might be given to those who were willing; that as to the articles proposed to him he begged to be excused subscribing to them; while he lived he never would abet superstition; and that, lastly, he hoped the archbishop would excuse what he had written. He knew his duty to his superiors, and would practice it; but in that case he thought a stronger obligation lay upon him."

The bishops, however, continued their persecutions, but their schemes were remarkably frustrated. Latimer being raised to the see of Worcester, in the year 1533, through Anne Boleyn, then the favourite wife of Henry, to whom, most

T

probably, he was recommended by Lord Cromwell, he had now a more extensive field in which to promote the principles of the reformation. All the historians of those times mention him as remarkably zealous in the discharge of his office; in overlooking the clergy of his diocese he was active, warm, and resolute; he presided in his ecclesiastical court with the same spirit. In visiting he was frequent and observant; in ordaining, strict and wary; in preaching, indefatigable; and in reproving and exhorting, severe and persuasive.

In 1536 he was summoned to attend parliament and convocation, which gave him a further opportunity of promoting the reformation. Many alterations were made in religious matters, and a few months after the Bible was translated into English, and recommended to a general perusal.

Latimer, highly satisfied, now repaired to his diocese. He had no talents, as he said, for state affairs. His whole ambition was to discharge well the pastoral functions of a bishop. How very unqualified he was to act the courtier, the following story will show. It was the custom in those days for the bishops to make presents to the king on New Year's day, and many of them presented liberally, proportioning their gifts to their expectations. Among the rest, Latimer, being then in town, waited upon the king with his offering, but instead of a purse of gold, which was the common oblation, he presented a New Testament, with a leaf doubled down in a very conspicuous manner at this passage, " Whoremongers and adulterers God will judge."

In 1539 he was summoned again to attend

parliament. The bishop of Winchester, Gardiner, was his great enemy, and on one occasion, when the bishops were with the king, kneeled down and solemnly accused Latimer of a seditious sermon preached at court. Being called upon by the king, with some sternness, to vindicate himself, Latimer was so far from palliating what he had said, that he nobly justified it, and turning to the king said, with that noble unconcern which a good conscience inspires, " I never thought myself worthy, nor did I ever sue, to be a preacher before your grace, but I was called to it, and would be willing to give place to my betters. If it be your grace's pleasure to allow them for preachers, I can be content to bear their books after them; but if your grace allow me for a preacher, I would desire you to give me leave to discharge my conscience, and to frame my doctrine according to my audience. I had been a very dolt, indeed, to have preached so at the borders of your realm as I preached before your grace." The boldness of his answer baffled his accusers' malice; the severity of the king's countenance changed into a gracious smile, and the bishop was dismissed with that obliging freedom which this monarch never used but to those he esteemed.

However, as Latimer could not give his vote for the six papistical articles, he thought it wrong to hold any office in a church where such terms of communion were required, and therefore resigned his bishopric and retired into the country. But an unhappy accident carried him again into the tempestuous atmosphere of the court: he was so bruised

by the fall of a tree that he was obliged to seek
for better assistance than he could have where he
resided. With this view he repaired to London,
where he saw the fall of his patron, the lord Cromwell, a loss which he was soon made sensible of;
for Gardiner's emissaries quickly found him out,
and on a pretended charge he was sent to the
Tower, where, without any judicial examination,
he suffered a cruel imprisonment for the remaining
six years of king Henry's reign.

On the death of Henry the protestant interest
revived under his son Edward, and Latimer was
immediately set at liberty. An address was now
made to the protector to restore him to the
bishopric. The protector was very willing, and
proposed the thing to Mr. Latimer: but he,
thinking himself now unequal to it, chose rather
to accept an invitation to take up his residence
with archbishop Cranmer at Lambeth, where his
chief employment was to hear the complaints and
redress the grievances of the poor. His character
for services of this kind was so universally known
that strangers from every part of England resorted
to him.

Thus he spent more than two years, during
which time he assisted the archbishop in composing
the homilies which were set forth by authority in
the reign of king Edward: he also preached the
Lent sermons before his majesty during the first
three years of his reign.

Upon the revolution which happened at court
after the death of the duke of Somerset, he retired
into the country, and made use of the king's

licence as a general preacher, where he thought
his labours might be most serviceable. He was
thus employed during the remainder of that reign,
and in the beginning of the next; but as soon as
the re-introduction of popery was resolved on, the
bishop of Winchester, who was now prime minister,
sent a message to cite him before the council. He
had notice of this some hours before the messenger's
arrival, but he made no use of the intelligence.
The messenger found him equipped for his journey,
at which, expressing his surprise, Mr. Latimer told
him that he was as ready to attend him to London
to answer for his faith as he ever was to take any
journey in his life, and that he doubted not but
that God, who had already enabled him to preach
the word before two princes, would enable him to
witness the same before a third. The messenger
then told him that he had no orders to seize his
person, and, giving him a letter, departed. However, finding it a citation from the council, he set
out immediately. As he passed through Smithfield
he said, cheerfully, " This place of burning hath
long groaned for me." The next morning he
waited upon the council, who, having loaded him
with many reproaches, sent him to the Tower,
from whence, after some time, he was removed to
Oxford.

NICHOLAS RIDLEY, bishop of London, received the
earliest part of his education at Newcastle-upon-
Tyne, from whence he went to Cambridge, where
his great learning and distinguished abilities so
recommended him that he was made master of
Pembroke Hall.

After being some years in this office he travelled into various parts of Europe. On his return he was made chaplain to Henry VIII. and bishop of Rochester, from which he was translated to the see of London by Edward VI.

In private life he was pious, humane, and affable; in public he was learned, sound, and eloquent, diligent in his duty, and very popular as a preacher.

He had been educated in the Roman catholic religion, but was brought over to the reformed faith by reading Bertram's book on the sacraments, and was confirmed in the same by frequent conferences with Cranmer and Peter Martyr.

On the accession of queen Mary he shared the same fate with others who professed the truth of the gospel. Being accused of heresy, he was sent prisoner to the Tower, and afterwards to Bocardo prison, in Oxford, from whence he was committed to the custody of Mr. Irish, mayor of that city, in whose house he remained till the day of his execution.

On the 30th September, 1555, these two eminent prelates were cited to appear in the divinity-school at Oxford. Dr. Ridley was first examined, and severely reprimanded by the bishop of London because when he heard the "cardinal's grace" and the "pope's holiness" mentioned in the commission he kept on his cap. The words of the bishop were to this effect: "Mr. Ridley, if you will not be uncovered in respect to the pope, and the cardinal his legate, by whose authority we sit in commission, your cap shall be taken off."

The bishop of Lincoln then made a formal harangue, in which he entreated Ridley to return to the holy mother-church; insisted on the antiquity and authority of the see of Rome, and of the pope as the immediate successor of St. Peter. Dr. Ridley, in return, strenuously opposed the arguments of the bishop, and boldly vindicated the doctrines of the reformation. He was then ordered to appear the following day in St. Mary's church.

When Latimer was brought into court, the bishop of Lincoln warmly exhorted him to return to the church from which he had revolted. His replies not being satisfactory, he was ordered to appear in St. Mary's church at the same time with Dr. Ridley.

On the day appointed the commissioners met, when Dr. Ridley being first brought before them, the bishop of Lincoln began to repeat the proceedings of the former meeting, assuring him that he had full liberty to make what alterations he pleased in his answers, and to deliver the same in writing.

After some debate, **Dr. Ridley** took out a paper and began to read, but the bishop ordered the beadle to take the writing from him. The doctor desired permission to read on, declaring the contents were only his answers, but the bishop and others having privately reviewed it, would not permit it to be read in open court.

The bishop of Gloucester, affecting much concern for Dr. Ridley, urged him not to indulge an obstinate temper, but to return to the unity of the holy catholic church.

Dr. Ridley coolly replied he was not vain of his own understanding, but was fully persuaded that the religion he professed was founded on God's most holy and infallible church, and therefore he could not abandon or deny the same. He desired to declare his reasons why he could not, with a safe conscience, admit of the popish supremacy: but his request was denied.

The bishop, finding him inflexible, thus addressed him: " Dr. Ridley, it is with the utmost concern that I observe your stubbornness and obstinacy in persisting in damnable - errors and heresies; but unless you recant I must proceed to the other part of my commission, though very much against my desire." Ridley not making any reply, sentence of condemnation was read, after which he was carried back to confinement.

When Latimer was brought before the court the bishop of Lincoln informed him that, though they had already taken his answers, yet they had given him time to consider the same, and would permit him to make what alterations he should deem fit, hoping by such means to reclaim him from his errors and bring him over to the faith of the holy catholic church. But he deviated not in a single point from the answers he had already given.

Being again warned to recant, he refused, declaring that he never would deny God's truth, which he was ready to seal with his blood. Sentence of condemnation was then pronounced against him, and he was committed to the custody of the mayor.

The account of the degradation of Ridley, his behaviour before and at the place of execution, is interesting; we therefore give it at length :—

"On the 15th of October Dr. Brooks, bishop of Gloucester, and the vice-chancellor of Oxford, Dr. Marshall, with some of the chief and heads of the same university, and many others, came to the house of the mayor, where Dr. Ridley was a prisoner. The bishop of Gloucester then said to him that the queen's majesty did again offer unto him, by them, her gracious mercy, if he would receive it and come home again to the faith in which he was baptized. He further said that if he would not recant they must needs proceed according to the law. 'But,' said he, 'we have oftentimes requested that you would recant your fantastical and devilish opinions, which hitherto you have not, although you might in so doing win many. Therefore, good Mr. Ridley, consider the danger that shall ensue both of body and soul if you shall so wilfully cast yourself away.'

"'My lord,' said Dr. Ridley, 'you know my mind fully herein; and as for my doctrine, my conscience assureth me that it is sound, and according to God's word (to his glory be it spoken); which doctrine, the Lord God being my helper, I will maintain so long as my tongue shall move and breath is within my body; in confirmation thereof I am willing to seal the same with my blood.'

"*Brooks.* It were best, Mr. Ridley, not to do so. For you know well enough that whosoever is out of the catholic church cannot be saved. Therefore, I say, that while you have mercy offered you, receive it, and confess the pope to be the chief head of the church.

"*Ridley.* I marvel that you will trouble me with such vain and foolish talk. You know my mind concerning the usurped authority of that anti-christ.

"And here he would have reasoned with the bishop, but was not suffered; the bishop told him, 'If he would not hold his peace, he should be compelled. And seeing,' saith he, 'that you will not receive the queen's mercy, we must, against our wills, proceed to degrade and deprive you of the priesthood. For we take you for no bishop, and, therefore, will the sooner have done with you: so, committing you to the secular power, you know what doth follow.'

"*Ridley.* Do with me as it shall please God to suffer you; I am well content to abide the same.

"*Brooks.* Put off your cap, and put upon you this surplice.

"*Ridley.* Not I, truly.

"*Brooks.* But you must.

"*Ridley.* I will not.

"*Brooks.* You must; therefore make no more ado, but put this surplice upon you.

"*Ridley.* Truly, if it come upon me it shall be against my will.

"*Brooks.* Will you not put it upon you?"

"*Ridley.* No, that I will not.

"*Brooks.* It shall be put upon you by one or other.

"*Ridley.* Do therein as it shall please you; I am well content with that, and more than that;

the servant is not above his master. If they dealt so cruelly with our Saviour Christ, and he suffered patiently, how much does it become us, his servants!" In saying these words, they put upon him a surplice, with all the trinkets appertaining to the mass. As they were about this, Dr. Ridley vehemently inveighed against the Romish bishop, and all that foolish apparel, calling the first antichrist, and the last, foolish and abominable, 'yea, too foolish for a device in a play.'

" *Brooks.* You had best hold your peace, lest your mouth be stopped. One Edridge, standing by, then said, 'Sir, the law is that he should be gagged, therefore let him be gagged.' At which words Dr. Ridley, looking earnestly upon him, shook his head at him, and made no answer.

" When they came to that place where Dr. Ridley should hold the chalice and the wafer-cake, Dr. Ridley said, 'They shall not come into my hands: for if they do, they shall fall to the ground for me.' Then one was appointed to hold them, while bishop Brooks read touching the degradation of spiritual persons, according to the pope's law. They then put the book into his hand, and read in Latin, 'We do take from thee the office of preaching the gospel,' &c. At which words Dr. Ridley gave a great sigh, and, looking up towards heaven, said, ' O Lord God, forgive them this their wickedness.' Having put on him the mass-gear, they began to take it away (beginning with the uppermost garment), again reading in Latin according to the pope's law. When all was taken from him, saving only the surplice, Dr. Ridley said, ' What power be you of, that you can take from a man that which he never had? I never was a singer: you take from me that which I never had.'

"So when this ridiculous degradation was ended, Dr. Ridley said to Dr. Brooks, 'Have you done? If you have, then give me leave to talk a little concerning these matters.' Brooks answered, 'Mr. Ridley, we must not talk with you; you are out of the church, and our law is that we must not talk with any out of the church.' Then Dr. Ridley said, 'Seeing that you will not suffer me to talk, neither will vouchsafe to hear me, what remedy but patience? I refer my cause to my heavenly Father, who will reform things that be amiss when it shall please him.'

"They were then going, when Ridley said, 'My lord, I wish you would vouchsafe to read over a little book of Bertram's writing concerning the sacrament. I promise you you will find much good learning therein.' To which Dr. Brooks made no answer, but was going away. Then said Dr. Ridley, 'Oh, I perceive you cannot away with this manner of talk. Well, as it is to no purpose, I will say no more; I will speak of worldly affairs. I pray you, therefore, my lord, hear me, and be a means to the queen's majesty in behalf of a great many poor men, especially my poor sister and her husband, who standeth there. They had a poor living granted unto them by me when I was in the see of London, which is taken from them by him that occupieth the same room without either law or conscience. I have a supplication to her majesty on their behalf. You shall hear it.' Then he read

the same, and when he came to the place that
spake of his sister by name he wept, so that for
a time he could not speak.   But recovering himself,
he said, 'This is nature that moveth me, but I
have now done;' and with that he finished it and
delivered it to his brother, commanding him to put
it up to the queen's majesty, and to sue not only
for himself, but also for such as had any leases or
grants by him and were put from them by Dr.
Bonner.   Dr. Brooks said, 'Indeed, Mr. Ridley,
your request in this supplication is very right;
therefore I must, in conscience, speak to the
queen's majesty for them.'

"*Ridley.* 'I pray, for God's sake, so do.'

"*Brooks.* 'I think your request will be granted,
except one thing hinder it, and that is because you
do not allow the queen's proceedings, but obsti-
nately withstand the same.'

"*Ridley.* 'What remedy?   I can do no more
than speak and write.   I trust I have discharged
my conscience therein, and God's will be done.'

"*Brooks.* 'I will do my best.'

"The degradation being concluded, Dr. Brooks
called the bailiffs, delivering to them Dr. Ridley,
with this charge, to keep him safely from any man
speaking with him, and to bring him to the place
of execution when commanded.   Then Dr. Ridley
said, 'I thank God there is none of you able to lay
to my charge any open or notorious crime, for if
you could it would surely be done, I see very
well.'   Whereunto Brooks said he played the part
of a proud pharisee, exalting himself.

"Dr. Ridley said, 'No, I confess myself to be a

miserable sinner, and have great need of God's help
and mercy, and do daily cry for the same; therefore I pray you have no such opinion of me.'   Then
they departed, and in going away a certain warden
of a college advised Dr. Ridley to repent and forsake his erroneous opinions.  'Sir,' said the doctor,
'repent *you*, for you are out of the truth; and I
pray God (if it be his blessed will) have mercy
upon you and grant you understanding of his
word.'   Then the warden, being in a passion,
said, 'I trust that I shall never be of your devilish
opinion, neither yet be in that place whither you
shall go; thou art the most obstinate and wilful
man that I ever heard talk.'

"On the night before he suffered, as he sat at
supper at the house of Mr. Irish, he invited his
hostess, and the rest at the table, to his marriage,
for, said he, to-morrow I must be married; and so
showed himself to be as merry as ever.   He then
asked his brother whether he thought his sister
could find it in her heart to be there.   He
answered, 'Yes, I dare say, with all her heart.'
At which he said he was glad to hear of her
sincerity.   At this discourse Mrs. Irish wept.   But
Dr. Ridley comforted her, saying, 'Oh, Mrs. Irish,
you love me not; for in that you weep, it doth
appear you will not be at my marriage, neither are
content therewith.   Indeed you are not so much
my friend as I thought you had been.   But quiet
yourself; though my breakfast may be somewhat
sharp and painful, yet I am sure my supper will be
more pleasant and sweet.'

"When they arose from the table, his brother

offered to stay all night with him.  But he said,
'No, no, that you shall not.  For I intend (God
willing) to sleep as quietly to-night as ever I did.'
On this his brother departed, exhorting him to be
of good cheer, and to take his cross quietly, for the
reward was great, &c.

## "Burning of Ridley and Latimer.

"On the north side of Oxford, in the ditch over
against Baliol College, the place of execution was
appointed; and for fear of any tumult, the lord
Williams was commanded by the queen's letters,
and the households of the city, to be there assistant,
sufficiently appointed; when everything was ready,
the prisoners were brought forth by the mayor
and bailiffs.

"Dr. Ridley had on a black gown furred, such
as he used to wear when a bishop; a tippet of
velvet furred, a velvet nightcap, with a corner cap,
and slippers on his feet.  He walked to the stake
between the mayor and an alderman, &c.

"After him came Mr. Latimer, in a poor Bristol
frieze frock much worn, with his buttoned cap and
kerchief on his head, all ready to the fire, a new
long shroud hanging down to the feet: which sight
excited sorrow in the spectators, beholding, on the
one side, the honour they sometime had: and on
the other, the calamity into which they had fallen.

"Dr. Ridley, as he passed toward Bocardo,
looked up where Dr. Cranmer lay, hoping to have
seen him at the glass window and spoken to him.
But Dr. Cranmer was then engaged in dispute with

friar Soto and his fellows, so that he could not see him. Dr. Ridley, then looking back, saw Mr. Latimer coming after. Unto whom he said, 'Oh, are you there?' 'Yea,' said Mr. Latimer, 'have after you as soon as I can.' So, he following, at length they came to the stake. Dr. Ridley first entered the place, and earnestly held up both his hands towards heaven; then seeing Mr. Latimer, with a cheerful look he ran to him, and embraced him, saying, 'Be of good heart, brother, for God will assuage the fury of the flame, or else strengthen us to abide it.'

"He then went to the stake, and kneeling down, prayed with great fervour; while Mr. Latimer, following, kneeled also, and prayed as earnestly as he. After this, they arose and conversed together, and while thus employed, Dr. Smith began his sermon to them upon this text of St. Paul, 'If I yield my body to the fire to be burnt, and have not charity, I shall gain nothing thereby:' wherein he alleged, that the goodness of the cause, and not the order of death, maketh the holiness of the person; which he confirmed by the examples of Judas, and of a woman in Oxford who of late hanged herself, for that they and such-like might then be adjudged righteous, which desperately destroyed themselves, as he feared those men who stood before him would do. He then charged the people to beware of them, for they were heretics, and died out of the church. He ended with an exhortation to them to recant and come home again to the church. His sermon scarcely lasted a quarter of an hour.

"At its conclusion, Dr. Ridley said to Mr. Latimer, 'Will you begin to answer the sermon, or shall I?' Mr. Latimer said, 'Begin you first, I pray you.' 'I will,' said Dr. Ridley.

"He then, with Mr. Latimer, kneeled to my lord Williams, the vice-chancellor of Oxford, and the other commissioners, who sat upon a form, and said, "I beseech you, my lord, even for Christ's sake, that I may speak but two or three words:' and whilst my lord bent his head to the mayor and vice-chancellor to know whether he might have leave to speak, the bailiffs and Dr. Marshall, the vice-chancellor, ran hastily unto him, and with their hands stopping his mouth, said, "Mr. Ridley, if you will revoke your erroneous opinions you shall not only have liberty so to do, but also your life.' 'Not otherwise?' said Dr. Ridley. 'No,' answered Dr. Marshall; 'therefore if you will not do so, there is no remedy: you must suffer for your deserts.' 'Well,' said the martyr, 'so long as the breath is in my body I will never deny my Lord Christ and his known truth: God's will be done in me:' with that he rose and said with a loud voice, 'I commit our cause to Almighty God, who will judge all, without respect of persons.' To which Mr. Latimer added his old saying, 'Well, there is nothing hid but it shall be opened.' They were then commanded to prepare immediately for the stake.

"With all meekness they obeyed. Dr. Ridley gave his gown and tippet to his brother-in-law, Mr. Shipside, who all the time of his imprisonment, although he was not suffered to come to him, was there at his own charge to provide him necessaries, which from time to time he sent him by the serjeant. Some of his apparel he also gave away, the other the bailiffs took.

"He likewise made presents of other small things to gentlemen standing by, divers of them pitifully weeping; to sir Henry Lea he gave a new groat; to my lord Williams, gentleman, some napkins, &c., and happy was he who could get the least trifle for a remembrance of this good man.

" Mr. Latimer quietly suffered his keeper to pull off his hose and his other apparel, which was very simple; and being stripped to his shroud, he seemed as comely a person as one could well see.

" Then Dr. Ridley, standing as yet in his trouse, said to his brother, ' It were best for me to go in my trouse still.' ' No,' said Mr. Latimer, ' it will put you to more pain; and it will do a poor man good.' Whereunto Dr. Ridley said, ' Be it in the name of God,' and so unlaced himself. Then being in his shirt, he held up his hand and said, ' O heavenly Father, I give unto thee most hearty thanks, that thou hast called me to be a professor of thee, even unto death; I beseech thee, Lord God, have mercy on this realm of England, and deliver it from all her enemies.'

" The smith then took a chain of iron, and brought it about both their middles; and as he was knocking in the staple Dr. Ridley took the chain in his hand, and looking aside to the smith, said, ' Good fellow, knock it in hard, for the flesh will have its course.' Then his brother brought him a bag of gunpowder, and tied it about his neck.

Dr. Ridley asked him what it was. He answered, 'Gunpowder.' 'Then,' said he, 'I take it to be sent of God, therefore I will receive it. And have you any,' said he, 'for my brother?' (meaning Mr. Latimer). 'Yea, sir, that I have,' said he. 'Then give it unto him,' said he, 'in time, lest you come too late.' So his brother carried it to Mr. Latimer.

"They then brought a lighted fagot, and laid it at Dr. Ridley's feet; upon which Mr. Latimer said, 'BE OF GOOD COMFORT, MR. RIDLEY, AND PLAY THE MAN; WE SHALL THIS DAY LIGHT SUCH A CANDLE BY GOD'S GRACE IN ENGLAND AS I TRUST NEVER SHALL BE PUT OUT.'

"When Dr. Ridley saw the fire flaming up towards him he cried with an amazing loud voice, 'Into thy hands, O Lord, I commend my spirit; Lord receive my spirit:' and continued often to repeat, 'Lord, Lord, receive my spirit.' Mr. Latimer cried as vehemently, 'O Father of heaven, receive my soul.' After which he soon died, seemingly with little pain.

"But Dr. Ridley, from the ill-making of the fire, the fagots being green, and piled too high, so that the flames, which burned fiercely beneath, could not well get to him, was put to such exquisite pain that he desired them, for God's sake, to let the fire come unto him. His brother-in-law hearing him, but not very well understanding, to rid him of his pain, and not well knowing what he did, heaped fagots upon him, so that he quite covered him. This made the fire burn so vehement beneath that it burned all his nether parts before it touched the upper, and made him struggle under the fagots, and often desire them to let the fire come unto him, saying, 'I cannot burn.' In such pains he laboured till one of the standers-by pulled the fagots from above, and where Dr. Ridley saw the fire flame up he wrested himself to that side. At last the fire touched the gunpowder, and he was seen to stir no more, but burned on the other side, falling down at Mr. Latimer's feet, his body being divided.

"The dreadful sight filled almost every eye with tears. Some took it grievously to see their deaths whose lives they had held so dear. Some pitied their persons, who thought their souls had no need thereof. But the sorrow of his brother, whose anxiety led him to attempt to put a speedy end to his sufferings, but who so unhappily prolonged them, surpassed that of all. So violent was his grief that the spectators pitied him almost as much as they did the martyr."

## The Sufferings and Martyrdom of Thomas Cranmer, Archbishop of Canterbury.

This eminent prelate was born at Aslacton, in Nottinghamshire, on the 2nd of July, 1489. Having completed his studies at the university, he took the usual degrees, was chosen fellow of Jesus College, and became celebrated for his learning and abilities. In 1521, by marrying, he forfeited his fellowship; but his wife dying in child-bed, he was re-elected. In 1523 he was chosen divinity lecturer in his own college, and appointed by the university one of the examiners in that science. In this office he principally inculcated the study of the holy Scriptures, then greatly neglected, as being indispensably necessary.

The plague breaking out at Cambridge, he removed to Waltham Abbey, where, meeting with Gardiner and Fox, the secretary and almoner of the king, that monarch's intended divorce of Catherine was mentioned, when Cranmer advised an application to the universities for their opinion in the case. These gentlemen introduced him to the king, who ordered him to write his thoughts on the subject, made him his chaplain, and admitted him into that favour and esteem which he never afterwards forfeited.

In 1530 the king sent him to dispute on the subject of the divorce at Paris, Rome, and other foreign parts. At Rome he delivered his book to the pope, offering to justify it in a public disputation, but none appeared to oppose him. The pope constituted him penitentiary-general of England, and dismissed him.

During the time he was abroad the great archbishop Warham died. Henry, convinced of Cranmer's merit, determined that he should succeed him. He was consecrated on March 30, 1533, and though he received the usual bulls from the pope, he protested against the oath of allegiance, etc., to him; for he had conversed freely with the reformed in Germany, had read Luther's books, and was zealously attached to the glorious cause of the reformation.

The first service he did the king as archbishop was pronouncing the sentence of his divorce from

queen Catherine; the next was joining his hand
with Anne Boleyn, from which marriage Elizabeth
was born, to whom he stood godfather.

As the queen was greatly interested in the
reformation, its friends began to conceive high
hopes. But the fickle disposition of the king and
the unhappy end of Anne alarmed their fears. No
ill effects, however, ensued; the pope's supremacy
was universally exploded; monasteries, etc., destroyed, upon the fullest detection of the most
abominable vices and wickedness existing in them;
that valuable book the " Erudition of a Christian
Man" was set forth with public authority; and the
sacred Scriptures at length, to the infinite joy of
the people, were not only translated, but introduced
into every parish.

Cranmer now made a collection of opinions from
the works of the ancient fathers and later doctors.
Shortly after he gave a shining proof of his disin-
terested constancy by his opposition to king
Henry's six bloody articles. He also published,
with an incomparable preface, the larger Bible, six
copies of which even Bonner—then newly consecrated bishop of London—caused to be fixed, for
the perusal of the people, in his cathedral of St.
Paul's.

The enemies of the reformation, however, were
restless; and Henry, alas! was no protestant in his
heart. Cromwell fell a sacrifice to them, and they
aimed their malignant shafts at Cranmer. Gardiner, in particular, was indefatigable; he had him
accused in parliament, and several lords of the privy
council moved the king to commit him to the

Tower. The king perceived their malice, and one evening ordered his barge to be rowed to Lambeth. The archbishop coming down to pay his respects, Henry acquainted him with the accusation, and spoke of his opposition to the six articles. The archbishop modestly replied that he must confess himself to be still of the same opinion, but was not conscious of having offended against them. The king then, with an air of pleasantry, asked him if his bedchamber could stand the test of these articles? The archbishop confessed that he was married in Germany before his promotion; but he assured the king that, on the passing of that act he had sent his wife abroad to her friends. His majesty was so charmed with his openness and integrity, that he discovered the whole plot laid against him, and gave him a ring of great value to produce on any future emergency.

A few days after this, Cranmer's enemies summoned him before the council, when they suffered him to wait in the lobby amongst the servants; treated him on his admission with haughty contempt, and would have sent him to the Tower. But he produced the ring, which changed their tone; and while his enemies received a severe reprimand from Henry, Cranmer gained the highest degree of favour. On this occasion he showed that lenity and mildness for which he was so much distinguished; he never persecuted any of his enemies, but freely forgave even the inveterate Gardiner, on his writing a supplicatory letter to him. The same lenity he showed towards Dr. Thornton, the suffragan of Dover, and Dr. Barber.

who, though entertained in his family, entrusted with his secrets, and indebted to him for many favours, had ungratefully conspired with Gardiner to take away his life.

When Cranmer discovered their treachery he took them into his study, and telling them that he had been basely accused by some in whom he had reposed the greatest confidence, asked how he should behave towards them. They, not suspecting themselves to be concerned, replied that such vile villains ought to be prosecuted with the greatest rigour, nay, deserved to die without mercy. At this the archbishop, lifting up his hands, cried out, " Merciful God! whom may a man trust ?" And then, showing the letters by which he had discovered their treachery, asked if they knew them. They were now in the utmost confusion, and, falling on their knees, humbly sued for forgiveness. The archbishop said that he freely forgave them, but that they must not expect him ever to trust them for the future.

We may here relate another pleasant instance of his readiness to forgive injuries :—

The archbishop's first wife—whom he married at Cambridge—was kinswoman to the hostess at the Dolphin inn, and boarded there. As he often resorted thither on that account, the popish party raised a story that he had been ostler at the inn, and had never had a learned education. This idle story a Yorkshire priest asserted in an ale-house, railing at the archbishop, saying he had no more learning than a goose. Some people informed Lord Cromwell of this, and the priest was committed to

Fleet prison. When he had been there nine or ten weeks he sent to the archbishop to beg his pardon and sue for a discharge. The archbishop instantly summoned him, and, after a gentle reproof, asked whether he knew him. He answered, "No." The archbishop then asked why he should make so free with his character. The priest excused himself by saying he was in liquor, but this, Cranmer told him, was a double fault. He then told him that if he was inclined to try what a scholar he was, he should have liberty to oppose him in whatever science he pleased. The priest humbly asked pardon, confessed himself to be ignorant, and to understand nothing but his mother-tongue. "No doubt, then," said Cranmer, "you are well versed in the English Bible, and can answer any questions out of that. Pray tell me who was David's father?" The priest, after considering for some time, at last told the archbishop he could not recollect. "Tell me, then," said Cranmer, "who was Solomon's father?" The poor priest replied that he had no skill in genealogies, and could not tell. The archbishop then, advising him to frequent alehouses less and his study more, sent him home to his cure.

These instances show Cranmer's clement temper. Indeed, he was blamed by many for his too great lenity. The king, who was a good discerner of men, remarking the implacable hatred of his enemies, changed his coat of arms from three cranes to three pelicans, feeding their young with their own blood, and told him that these birds should signify to him that he ought to be ready, like the pelican, to shed his blood for his young ones brought up in the faith of Christ; "for," said the king, "you will be tried at length if you stand to your tackling." The event proved the king to be no bad prophet.

In 1547 Henry died, and left his crown to his only son, Edward, Cranmer's godson, who had imbibed all the spirit of a reformer. This excellent young prince, influenced no less by his own inclinations than by the advice of Cranmer and other friends of the reformation, was diligent in endeavour to promote it. Homilies and a catechism were composed by the archbishop; Erasmus's Notes on the New Testament were translated and fixed up in the churches; the sacrament was administered in both kinds; and the liturgy read in the vulgar tongue. Ridley, the archbishop's great friend, one of the brightest lights of the reformation, was equally zealous in the cause. In concert with him, the archbishop drew up the forty-two articles of religion, and published a much-esteemed treatise entitled "A Defence of the True and Catholic Doctrine of the Sacrament of the Body and Blood of our Lord Jesus Christ."

But this prosperity was not long to continue. God was pleased to deprive the nation of king Edward in 1553, designing, in his wise providence, to perfect the new-born church of Christ in England by the blood of martyrs, as at the beginning he perfected the church in general. Anxious for the success of the reformation, and wrought upon by the duke of Northumberland, Edward had been persuaded to exclude his sisters, and to bequeath the crown to that duke's amiable daughter-in-law, the Lady Jane Grey. The archbishop did his utmost to oppose this alteration in the succession; but the king was overruled; the will was made, and subscribed by the council and the judges. The archbishop was sent for last of all, and required to subscribe, but he answered that he could not do so without perjury, having sworn to the entail of the crown on the two princesses, Mary and Elizabeth. To this the king replied that the judges, who ought to be regarded in this point, had assured him that, notwithstanding that entail, he might lawfully bequeath the crown to Lady Jane. The archbishop desired to discourse with them himself about it, and they all agreeing that he might lawfully subscribe the king's will, he at last set his hand to it.

Hence he thought himself obliged to join the Lady Jane; but her short-lived power soon expired. Mary and persecution then mounted the throne, and Cranmer could expect nothing less than attainder, deprivation, and death.

He was condemned for treason, and, with pretended clemency, pardoned; but, to gratify Gardiner's malice, and her own hatred to him for her mother's divorce, Mary gave orders to proceed against him for heresy. The Tower was crowded with prisoners; Cranmer, Ridley, Latimer, and Bradford were all put into one chamber. They blessed God for the opportunity of conversing and reading the Scriptures together, confirming one another in the faith, and exhorting to

constancy in professing it, and patience in suffering
for it. Happy society! blessed martyrs! rather to
be envied than the purpled tyrant, with the sword
deep drenched in blood, though encircled with all
the pageantry of power!

In April, 1554, the archbishop, with bishops
Ridley and Latimer, was removed from the Tower
to Oxford, to dispute with some select persons of
both universities. But how vain are disputations
where the fate of men is fixed and every word is
misconstrued! On April the 20th Cranmer was
brought to St. Mary's, before the queen's commissioners, and, refusing to subscribe to the popish
articles, sentence of condemnation was passed upon
him.

After this his servants were dismissed, and himself closely confined in Bocardo, the prison at
Oxford. But this sentence being void in law, as
the pope's authority was wanting, a new commission was sent from Rome in 1555, and in St.
Mary's church he was tried again. Here he was
well-nigh too strong for the judges; and if reason
and truth could have prevailed, there would have
been no doubt who should have been acquitted and
who condemned.

The February following a new commission was
given to bishops Bonner and Thirlby. When they
came down to Oxford they read their commission
from the pope, for not appearing before whom in
person, as they had cited him, Cranmer was
declared contumacious, though they themselves
had kept him a close prisoner. Bonner then,
in a scurrilous oration, insulted him in a very

unchristian manner, for which he was often rebuked by Thirlby, who wept, and declared that it was the most sorrowful scene he had beheld in his life. In the commission it was declared that the cause had been impartially heard at Rome, the witnesses on both sides examined, and the archbishop's counsel allowed to make the best defence for him they could. At this he could not help crying out, "Good God! what lies are these—that I, being in prison, and not suffered to have counsel or advocate at home, should produce witnesses and appoint my counsel at Rome. God will punish this shameless and open lying!"

When Bonner had finished his invective, they proceeded to degrade him; and that they might make him as ridiculous as they could, the episcopal habit which they put on him was made of canvas and old rags. Bonner, by way of mockery, called him "Mr. Canterbury," and the like. He bore this treatment with patience; told them the degradation gave him no concern, for he had long despised these ornaments; but when they came to take away his crozier, he held it fast, saying to Thirlby, "I appeal to the next general council."

When they had stripped him of his habits, they put on him a poor yeoman-beadle's gown, threadbare and ill-shaped, and a townsman's cap, and in this manner delivered him to the secular power to be carried back to prison, where he was kept entirely destitute and totally secluded from his friends. Nay, such was the fury of his enemies, that a gentleman was taken into custody by

Bonner, and narrowly escaped a trial, for giving him money to buy him a dinner.

Cranmer had now been imprisoned almost three years, and death should have soon followed his degradation; but his enemies reserved him for greater misery and insult. Every means was employed to shake his constancy; but he held fast the faith. Even when he saw the barbarous martyrdom of his dear companions, Ridley and Latimer, he was so far from shrinking that he prayed God, by their example, to animate him to a patient expectation and endurance of the same fiery trial.

The papists at length determined to try how gentle methods would do with Cranmer. They accordingly removed him from prison to the lodgings of the dean of Christ church, where they urged every persuasive and affecting argument; and, indeed, too much melted his gentle nature by the false sunshine of pretended respect. As, however, he withstood every temptation, they removed him to the most loathsome part of the prison, and treated him with the most unparalleled severity. This was more than the infirmities of so old a man could bear: the frailty of nature prevailed; and he was induced to sign the following recantation.

"I, Thomas Cranmer, late archbishop of Canterbury, do renounce, abhor, and detest all manner of heresies and errors of Luther and Zuinglius, and all other teachings which are contrary to sound and true doctrine. And I believe most constantly in my heart, and with my mouth I confess one holy and Catholic church visible, without which there is no salvation; and therefore I acknowledge the bishop of Rome to be supreme head on earth, whom I acknowledge to be the highest bishop and pope, and Christ's vicar, unto whom all Christian people ought to be subject.

"I believe and worship in the sacrament of the altar, the very body and blood of Christ being contained most truly in the form of bread and wine; the bread through the mighty power of God being turned into the body of our Saviour Jesus Christ, and the wine into his blood.

"And as to the other six sacraments, I believe and hold as the universal church holdeth, and the church of Rome judgeth and determineth.

"I believe also that there is a purgatory, where souls departed are punished for a time, for whom the church doth godly and wholesomely pray, like as it doth honour saints and make prayers to them.

"Finally, in all things I profess that I do not otherwise believe than as the catholic church and church of Rome holdeth and teacheth. I am sorry that ever I held or thought otherwise. And I beseech Almighty God, that of his mercy he will vouchsafe to forgive me whatsoever I have offended against God or his church.

"And all such as have been deceived either by mine example or doctrine, I require them, by the blood of Jesus Christ, that they will return to the unity of the church, that we may be all of one mind, without schism or division.

"And to conclude, as I submit myself to the catholic church of Christ, and to the supreme head thereof, so I submit myself unto the most excellent majesties of Philip and Mary, king and queen of this realm of England, etc., and to all other their laws and ordinances, being ready always to obey them. And God is my witness, that I have not done this for favour or fear of any person, but willingly and of my own conscience, as to the instruction of others."

This recantation of the archbishop was immediately printed, and distributed throughout the country. All this time, Cranmer had no certain assurance of his life, although it was faithfully promised him by the doctors; but after they had gained their purpose, they committed the rest to chance, as usual with men of their religion. The queen, having now an opportunity for revenge, received his recantation very gladly; but insisted on putting him to death.

Now was Dr. Cranmer in a miserable case, having neither quietness in his own conscience, nor yet any help in his adversaries'. Besides this, on the one side was praise, on the other side scorn, on both sides danger, so that he could neither die honestly nor yet honestly live. And whereas he sought profit, he fell into double disprofit, that neither with good men he could avoid secret shame, nor yet with evil men the note of dissimulation.

Meantime the queen, taking counsel how to despatch Cranmer, who knew not of her hate, and was not expecting death, appointed that Dr. Cole, against the 21st of March, should prepare a sermon for his burning. Soon after, other worshipful men and justices were commanded to be at Oxford on the same day, with their servants and retinue, lest Cranmer's death should raise any tumult. Dr. Cole now returned to Oxford. As the day of execution drew near, he came into the prison to Dr. Cranmer, to try whether he abode in the catholic faith. Cranmer told him that by God's grace he would be daily more confirmed in the catholic faith. The day following Cole repaired to him again, but as yet told him not of his death that was prepared. On this occasion he asked him if he had any money; when he had answered that he had none, Cole delivered to him fifteen crowns to give to the poor, to whom he would : and exhorting him to constancy in the faith, departed.

The archbishop now began to surmise what they were about. There came to him the Spanish friar, witness of his recantation, bringing a paper with articles, earnestly desiring him to write it and sign it with his name; which when he had done, the friar desired that he would write another copy, which should remain with him, and that he did also. But seeing now whereunto their devices tended, and that the time was at hand in which he could no longer dissemble, he put his prayer and exhortation, written in another paper, secretly into his bosom, intending to recite them to the people before he should make the last profession of his faith; fearing if he made the confession of his faith first, they would not afterwards suffer him to exhort the people.

Soon after, about nine o'clock, the lord Williams, sir Thomas Bridges, sir John Brown, and the other justices, with certain noblemen of the queen's council, came to Oxford with a great train of waiting-men. There was besides a great multitude, and greater expectation : they of the pope's side being in great hope to hear something of Cranmer that should

W

establish their opinion: other endued with a better mind, not doubting that he who for so many years had sent forth the true doctrine of the gospel, would confess it now in the last act of his life.

Dr. Cranmer at last came from the prison of Bocardo to St. Mary's church. The mayor went before, next were the aldermen; after them Cranmer between two friars, who, mumbling certain Psalms, answered one another until they came to the church door, and there began the song of Simeon, " *Nunc dimittis;* " then, entering into the church, they brought him to a stage set over against the pulpit, on which he stood, waiting until Dr. Cole made ready for his sermon.

This was indeed a sorrowful spectacle to all Christian eyes that beheld it. He that lately was archbishop, metropolitan, and primate of England, and the king's privy counsellor, being now in a ragged gown, with an old square cap, exposed to the contempt of all.

In this habit, when he had stood a good space upon the stage, turning to a pillar near adjoining, he lifted up his hands, and prayed. At length Dr. Cole coming into the pulpit, and beginning his sermon, entered first into mention of Tobias and Zachary, whom he praised for their perseverance in the true worshipping of God; he then divided his sermon into three parts, intending to speak first of the mercy of God: secondly, of his justice to be showed: and last of all, how the prince's secrets are not to be opened. But he soon took occasion, with many hot words, to reprove Cranmer, that he, being endued with wholesome and catholic doctrine, fell into pernicious error;

which he had not only defended by his writings, but also allured other men to do the like.

After Cole had ended his sermon, he called back the people to prayers. "Brethren," said he, "lest any man should doubt of this man's repentance, you shall hear him speak before you; and therefore I pray you, Mr. Cranmer, to perform that now which you promised: namely, that you would openly make a true profession of your faith, that all men may understand that you are catholic indeed." "I will do it," said the archbishop, "and that with a good will." Then rising up, and putting off his cap, he said:—

"Good christian people, my dearly beloved brethren and sisters in Christ, I beseech you most heartily to pray for me to Almighty God that he will forgive me all my sins and offences, which be many without number and great above measure. But yet one thing grieveth my conscience more than all the rest, whereof, God willing, I intend to speak more hereafter. But how great and many soever my sins may be, I beseech you to pray to God of his mercy to forgive them all." And here kneeling, he prayed:

"O Father of heaven, O Son of God, Redeemer of the world, O Holy Ghost, three persons and one God, have mercy upon me, most wretched caitiff and miserable sinner. I have offended against heaven and earth more than my tongue can express. Whither, then, may I go, or whither shall I flee? To heaven I may be ashamed to lift mine eyes, and in earth I find no place of refuge or succour. To thee, therefore, O Lord, do

I run; to thee do I humble myself, saying, O Lord, my God, my sins be great, but yet have mercy upon me for thy great mercy. The great mystery that God became man was not wrought for little or few offences. Thou didst not give thy Son, O heavenly Father, unto death for small sins only, but for all the greatest sins of the world, so that the sinner return to thee with his whole heart, as I do at this present. Wherefore, have mercy on me, O God, whose property is always to have mercy; have mercy upon me, O Lord, for thy great mercy. I crave nothing for mine own merits, but for thy name's sake, that it may be hallowed thereby, and for thy Son Jesus Christ's sake. And now, O Father of heaven, hallowed be thy name," etc. Then rising, he said :—

" Every man desireth at the time of his death to give some good exhortation, that others may be the better thereby; so I beseech God grant me grace that I may speak something at this my departing, whereby God may be glorified and you edified.

" First, it is a great grief to see that so many so dote upon this false world, and so care for it that they care little or nothing for the love of God, or of the world to come. Therefore, this shall be my first exhortation, that you set your minds upon God and the world to come, and learn what this meaneth, 'That the love of this world is hatred against God.'

" The second exhortation is, that you obey your king and queen willingly and without murmuring, knowing that they are ministers appointed by God to rule and govern you; therefore, whosoever resisteth them, resisteth the ordinance of God.

"The third exhortation is, that you love like brethren and sisters. For, alas! pity it is to see what hatred one christian man beareth to another, taking each other as strangers and mortal enemies. But I pray you learn to do good to all men as much as in you lieth. For whosoever hateth any person, and goeth about maliciously to hurt him, surely God is not with that man, although he think himself ever so much in God's favour.

"The fourth exhortation is to them that have the riches of this world, that they will consider well these three sayings: one of our Saviour, 'It is hard for a rich man to enter into the kingdom of heaven.' A sore saying, yet spoken by him who knoweth the truth. The second of St. John, 'He that hath the substance of this world and seeth his brother in necessity, and shutteth up his mercy from him, how can he say that he loveth God?' The third of St. James, 'Weep you and howl for the misery that shall come upon you; your riches do rot, your clothes be moth-eaten, your gold and silver doth canker and rust, and their rust shall bear witness against you, and consume you like fire; you gather a hoard of treasure of God's indignation against the last day.' Let them that be rich ponder well these three sentences; for if they ever had occasion to show their charity they have it now, the poor being so many, and victuals so dear.

"And now, forasmuch as I am come to the last end of my life, whereupon hangeth all my life past, and all my life to come, either to live with my master, Christ, for ever in joy, or else to be in pain for ever with wicked devils in hell, and I see before mine eyes presently either heaven ready to receive me, or else hell ready to swallow me up; I shall, therefore, declare unto you my faith without any dissimulation:

"First, I believe in God the Father Almighty, maker of all heaven and earth, &c. And I believe every article of the catholic faith, every word and sentence taught by our Saviour Jesus Christ, his apostles and prophets, in the Old and New Testament.

"And now I come to what troubleth my conscience more than anything that ever I did or said in my life, and that is, the setting abroad of a writing contrary to the truth, which now here I renounce and refuse, as written with my hand indeed, but contrary to what I thought in my heart, and written for fear of death, and to save my life, if it might be; all such papers which I have written or signed since my degradation I renounce as untrue. And forasmuch as my hand hath offended, it shall first be punished, for when I come to the fire it shall be first burned.

"And as for the pope, I refuse him, with all his false doctrine, as Christ's enemy and as anti-christ.

"And as for the sacrament, I believe as I have taught in my book against the bishop of Winchester; the doctrine my book teacheth shall stand at the last day before the judgment of God where the papistical doctrine shall be ashamed to show her face."

The standers-by were amazed. Some began to admonish him of his recantation and to accuse him of falsehood. It was strange to see the doctors beguiled of their hope. For it is not to be doubted that they looked for a glorious victory and a perpetual triumph by this man's retraction.

Then was an iron chain tied about Cranmer and the fire set unto him. When the wood was kindled and the fire began to burn near him, he stretched forth his right hand, which had signed his recantation, into the flames, and there held it so that the people might see it burnt to a coal before his body was touched. In short, he was so patient and constant in the midst of his tortures, that he seemed to move no more than the stake to which he was bound; his eyes were lifted up to heaven, and often he said, so long as his voice would suffer him, "this unworthy right hand!" and often using the words of Stephen, "Lord Jesus, receive my spirit," till the fury of the flames putting him to silence, he gave up the ghost.

Martyrdom of William Bongeor, Thomas Benhote, William Purchase, Agnes Silverside, Helen Ewring, Elizabeth Folk, William Munt, John Johnson, Alice Munt, and Rose Allen, at Colchester.

Amongst twenty-two persons brought from Colchester to London, and discharged on signing a confession, were William Munt, who resided at Muchbentley, Alice, his wife, and Rose Allen, her daughter. On coming home they again absented

themselves from the idolatrous service of the
popish church, and frequented the company of
persons who read the word of God and called on
his name through Christ. For this conduct they
were accused to the Lord Darcy, and compelled for
a while to withdraw. After a short time, however,
lulled into security, they returned. On the 7th of
March, 1557, about two o'clock in the morning,
Edmund Tyrrel (a descendant of the person who
murdered king Edward V. in the Tower of
London), with a number of attendants, came to
the door and told Mr. Munt that he and his wife
must go with him to Colchester castle.

This sudden surprise greatly affected Mrs. Munt,
who was much indisposed in consequence of the
cruel treatment she had before received from the
popish party; but after she had a little recovered
herself, she desired of Tyrrel that her daughter
might fetch her something to drink. This being
granted, Tyrrel advised the daughter to counsel
her father and mother to behave like good
christians; to which she replied, " Sir, they have
a better instructor than me; for the Holy Ghost
doth teach them, I hope, and will not suffer them
to err."

*Tyrrel.* Art thou still in that mind? It is time,
indeed, to look after such heretics.

*Rose.* Sir, with what you call heresy do I worship my Lord God; I tell you truth.

*Tyrrel.* Then I perceive you will burn, gossip,
with the rest, for company's sake.

*Rose.* No, sir, not for company's sake, but for
Christ's sake, if so I be compelled; and I hope, in

his mercy, if he call me to it, he will enable me to bear it.

The cruel Tyrrel then seized her wrist, and taking the lighted candle from her, held it under her hand, burning it across the back, till the sinews cracked; during which barbarous operation he said often to her, "Why wilt thou not cry? wilt thou not cry?" To which she constantly answered that "she thanked God she had no cause, but rather to rejoice. But," she said, "he had more cause to weep than she, if he considered the matter well." At last he thrust her violently from him, with much scurrilous language. She then went and carried her mother drink, as she was commanded.

Tyrrel then conducted them all to Colchester castle, together with John Johnson.

On the same morning they apprehended six others, namely, William Bongeor, Thomas Benhote, William Purchase, Agnes Silverside, Helen Ewring, and Elizabeth Folk, whom they sent to Motehill. After a few days they were brought, with many others, before several justices, priests, and officers, to be examined relative to their faith.

They were all condemned, and bishop Bonner sent down a warrant for their being burnt on the 2nd of August. As they were confined in different places, it was resolved that part of them should be executed in the former, and the rest in the latter part of that day. When those appointed for the morning arrived at the spot, they kneeled down and humbly addressed themselves to Almighty God, though they were interrupted by their popish enemies. They then arose, and were fastened to the stakes. They died with amazing fortitude, triumphing amid the flames, and exulting in hopes of the glory that awaited them.

In the afternoon of the day the others were brought to the same place. There they all kneeled down and prayed with the greatest fervency. After prayer they were fastened to the stakes and burnt, with their latest breath exhorting the people to beware of idolatry, and testifying their faith in Christ crucified.

Nearly 400 fell a sacrifice during the reign of Mary. There were burnt 5 bishops, 21 divines, 8 gentlemen, 84 artificers, 100 husbandmen, servants, and labourers, 26 wives, 20 widows, 9 virgins, 2 boys, and 2 infants; 64 more were persecuted for their religion, of whom 7 were whipped, 16 perished in prison, and 12 were buried in dunghills.

Such are the annals of England's apostles, who counted not their lives dear unto them so that they might finish their course with joy. Let us honour those heroes of spiritual progress and champions of our faith who were martyrs, and were baptized in blood because their genius or enlightenment forced them to be in advance of their day.

## The Death of Queen Mary—The Happy Accession of the Lady Elizabeth to the Throne of England.

On the 17th November, 1558, queen Mary died, in her forty-third year, after having reigned five years four months and eleven days. Her false

conception, and the melancholy that followed it, aggravated by the loss of Calais, brought on an illness which turned to a dropsy, and put an end to her unhappy reign.

Its history proves her excessive bigotry; to this she joined a cruel and vindictive temper, which she confounded with zeal for religion; but when it was not possible to unite them, she plainly showed that she was inclined to cruelty no less by nature than by zeal. It was her misfortune to be encouraged in this horrid disposition by all who approached her. King Philip was naturally morose; Gardiner was one of the most revengeful men living; Bonner was a fury; and the other bishops were chosen from the most cruel of the clergy. She left to her council the whole conduct of affairs, and gave herself up entirely to the humours of her clergy.

Her half-sister, the Lady Elizabeth, succeeded this bloody queen. Her accession gave infinite joy to the nation in general, but great mortification to the priests and the Romish party, who apprehended a new revolution in matters of religion. She passed through London amid all the joys that a people delivered from the terrors of fire and slavery could express. King Philip proposed marriage to her in vain; her answer being that she had espoused her kingdom. She gave orders that all who were imprisoned for religion should be set at liberty; upon which, a person observing that the four Evangelists were still captives, and that the people longed to see them set free, she replied that she would speak to her subjects to know their minds. A reformation being soon resolved upon, the queen desired that

the changes might be so managed as to occasion as little division as possible among her subjects; the final results of which were a new translation of the Scriptures, and the national establishment of the protestant religion. Queen Elizabeth died, in the seventieth year of her age and the forty-fifth of her reign, on the 24th of March, 1603.

---

And now to conclude this list of those who sealed with their lives their testimony of attachment to the Lord Jesus Christ. There are important lessons which it would be well for every one to learn. First, it behoves every British reader to be thankful to God that he lives in a country where he " can sit under his own vine and fig-tree, none daring to make him afraid." Secondly, we should never forget that our exemption from persecution for our religious belief was purchased by the lives of those heroic martyrs: and our admiration ought to be awakened for their steadfastness in the fiery trial. Thirdly, we should be thankful to God that we are not under the influence of popery, and its soul-destroying errors. Fourthly, we should be deeply impressed with the conviction that as our forefathers suffered so greatly for religious freedom, it is our duty to be prepared to suffer in the cause of him who gave up his life to redeem a guilty world. Fifthly, the triumphant deaths of the martyrs should increase the attachment of the followers of Jesus to that cause which they have espoused, and should strengthen their faith, their hope, and their joy in the Lord. Lastly, if any readers of the foregoing pages have not yet decided

to be on the Lord's side, surely the triumphant testimonies of those who laid down their lives for love
of Jesus, to the value of his religion, is a lesson so
impressive, that hard and stoical must be the heart
that does not feel its influence. May the traveller
Zionward be strengthened for his journey by perusing the contents of this volume; and may the wan-
derer be reclaimed from the error of his way; and
to God shall be all the glory. Amen.

FINIS.